BECOMING THE ARCHANGEL MICHAEL'S COMPANIONS

RUDOLF STEINER (1918)

BECOMING THE ARCHANGEL MICHAEL'S COMPANIONS

Rudolf Steiner's Challenge to the Younger Generation

Thirteen Lectures Held in Stuttgart
October 3-15, 1922

TRANSLATED BY RENÉ M. QUERIDO
INTRODUCTION BY CHRISTOPHER BAMFORD

RUDOLF STEINER

SteinerBooks

CW 217

SteinerBooks
Anthropsophic Press

402 Union Street #58, Hudson, New York 12534
www.steinerbooks.org

Translated from German by René M. Querido

This book is volume 217 in the Collected Works (CW) of Rudolf Steiner, published by SteinerBooks, 2020. It is a translation of *Paedagogischer Jugendkurs,* published by Rudolf Steiner Verlag, Dornach, Switzerland, 1961. Translated from shorthand reports unrevised by the lecturer.

Print ISBN: 978-0-88010-609-3

Printed in the United States of America

CONTENTS

3.

Stuttgart, October 5, 1922

The person of today considers only the waking consciousness between waking up and going to sleep, whereas in former times something from one's sleeping consciousness was carried over into the day. When salt, mercury, phosphorus, etc., were spoken of, one still had an etheric perception of these things. Since the fifteenth century the sleeping consciousness trickles into waking consciousness less and less. The development of culture from the educational point of view. Formerly a book stimulated productive forces in the human being; today everything is taken in formally, logically and inactively. Today's thinking is a product of the brain; to that extent materialism is correct. But it is a dead thinking, which must be distinguished from one that is alive. The results obtained by external observation with dead thinking cannot be taken into sleep. In sleep the human being of today is almost completely absorbed by the spirituality of nature, whereas previously the human being "was something" even in sleep. It does not depend on the words: one can even represent Theosophy in a materialistic way. Spirit is not to be spoken about, but in speaking, spirit is to be generated. Schematic Anthroposophy is spiritless. The Benedictine Father Mager about Anthroposophy. Only out of an inner penetration of the spirit can we re-enliven the culture of the present time.

pages 25–36

4.

Stuttgart, October 6, 1922

The philosophers as "thermometers" of the spiritual condition of their time. Spencer's *Principle of Ethics* in which it is proven that ethical distinctions cannot be based on moral intuitions, feelings, etc., but that ethics can only be a matter of what applies in practice to the particular situation in society. In contrast to this, *Intuitive Thinking as a Spiritual Path* presents the view that anything else besides the immediate moral intuitions revealed in the human soul can no longer be considered authoritative, since now for several decades the human soul has confronted "the nothingness" as regards the spirit. Nietzsche's path: philology, Schopenhauer, Wagner. Nietzsche against the Socratic method. His rejection of the ideals of his time, because he recognized they had turned into empty phrases. Nietzsche and Paul Rée, who apply the natural scientific discoveries of the time to morality. This led Nietzsche to the ideas of the super human and of the eternal recurrence of the same. Youth today seek for the living spirit, which, however, is not to be found in the intellectual sphere. The Youth Movement's tendency to use clichés, or empty phrases. The need to develop a feeling for the truth. Empty phrases, convention and routine must be overcome through truth, a direct relationship between human beings and through a spiritual element in everyday activities.

pages 37–49

5.

STUTTGART, OCTOBER 7, 1922

Formerly, moral intuitions were given to groups of people, now the individual has to achieve them. The primal revelation has dried up; passive forces can no longer bring about a real connection with the spirit. Observing, experimenting, and thinking do not require inner activity. Only in *active* thinking does thinking enter into the will; out of this arises productive moral imagination. Intellectual thinking stands in relation to living thinking like a corpse to the living human being. Therefore the actual object of knowledge is what is dead. In this way science can be carried on, but not the education of youth. The intellectualism handed down to them by the older generation is like a stake in their flesh. The moral intuitions in *Intuitive Thinking as a Spiritual Path* are the beginning of the living thinking that can once again grasp the spirit. We have to learn to carry self-active living wisdom, which worked in us before birth and in our childhood, into the died-out thinking. In this sense the words in the Bible, "lest you become as little children ..." are relevant today. The Youth Movement should have the aim that childhood, that is to say, the spirit, is carried over into the later years. As a final consequence a spiritual science arises in which anthropology becomes Anthroposophy.

pages 50–61

6.

STUTTGART, OCTOBER 8, 1922

Comprehending the basic character of our time pedagogically. A new attitude is necessary towards the younger generation, one that arises from a consciousness of the pre-earthly existence of the soul. The solution to the world's riddle is in the words "Human Being, know thou thyself." The world is the question, and the human being the answer. The necessary transformation of the old moral impulses: moral love within and mutual trust on the outside. Kantian concept of duty and ethical individualism. The joy of trust and the pain of mistrust towards others will infinitely increase in the future. Knowledge of the human being must become the basic principle of pedagogy in the future. Through moral intuitions that have been worked for, rather than God-given, all of life will once more be imbued with a religious impulse. While we meet other people with human trust, we must stand before children with trust in God. Thus the moral element will again become a religious one. The Youth Movement must have a Janus-head, the two-faced Roman god, which on the one hand looks at youth's own demands on their elders, on the other hand at the demands that coming generations will make on those who are now young. The Youth Movement cannot be only oppositional, but must creatively look ahead.

pages 62–71

7.

STUTTGART, OCTOBER 9, 1922

The fatigue of the youth. Young people no longer become tired in the right way. Science of today does not require any inner participation. Reading the writings of a mediaeval thinker requires the greatest soul effort. The split of today's seeker of knowledge into that of scientist and of human being, both strictly separated. In every child is a hidden human being who rejects what a teacher reads from a book. Where did people direct the soul forces that were not addressed? The young ones became enraged (Youth Movement), the older ones looked for a sedative in Theosophy, as it was then often practiced. The longing for something new can only be satisfied by spiritual science. The four ways to knowledge in the old Brahman schools. Today's way: trusting that what is communicated by another person can become the source of one's own soul-spiritual experience.

pages 72–83

8.

STUTTGART, OCTOBER 10, 1922

The historical development of humanity from revealed to self-generated thoughts. We only have an external history, no history of feeling, thought, or the soul. The year 333. Nominalism and Realism. The tragedy of the Middle Ages: the vanishing connection between human thoughts and the spiritual world. In recent times picking up thoughts from the outer sense world has replaced inner thought formation. Kepler as representative of two worlds. The last echoes of a feeling for the divine-spiritual nature of thinking were lost in the nineteenth century (Henle, Burdach, Hyrtl). The appearance of psychology without soul. The connection between what is microscopic and macrocosmic development became a perceptual problem for many people of depth. Professor Fortlage. Anthroposophical literature requires active thinking in which the heart also participates, not only the head. Through the activity of the will brought into thinking we recapture the divine nature of thinking.

pages 84–95

9.

STUTTGART, OCTOBER 11, 1922

The bridge connecting human beings is missing. Young people want to judge everything. This is only possible with the intellect. Life situations can only be judged with active thinking, which cannot be acquired before the eighteenth year. Formerly education did not depend on knowledge confirmed by diplomas, but on ability. The teacher earned authority by giving proof of ability. Grammar, rhetoric, dialectic, and instruction in the arts. Today all education must be imbued with an artistic element. Truth can be captured only through beauty. The human being cannot be understood intellectually. Concepts appropriate for outer nature are adequate only for the physical body. Even the lowest supersensible member, the etheric body, can be understood only out of an artistic soul experience. A genuine youth movement will not be an opposition, but a movement that is drawn towards the teachers. This can happen when, from the side of the older generation, the youth are met with truth in the form of beauty. Then, not the passive intellect, but the active will is addressed.

pages 96–106

10.

STUTTGART, OCTOBER 12, 1922

With regard to the intellect, the maturity of a person plays no part. Concepts can be discussed by anyone with anyone else. The history of the soul development of humanity and of the individual. Rhythmical progression. Examples from Goethe's life. Thousands of years ago these rhythms and sudden changes were experienced just as strongly throughout life as they now are only in childhood (change of teeth, adolescence, etc.) Older people experienced the withering of the body and the freeing of the soul (Patriarchs). People have increasingly lost consciousness of this, and it must be regained. The spiritual element that formerly sprouted forth naturally with age must now be acquired through inner effort. Advances in intellectualism will only be experienced through practice, but no longer as a deepening. Spiritual science requires soul cooperation. Pure thinking, in the sense of *Intuitive Thinking as a Spiritual Path*, is at the same time pure willing. Through pure thinking a new inner person is born who can bring an unfolding of the will out of the spirit. This activity is identical with artistic activity. The pedagogue of today needs an artistic constitution in order to develop a new relationship between teacher and student. Through this the student can once more come in a natural way to look up to the teacher.

pages 107–119

11.

STUTTGART, OCTOBER 13, 1922

In the subconscious of the human being lives the need to experience the world not only with the head, but with the whole being. The modern individual has this capacity only until the change of teeth. The infant is entirely sense organ. One cannot educate human beings with abstract scientific content; education is possible only if one approaches them in an artistic way.

The "philosophy of freedom" as a means to take hold of the human individuality. One cannot be an educator by knowing a lot, but by giving the student something as a human being. The essential thing between the change of teeth and adolescence is the soul configuration of the teacher. Praying and blessing in their causal relationship to each other. The child must get pictures capable of growth, not abstract definitions, which would be like tying them up inside an apparatus. We must develop an art of education through which people learn to live with one another once more.

pages 120–132

12.

STUTTGART, OCTOBER 14, 1922

Only in our own time do individual "I"s confront one another unveiled. In the Indian cultural epoch sense perception also revealed the spiritual. The aim of the Mysteries: in a roundabout way via the soul-spiritual to make the sense-perceptible understandable by the soul of the human being. Persian epoch: perception of the human being as a light-form. Egypto-Chaldean epoch: the human being began to see the exterior with the senses and the interior soul-spiritually. Greek epoch: distinct separation of the bodily-corporeal and the soul-spiritual. Until the Greek epoch the "I" was still perceived through sheaths. Perception of the unsheathed "I" creates fear among humanity in more recent times (examples: Francis Bacon, Shakespeare, and Jean Paul). Anthroposophical pedagogy does not want to instruct but to characterize human beings. Actually, education should not be talked *about.* We can only educate with the mobile human forces that are active in us in childhood. The real pedagogue can be neither a philistine nor a pedant.

pages 133–144

13.

STUTTGART, OCTOBER 15, 1922

The transition from revealed concepts to those worked out from outer nature. The concepts dying out within have been re-enlivened by outer nature. The thinking derived from nature is not adequate for understanding the human being. With the development of natural science, anthropology has fallen into decline. The dragon devours the soul life of the human being. The dragon can therefore have a powerful effect, since the human being no longer comprehends its being. The belief that matter is preserved in the human organism is proof of the complete misunderstanding of what the human being is. In fact, matter is being continually destroyed and newly created in the human being. The dragon must be vanquished in that we recognize that Michael also comes from outside. Every science today is a metamorphosis of the dragon. The only remedy against the dragon: to penetrate oneself through and through with the true knowledge of the spiritual being of the world. By means of a living, artistically conducted education of the youth we will prepare the vehicle for Michael to enter into our civilization. This is the real, basic impulse of every educational doctrine. The spiritual is something alive that is not like the bones, but the blood. The vessels in which this blood runs are the young people growing up. Only when the child becomes our educator, in bringing messages down from the spiritual world, will the child also be prepared to receive the messages from adults about life on the Earth. This course was meant, above all, to speak *to the hearts.*

INTRODUCTION

CHRISTOPHER BAMFORD

These lectures—the "pedagogical youth course"—hold a special place in Anthroposophical literature. Even though Rudolf Steiner was speaking in 1922, which seems a long time ago, he was in a unique way and for the first time then, as still today, addressing a new generation: *us*. The lectures thereby mark a momentary and astonishing second birth of Steiner's teaching, unencumbered by the contextual Theosophical trappings with which he began. Spontaneous, intimate, direct, and still amazingly fresh and new, this lecture course has always had an extraordinary power to speak to those who approach Anthroposophy without preconceived ideas, drawn simply by their souls' needs. It was so among the first generation of young people who turned to Anthroposophy, and it is still true today.

Historically, Steiner was addressing bright, educated, and passionate eighteen- to twenty-five-year-olds, who were seeking meaning and authenticity in a world that seemed to them desperately intent on falsity and lies. On the cusp of their adult lives, they had just witnessed and endured the apparent collapse of Western civilization in the bloodiest conflict, and then the most duplicitous peace, the world had yet seen. Wide-awake, energetic, committed to the recovery of spiritual meaning in human life, they wanted to do something about it. Further wars and greater loss of meaning and value, accelerated by the increasing dominance of technological egotism, have extended and consolidated the crisis. But the lessons, never learned, were and are the same. Their world is our world.

Unlike those who joined Steiner in 1900, when he started teaching, the new generation came to Anthroposophy innocently, out of their hearts' needs, without any connection either to traditional esotericism or to the remarkable spiritual happenings of the last third of the nineteenth century. They knew little if anything about Spiritualism, Theosophy, Masonry, Ritual Magic, or any of the other movements—including the Temperance Society—from which the first Anthroposophists were drawn. The older generation of Anthroposophists seemed to them entirely from another world, another culture, with which they could find little shared ground—and the feeling was mutual.

They did not think of themselves primarily as aspirant esotericists. They were spiritually-open activists, true philosophers, who sought to become spiritual, social, scientific, and philosophical *pioneers*. They wanted to change the world and change themselves. They saw that if it were allowed to continue unchecked, "life as usual" would result only in the progressive dehumanization of humanity, the gradual destruction of the earth, and the alienation of the gods and consequent loss of any and all transcendent purpose to life. They understood that a radical change in human "being" was necessary—as we do still today.

For these reasons, then, we may say that Rudolf Steiner is truly addressing us as spiritually independent free individuals interested in and drawn to what he has to say not so much for its esoteric "information" (interesting and vital as it may be) as for the humanity and divine-spiritual-cosmic wholeness of his worldview and the gift of the spiritual ferment or praxis—the new heart thinking—by which humanity can be empowered to change itself and begin the process of healing the world.

Naturally, Steiner welcomed the opportunity to speak to such a group. He had been waiting for this moment, for these young people, all his life. Whatever and whoever else he was, Steiner himself had always possessed a radical, even revolutionary side. Like those who came to him, he had no patience for conventional values and conventional thinking. Conventionality—synonymous with sleep—was one of the few things that irritated him. He saw conventionality as a symptom of a potentially fatal disease, one carried preeminently by the bourgeoisie, whose unthinking espousal of egotism, utility, and comfort as primary virtues dominated not only social and cultural life but also and above all academic, artistic, scientific, and even religious life.

Steiner had always sought to lay the ground for a *global transformation* that would overcome all egotistic divides: between subject and object, self and other, individual and community, spirit and matter, nature and cosmos, and cosmos and divinity. As *The Philosophy of Freedom*† (1894) makes very clear, he never separated the necessary epistemological transformation in *how we know* (monism or non-dualism) from either the ethical transformation of *how we act* (ethical individualism) or its social consequences in *how we live together* (basically, a kind of anarchism). It does not take much to read Steiner's non-dualist, individualist, quasi-anarchist philosophy between the lines of his biography. One finds his radical affinities delineated quite explicitly in his *Autobiography* as he unfolds his sympathies: with Nietzsche's "transvaluation of all values;" Max Stirner's radical individualism, as well as the "individualistic anarchism" of his friend and fellow Stirnerian J. H. Mackay; and, finally, his commitment to teaching at the leftist Workers' College.

When the spiritual world graciously offered him the opportunity to work through Theosophy, Steiner had to lay aside this social-cultural side of his mission. Certainly, the vast and initiatory field of opportunity opened up by Theosophy (and the other esoteric movements that flowed into it) more than compensated for what he had to give up in terms of radical social activism. Yet we can be sure that when young people were drawn to Anthroposophy out of the same radical, activist mood of soul which more than forty years before had led him to it, he was enormously heartened, as is evident in his total commitment to working with them.

* * *

What is remarkable is that from Steiner's beginning to teach in 1900, it took about twenty years for a new generation of young people to be drawn to him. Put another way, those who came to him when they did (1918–1922) were born at about the time when he began to teach. This was not a coincidence. For Steiner, 1900 marked a supremely important moment in human evolution. Those born after that date would be different from those born before it. To be able to grasp his teaching in the truly new way he intended it to be understood, a person would have to have grown to maturity in the post–Kali Yuga period. Therefore, when those whose destiny it was to do so stood before him, he understood with perfect clarity that here were people truly prepared to receive his teaching. But there is more to it than that.

* * *

Steiner was born in 1861. He was thus forty when, in 1901, he stepped onto the world stage as a spiritual teacher within the world of the Theosophical Society, which had been founded a quarter of a century earlier by Madame Blavatsky (1831-1891). Steiner, in other words, grew out of the nineteenth century, as did all those "homeless souls" who initially followed him. Hence, though younger people were continuously drawn into the orbit of Theosophy/Anthroposophy during the period leading up to World War I, it was not really until the epochal moment following the end of the war in 1918 that a truly *new* generation—that is, a generation born after 1900—passionately and in large numbers began to seek in Anthroposophy (and even in a spontaneous, frank, and direct way from Steiner himself) what their hearts and souls felt that the times were calling for. Although all this may still seem as if it took place a long time ago, we in the twenty-first century share a common destiny with that generation. When Steiner speaks to them, he is also speaking to us, as indeed he well knew. For that generation was the beginning of a new movement on the spiral of human evolution.

An event of signal importance in human cultural evolution—in the evolution of human consciousness generally—occurred around the turn of the twentieth century. In the language of Indian tradition, the Kali Yuga, the Dark Age or "Age of Iron," came to a close, giving way, in principle at least, to the possibility of the beginning of a return, on a higher turn of the evolutionary spiral, to a new Age of Light. Referring to the same cosmic-earthly-human phenomenon, Steiner also often spoke of the spiritual fact that as the twentieth century progressed into the twenty-first, humanity would begin increasingly to cross the threshold into the spiritual world. That is, in contrast to the previous millennia—during which humanity had been progressively cut off from spiritual reality to the point that few people had any experience of it and most lived lives wholly immured to it, so that for them it had no existence at all—with the turn of the twentieth century, humanity would find itself more and more living out of and connected to the spiritual world. The speed of generational change, culminating in the now apparently widespread belief that wholly new kinds of children are being born today—"indigo" or "star" children—would seem to attest to this reality.

Coincident with these changes, and integral to our ability to deal with them, is a second cosmic-spiritual phenomenon also much referred to by Steiner and central both to the particular lectures printed here and to Anthroposophy in general: namely, the accession to the regency of evolving human consciousness by the archangel Michael in November 1879. The tradition of the archangelic "regents of the age" has been an accepted part of the Western, Rosicrucian esoteric teaching since at least 1515, when Johannes Trithemius published his small *Treatise on the Seven Secondary Causes*. In this book of "mystical chronology," Trithemius, aligning the seven archangels or spirits with the planets, describes how each spirit, in turn, sequentially rules the universe for a period of 354 years and 4 months, according to the following rhythm: 1: Oriphiel (Saturn), 2: Anael (Venus), 3: Zachariel (Jupiter), 4: Raphael (Mercury), 5: Samael (Mars), 6: Gabriel (Moon), and 7: Michael (Sun). Tracing the regencies from creation into what is for him the future, Trithemius concludes his *Treatise*:

> Gabriel, Angel of the Moon, will take up the direction of the world again on June 4 of the year of creation ... the year 1525 of the Christian Era. Gabriel will then govern the world for 354 years and 4 months until the year ... of the Lord 1879, the eighth month.

While differing slightly in his calculations and without going back to the beginning of creation, Steiner confirmed and taught out of his own experience that the age we live in is the Michael age. More than that, he placed his own striving and the deepest meaning of the teaching and practice of Anthroposophy under the sign and aegis of this same archangel Michael, who is "the messenger of Christ" and who stands for "the inflow of spiritual life into the sense world." The archangel Michael, now our "Time Spirit," is the spirit of inner strength. He makes it possible for human beings to go beyond the duality of an abstract spirituality on the one hand and a literalized material world on the other in order to see *matter penetrated everywhere by spirit*: "the flesh becoming Word and learning to dwell in the Kingdom of the Word."

Rudolf Steiner speaks of this process in many ways—above all, perhaps, as "Michaelic thinking," that is, the thinking of the enchristened heart that allows us to think (cognize) the invisible in the visible so that we realize that we, too, are invisible, supersensible beings. He also stresses that it is Michael's task and nature to reveal nothing to us unless we bring to him something of our own earthly spiritual work. In this sense, Michael is a mediator: bringing knowledge of the spirit in return for our work, he ensures that we can properly (consciously) appropriate what we are given, rather than opening ourselves to the risk of being overcome by it. Thus we are in a new age in which, historically, much is at stake.

* * *

From this point of view, the nineteenth century, especially the second half, when materialism reached its apogee, marks a kind of endpoint of nothingness in the human soul that continues to echo into the present. Beginning in the 1870s (let us say with Nietzsche), powerful and devastating symptoms of what amounts to a kind of bankruptcy or sleep—an abdication of human responsibility, in which the authentic human self-image is submerged, as it were, in a dark flood of undigested materialism—were already clear and self-evident to those who were still awake. Among the latter, considering only the German-speaking world, thinkers like Martin Heidegger, Franz Rosenzweig, Martin Buber, and Walter Benjamin come to mind. All saw the same signs and spoke of them in similar ways to Steiner who, likewise awake to these signs, speaks of three symptoms of human sleep.

First, there is what he calls the reign of the "empty phrase," banality, the cliché—manifesting in the social domain as meaningless chatter and gossip, and among so-called intellectuals in pseudo-scientific jargon, or language reduced to pure nominalism or information. Rigorous thinking chiseled into logical, elegant speech becomes increasingly rare. Second, there is a new emptiness in human relationships. Human beings no longer meet each other. One soul never truly encounters another soul. They pass each other by, like ships in the night, interested only in themselves and their own "point of view." Few people show any interest in each other, and fewer still are interested in the other for the other's sake. It is an age of terrifying egotism. Third, no one truly thinks anymore. Thinking has become cold and automatic, a pale shadow, without passion or will, disconnected from the heart. Steiner calls this residue of the nineteenth century "a spiritual ice age."

* * *

Against this "ice age," the new souls incarnating would react. As they did so, they would find that the path was being prepared for them in different ways. On October 17, 1901, for instance, Steiner began the series of lectures at the Theosophical Library that would become his turning-point work, *Christianity as Mystical Fact*. Synchronously, however, as these lectures were unfolding, on November 4, in the back room of a pub in another suburb of Berlin, the German Youth Movement, soon to become the famous *Wandervogel*, was born. Twenty years later, when young people, many of whom were affiliated with it, began to turn to Anthroposophy, Steiner would praise it as an "international movement of elemental forces born from the heights."

The Youth Movement arose first as a reaction against what members saw as a deadly mix of stifling materialism, which made industrial capitalism the only value, coupled and conflated with the suffocating aridity of Prussian formality, which valued loyalty and service to Kaiser and the Reich above individual freedom and the pursuit of happiness and self-fulfillment. As a protest against the general meaninglessness of life and human relations, the movement's chosen form, deeply colored by Romanticism and a Pre-Raphaelite-like medievalism, was an idealistic reversion to "simpler" values.

At first, the Youth Movement was mostly limited to teenage boys, but gradually it extended its range to younger adults and even sympathetic older people. Comprised of many different, separate initiatives, it slowly created its own shared culture for the "reformation of life" (*Lebensreform*): wandering or rambling in nature, hiking in groups, camping, learning basic survival skills, living and eating healthily, exercising, singing folk songs, dancing, and reciting together. Hence, its members became known as *Wandervogel*, or Wandering Birds, after the Wandering Scholars of the Middle Ages.

In October 1913, on the Hohe Meissner, a mountain to the south of Cassel sacred to the goddess Holle—Frau Holle of the fairy tale—all these groups came together, uniting for cultural transformation as visionary utopians and proto-hippies. They talked of Thomas Carlyle and Johann Gottlieb Fichte and quoted Johann von Goethe and Novalis, and they saw a new age of freedom dawning. The euphoria, however, would not last long. Internal squabbles led to inevitable politicization; long-brewing disputes soon led to separation of left- and right-wing elements. Then came World War I. In the chaos and uncertainty that followed, the political groupings only hardened further. At the same time, a new mystical streak emerged. There was a rediscovery both of Eastern wisdom and of the German mystics. It was a time of crisis (danger and opportunity), of great searching. For a brief moment before the inevitable die was cast, everything was possible.

Realizing this, Rudolf Steiner presciently and prophetically launched his movement for a Threefold Social Order. Europe was still at war, but it was already clear that the war would end and that the task of the peace would be to attempt to rebuild society on a new footing. In May 1917, in response to a call from Otto von Lerchenfeld, a German diplomat in Berlin, Steiner prepared two memoranda, which called for a radical rethinking of social life on the basis of which a true and lasting peace might be built.

The memoranda claimed that the time of the unitary, centralized, national political state—the dead weight of which had led to the conflict—was past. True peace and justice would require a radical threefold ordering of society. *Culturally*, it was imperative that individual, spiritual freedom not only be protected but also supported, encouraged, and enhanced in all possible ways. Such freedom, after all, was the source of all future good in the form of new ideas, as these ideas come to expression through art, science, philosophy, and other cultural pursuits. This cultural sphere of soul-spiritual freedom, though it was central, was but one sphere making up the whole social fabric. A second sphere was that of *economic life*, namely, the production, distribution, and consumption—the circulation—of goods and services. Freedom was clearly also necessary in this arena—not explicitly spiritual freedom but *freedom in community*, that is, association or "brotherhood." Finally, both the cultural and the economic spheres rested on a third sphere of political freedom, the freedom assured by *equality* in human rights under the law. In this way, Steiner transformed the celebrated motto of the French Revolution—*Liberté*, *Egalité*, *Fraternité*—into a clarion call for a threefold restructuring of society.

Although officially the memoranda came to nothing, as the war was ending Steiner took his message to the people. Cultural and spiritual renewal was the order of the day. The Association for the Threefold Social Organism was formed. Books and lectures were published. Steiner traveled indefatigably, giving public lectures to large numbers of people. All this effort fell on fertile soil. Eighty thousand copies of *Toward Social Renewal* were sold in the first year! But this was not all.

Growing out of the Threefold Social Movement, the first Waldorf school was born. Among the first to heed the call for social renewal had been Emil Molt, owner and director of the Waldorf Astoria cigarette factory in Stuttgart. In April 1919, Steiner talked to the factory workers about the threefold social order. Following his talk, Molt asked Steiner whether he would take on the establishment and leadership of a school for the workers' children: in September, the first Waldorf school opened its doors.

All this public, socially-oriented activity had to have radical consequences for Anthroposophy and the Anthroposophical Society. Among them, perhaps the most significant was the influx of educated, seeking, young people who wished above all to make a difference with their lives. In this way a kind of third, spiritual stream—beyond left and right—emerged where the *Wandervogel* had been; these were the young people who were drawn to Anthroposophy as a true *Lebensreform*. They wanted to develop spiritually as well as intellectually. They yearned to overcome the separation between everyday life and the disciplines of science, art, history, psychology, religion, and so on. They wanted spiritual life, professional life, and personal life to be a continuum, lived from the same source. On this basis, they wished to change the world. They envisioned Anthroposophy as a way of life—self- and world-transformation in one.

Suddenly, in the universities and colleges in Germany, Switzerland, and Austria, Anthroposophical student groups came into being. In the summer of 1920 the Union for Anthroposophical College Work was founded. "College" courses began to be held in the Goetheanum. All this youthful "academic" activity was not necessarily well received by the older members, who felt the foundations of their world and their understanding of Anthroposophy shaken. "New thinking" for them had ossified into mere contents. Steiner, for his part, was delighted with the epistemological clarity of the younger generation. They were friends indeed.

During the first members' meeting of the Anthroposophical Society after World War I—held on September 4, 1921, in Stuttgart—following the vote by a student from Tübingen University, Steiner exclaimed:

> Here a representative of the Youth Movement has spoken! Here sit a whole number of student representatives! My dear friends: That members of such a movement or organization have come to our Anthroposophical Society is something that we must look on as *epoch-making* in the history of our Anthroposophical Movement. We must do everything that may rightly be expected from the Anthroposophical Society."

Many of the young who were drawn to Anthroposophy were still strongly linked to the earlier *Wandervogel* movement and prized their freedom and independence: they wanted to pursue the "free spiritual life" offered by Anthroposophy in their own way. They were not satisfied—or happy—with the mood, tenor, and spirit of the Anthroposophical Society as they found it and very early sought to organize their own society. In March 1920 they had circulated a "Call for the Foundation of a Youth Branch." In April of that same year, one of their members, Otto Palmer, made their case at the Goetheanum. He began quite bluntly:

> If you want to understand this movement rightly, you must see it above all as a protest that has come alive among the youth against the old life of the branches.... In fact, something in the youth feels the need not to see Anthroposophy as a mere Sunday afternoon decoration. Rather, it wants to lead what we are given in Anthroposophy into life and translate it into practice.

He concluded, directly addressing the concerns of the older members:

> [The Youth Movement and its call for its own branch] really has to do with making the attempt to realize the freedom of spiritual life insofar as this can be done within such a limited framework. For this it is worth overcoming a certain fear that still rules in this regard that a free spiritual life of this kind will awaken counter-forces, which could and would make for difficulties. One can undertake such a task only if one believes that one has something living in oneself from which the powers can come that are in a position to overcome the counter-forces.

This was just the beginning. In April, Ehrenfried Pfeiffer wrote:

> The work in the Youth branch should proceed above all so that the youth can become the bearers of Anthroposophically-oriented spiritual science.... If we can make our action follow our will, then the struggle against the old thinking can be taken up everywhere. If the work of the Youth branch occurs in this way, then its outer form will come about by itself.

For the next two years (1920-1922), the struggle to establish a true working forum for the younger generation continued against rising and increasingly strident opposition from the older generation. By 1922 a turning point in orientation seemed to be called for. The fate and future of Anthroposophy appeared to hang in the balance. In retrospect, it is as if the spiritual world was guiding Rudolf Steiner in fateful anticipation of the traumatic conflagration—the burning of the Goetheanum over New Year 1922-1923—into what Marie Steiner called the "Year of

Destiny" (1923), which would conclude with the refounding of the Anthroposophical Society over the Holy Nights at the year's end.

As if in preparation for the great event, the year 1922 began with intense public activity. Rudolf Steiner undertook two major lecture tours, organized by a leading concert agency, which took him through twelve German cities. His theme in all but one was "the Being of Anthroposophy." He reported on February 11:

> In all these cities you could see that at this very moment a deep need was present in the wider circles of humanity to hear some news of the spiritual world....
>
> Let me remark, however, just this kind of lecture tour shows us how—though we have now worked intensely for two decades—we actually still stand at the beginning of our movement. Traveling from city to city, always talking on the same subject, and doing so out of the spiritual world, one notices how even though the theme is always the same, one actually must wrestle in each individual lecture to find the right words that make speech necessary in the moment. At least from my point of view, I cannot say that it was easier to give the same lecture over and over again. On the contrary, each time I had to give the lecture it became not easier but instead more difficult to give it the next time.

It was also exhausting. Besides the tours, Steiner gave countless other lectures, including for the first time since the war, lectures to large audiences in England and Holland. In fact, he gave more than seventy public lectures during this year. It was the last time he would do anything comparable. The following year he gave only eleven; and in 1924 only two. In other words, after 1922, he turned inward to focus on the ailing Anthroposophical Society and the Movement in itself. The reason was not the rising chaos in Germany, but much more that his intentions were not being actively taken up by the society, which, he said, was "asleep." Institutions were failing; difficulties were everywhere. Even the Goetheanum was having financial problems. At the same time, there was also much that was positive. The Whitsun East-West Congress in Vienna was a great success. The Christian Community was founded, after a year of preparation. Above all, there were the young people. One has the feeling that the turn inward, which would find its fulfillment in the Christmas Conference and the Foundation Stone Meditation, had its earthly beginning and inspiration in the Youth Movement, epitomized by the lectures collected here.

* * *

In March 1921, in a question-and-answer session after a course in Stuttgart, Steiner made clear why he expected so much from these young people. Asked about the spiritual meaning of the Youth Movement, he said in part:

> If we approach the Youth Movement with the historical knowledge of spiritual science, we recognize its connection to the reversal that took place within individuals and in human history at the end of the nineteenth century. We can come to this conclusion by observing the qualities of statements made by people who were adolescents or children at that time. Having observed such statements closely, I have come to realize that the Youth Movement is indeed related to the great reversal at the end of the nineteenth century. It is one of the symptoms of the dawning of a new era....
>
> This universally human impulse appears to be alive in the hearts of those who turned to the Youth Movement. Their hearts are illumined by this tremendously important turning point at the end of the nineteenth century. It is not always especially important to get into discussion on such matters, but it is important to recognize the significant impulses at work and to acknowledge that those who joined the Youth Movement sensed the presence of these impulses.

Later, in the same question-and-answer session, which was equally revealing, he spoke to them of Anthroposophy:

> Anthroposophy is not simply a matter of assuming a worldview. Being an Anthroposophist involves participating with your whole being....

> There are many different routes to Anthroposophy. We must move beyond collisions with individual Anthroposophists to attempting to experience Anthroposophy as such. At present, Anthroposophy is actually the only non-dogmatic worldview, the only one that is not set on very specific ways of doing things and makes an effort to take a variety of perspectives. Anthroposophy's main concern is life, not the forms things assume....
>
> I see Anthroposophy as something living, something capable of transforming individuals into beings different from what they were before. Through the substance of Anthroposophy, we become free. After a brief period of development, we become really free human beings. A question that has passed through life cannot be resolved by thinking about it. If tackled from the perspective of freedom, however, it will be solved through real life. We must not be concerned about possible undesirable social consequences. Suppose we want to understand how conception results in the birth of a male or a female being. If this ever became a matter of rational control, there would surely be fewer men than women on Earth. Despite the fact that this process manifests as the sum of many individual incidents, the inner laws governing it ensure social balance.... Our life cannot be transformed all at once, and change certainly cannot be programmed. But we can prepare for change by developing an independent attitude as a basis. This problem must be solved on an individual basis....
>
> In the future, any task an individual undertakes will be a common task, and everyone will have to make common tasks their own. It will not work any other way. But we can only accomplish this through association, not through organization.

In these remarks, the future path of Anthroposophy, as Steiner saw it, is clear. Over the next two years, his vision would deepen and gain true esoteric foundations. To uncover these foundations, Steiner would work, as always, out of a twofold sense of responsibility to the Earth and to the Spirit—two calls, which may perhaps be distinguished but cannot be divided. That is to say, Steiner strove always to be open and receptive to the gifts and calls of the spiritual world, while at the same time at all times being receptive, attentive, and true to the gifts and calls of the earthly world—which endlessly brought him questions and true human soul needs. Chief among the latter were the soul needs and questions presented to him by those young people born after the end of the Kali Yuga and called to be members of the Michael's school with whom he continued to work patiently and expectantly.

* * *

A turning point came following the East-West Congress (June 1922), when a group of young people (Ernst Lehrs, Fritz Kubler, and René Maikowski) came to Dornach to speak to Rudolf Steiner. It was agreed at that time to hold a large meeting in October. Ernst Lehrs wrote to Steiner to report on his travels among the youth in preparation for the meeting. To his great joy, he found everywhere a "new feature," coming from a shared impulse. He writes: "The insight has arisen universally and is confirmed in our circles that any attempt to work together in the consciousness soul epoch must become a 'working alongside one another'." Such working alongside one another would lead to a conscious brotherhood-sisterhood. In this sense, scientists, artists, and teachers must work together to build community. Learning and teaching, education and self-education, must become one in the highest sense. In Berlin a group had been studying *Mystics after Modernism*. They had been struck by the chapter on the Friend of God from the Highlands and his circle of twelve. Just such a circle, Lehrs stressed, represented the deepest desire of the young. For them, Rudolf Steiner was another such Friend of God.

* * *

In the beginning of October, about eighty young people between the ages of eighteen and twenty-five gathered in the Anthroposophical Society building in Stuttgart to meet with Steiner. There were a few older people. Pointedly, older members were generally not invited, which naturally increased their pain and alienation. Asked about this, Steiner replied that he did not know what the young people wanted. A few had come to see him; they had talked about everything imaginable. He had agreed to meet with them for a lecture course. What it was to be about, he had no idea.

Again, older members were shocked. How could he agree to do such a thing? Steiner explained that the young people thought a rigid program was somewhat antiquated, and he completely agreed with them! They wanted the program to emerge from the work that they would do together. Steiner asked for questions to orient his first lecture. Afterward, out of discussions and intimate conversations, the second lecture would develop, and so on. In this way, as the young people wanted, the course would arise in a living way without a fixed program—the themes that Steiner would address would be those in everyone's heart and mind.

Early on, during the course of the lectures, it had become clear that two groups, or two kinds of needs, were present in the gathering. One was primarily concerned with the question of building a true esoteric community; the other was uninterested in that and wanted Steiner to address purely and exclusively pedagogical questions. Both themes then run through the lectures published here: "Becoming the Archangel Michael's Companions" speaks to the first theme and the "Pedagogical Youth Course" to the second. In a real sense, of course, the two are one. To become a true teacher is to become one of Michael's companions; to become a companion of Michael is to be a true teacher in the widest and most healing sense.

Much came from the two groups: on the one hand, passionately-committed and spiritually-seeking teachers for the growing Waldorf movement and, on the other, growing out of long, intimate discussions with Steiner, an esoteric "Youth Circle" made up initially of twelve members. Their last discussion was on October 12. On October 16, the day after the meeting closed, Rudolf Steiner formulated a vow for the circle, and it was officially founded. Also flowing from this meeting and the entire youth movement was the foundation in March 1923 of a "Free Anthroposophical Society," primarily for young people, within the General Society.

* * *

The lecture hall in Stuttgart had a stage with steps leading up to it at both ends and a balustrade that could be lowered for Eurythmy performances. To the left was a curved indentation behind which the speaker usually spoke. Steiner, however, did not do so. He began by standing in the middle, behind the balustrade. Soon he started to walk back and forth animatedly. His gestures, too, became increasingly lively, his hands moving continuously to illustrate what he said in dynamic, intensely communicative ways.

Each lecture began slowly, peacefully laying thought upon thought to rise at the end to a thrilling urgency that spoke directly to his audience, bringing "soul clarity" to what lived in the depths of their souls—demonstrating that what they sought was truly there within them, "in the common center of true adulthood." In the deepest part of human nature, something was coming to birth. Out of the darkness and nihilism into which the nineteenth century had plunged humanity, human beings had now to reach out, from their own willing, feeling, and thinking, and make a new, free, individual connection with the spiritual world.

The key—the demand of the age—was to make one's cognitive capacities come alive. To the extent that our thinking, feeling, and willing is *living* and not brain-based and body-based (dead, automatic, and asleep), the spiritual world can enter into relationship with us, for *spirit is life*. It is also always *individual* in the process of cognition, which is the process of encountering an "other," including another human being:

> Real experience of the spiritual, wherever we meet it, always becomes individual.... In going through life and meeting individuals, we must always have an open heart, an open mind for the individual. We should be able to unfold a completely new human feeling for every individual we meet. We do justice to a human being only when we see in the person an entirely new personality. If we come with a general idea in our heads, saying that a human being should be like this or that, then we are being unjust to the individual. With every definition of a human being we really put up a screen to make the human being invisible. (Lecture 4)

Another way of saying this is that we need a feeling for the truth. "Truth is the alpha and omega of what we need today." We need truth and honesty in every aspect of our being—in our thinking; in our language (in how we speak and relate to one another); and in our actions.

> In our time the soul must strive beyond empty phrase, convention, and routine; beyond the empty phrase to a grasp of truth; beyond convention to a direct, elementary warmhearted relationship between one human being and another; beyond routine to the state in which the spirit lives in every single action, so that we no longer act automatically but that the spirit lives in the most ordinary, everyday actions. We must come to spirituality in action, to the immediate experience of human beings in their relations to one another and to an honest, upright experience of truth. (Lecture 4)

This is the meaning of the *Philosophy of Freedom*. Another way of putting it is this: "Except ye become as little children, ye cannot enter the Kingdom of Heaven."

> For it is always the Kingdom of Heaven that one is seeking. But if one does not become like the child before puberty, one cannot enter the Kingdom of Heaven. Childlikeness, youthfulness, must be brought into dead thinking. Thereby it becomes alive; it comes once more to intuitions. Thus we learn to speak out of the primal wisdom of the child....
>
> In this sense we must return to childhood and learn a new language. The language we learn in the first years of childhood gradually becomes dead, because it is permeated by dead intellectual concepts. We must quicken it to new life. We must find something that strikes into what we are thinking, just as when we learned to speak, an impulse arose in us out of the unconscious.... We must learn to open our mouths by letting our lips be moved by the spirit. Then we shall become children again, that is to say, we shall carry childhood on into our later years. And that is what we

> must do. If a youth movement wants to have truth and not only phraseology, then such a movement is imbued of necessity with the longing for the human mouth to be opened by the spirit, a longing for the quickening of human speech by the spirit, which wells forth from the individual. As a first step, individual moral intuitions must be brought out of the human individuality.... as a result, the true Science of the Spirit, which makes all anthropology into Anthroposophy, is born. (Lecture 5)

It is difficult to give a sense of the vitality and intimacy of these lectures. Bearing in mind his double mission—to address the inner work necessary for the formation of an esoteric circle and the pressing task of the new art of teaching or pedagogy exemplified by the growing Waldorf school movement—Rudolf Steiner moves continuously and seamlessly between its two poles, now focusing on one and now on the other. In the last lecture, the two poles become one in the "conquering of the dragon":

> Previous civilizations understood the kingdoms of nature as arising out of humanity; modern civilization grasps humanity as arising out of nature, as the highest animal. It does not grasp to what extent animals are imperfect humans. If we fill our soul with what our thinking has become through nature, there appears in the picture of the human-devouring dragon that which is the most potent factor in modern civilization. Humanity feels itself confronting a being who is devouring it. (Lecture 13)

This being, the dragon, has now become objective. It meets us from outside in every aspect of our lives and devours us as beings of soul. Every science has become a metamorphosis of the dragon, so that the dragon everywhere rears up to meet us, not only in technology and scientific thinking but also in the social organism and in our soul lives. All human life today proceeds from this dragon, which can be overcome only in freedom and by becoming aware of how Michael, whose age we live in, also comes to us from outside. Therefore, in Lecture 13, Steiner issues a call to arms:

> We must acquire the vision of Michael ... who shows us that, by uniting ourselves with the spiritual world, we can bring life again into a dead world through our moral impulses.

Then, with utmost seriousness, Rudolf Steiner places the radiant, powerful image of Michael before us. He stresses how Michael depends on us to overcome the dragon. With the forces we develop inwardly and in freedom, we—together with Michael—will overcome the dragon. But it is we who must build the chariot, the vehicle for Michael. *We must become Michael's companions.* Only then shall we participate in what can lead to progress and bring peace.

Further Reading:

Lacquer, Walter Z. *Young Germany: A History of the German Youth Movement.* New York: Basic Books, 1962.

Steiner, Rudolf. *Der Erkenntnis-Aufgabe der Jugend* ["The cognitive task of youth: addresses, question and answer sessions, articles, and reports from 1920-1924, to supplement the "Pedagogic Youth Course of 1922"] Forthcoming as: *Youth and the Etheric Heart* (CW 217a). Great Barrington: SteinerBooks, 2007.

Preface

The younger generation is always faced with the dilemma of being heir to the old while about to become a guide for the new. Never did this dilemma seem greater than after the turn of this century when Rudolf Steiner spoke; for us today it looms even larger, with no end of its precipitate growth in sight. Uncountable remedies have been offered, and self-appointed pundits of many nations, creeds and convictions continue to peddle their wares. Instant diagnosis is followed by suggestions of all kinds of therapies—from more money to nihilistic revolutions. To be "deeply involved" is the demand of the day, but this is naturally followed by the question as to how to be so without losing one's identity. If a fresh view can be maintained, despite the "systems" that tend to make us into interchangeable items within a catalogued society, the problem of providing the incentive for this fresh view is somewhat like that faced by the inexperienced gardener who lifts each sprouting plant from its seedbed to check on its root development. The very manner of growth—first a stillness, then a sprouting, a sudden spurt of leafing followed by a pause before further growth—a way necessary for all living things in order to be alive and to be themselves, is even less within our understanding today than at the time these lectures were given.

Therefore these lectures are not less applicable today. Readers, provided they can be *guided* by the circumspect sequence of the thoughts and images contained therein, will be stirred as well as strangely quieted. Here we are *led*, not thrust forward or backward; here we are guided, not badgered, threatened or left directionless. Yet the direction we receive is not merely a signpost to all too obvious and all too fallible remedies. Rather, we are enabled to begin assembling convictions from within until the conflux of such inner preparedness can meet with the final image of "the chariot of Michael."

To achieve the image of this chariot, however, demands a new education. By its nature it signifies not so much the content and circumference of material as the way in which it becomes, as conveyance, a transmitter of substance. We may time and again consult one single paragraph, to know what was meant then and is still implied for us today:

> The great transition to this newer age consists in human meeting human free of sheaths—according to each person's disposition, to what the soul demands; but the capacities for this untrammeled encounter have not yet been acquired. Above all we have not yet acquired the possibility for a relation between ego and ego. But this must be prepared for by education. That is why the question of education is of such burning importance.

As can readily be felt throughout, this cycle of lectures was given to a group of young people in whom an active current—sometimes even causing divisions—was to be carried into the inner meaning of education. Destiny spoke throughout their sometimes-heated discussions, awakening one and beclouding another. The call to carry a new education out into this world—an education for life, for the spirit in humankind and in the universe—had begun to sound. It was the year of challenge, 1922, and Rudolf Steiner responded to it, traveling and lecturing untiringly—from the East-West Congress in Vienna to his visits to England. At Stuttgart, where these particular lectures were given, the young listeners had to develop a new ear to perceive something of a new dawn of the spirit, even while Rudolf Steiner was speaking to them—surveying, explaining, developing and guiding them toward an understanding of themselves in their present world-situation. In this new dawn some of those listeners, like the readers of these lectures today, could understand the necessity for self-education as the preliminary to all other education. And from their desire to become educators, to be able to dispense true nourishment, they began to recognize that in order to grow such food demands that the plough first be turned inward and seeds of spirit sown. Eventually—in good time and according to the rhythms of growth, with the power of the sun and the moon and the stars—a harvest may mature, which will yield bread, not stones, in people's relationship to each other.

This cycle of lectures to the younger generation speaks of a pathway to a Michaelic harvest for ears which have the good will to hear. If they only now appear in English—forty-five years after the sowing—we should neither be disheartened by the slowness of growth nor complacent about the fruits already gathered. Much rather, when we have read, listened and heard, and have become better aware of the pathway, may we continue toward that universal harvest with greater singleness of purpose, without dismay and, however lonely, with a certainty of spirit-companionship transcending all generations.

Carlo Pietzner
Easter 1967

BECOMING THE ARCHANGEL MICHAEL'S COMPANIONS

Rudolf Steiner

1

STUTTGART, OCTOBER 3, 1922

FIRST of all want to say a few words of greeting this evening to express the feelings which your gathering has aroused in me. Your speaker described in a most sympathetic way the impulses that have brought you together here. Much of what I shall have to say in the coming days will inevitably be a kind of interpretation of what is more or less strongly present within you in the form of inner experiences that you want to bring to real soul clarity. I stress *soul* clarity in contrast to a merely conceptual understanding.

You have been brought together by what lives in the depths of your souls. It must be sought there. Forces have taken hold of these soul depths which, in the specific way they are working now, are quite recent. These forces—in the way they are working in you—are scarcely older than this century. They are forces which already today reveal themselves very clearly to anyone who can see them, but in the near future they will become ever more apparent. In the next few days we shall describe these forces in their most intimate nature, as well as the opposite tendencies that preceded them and had become "out-of-date" by the last third of the nineteenth century. But today, I shall speak about these forces in their more outer aspect.

I think you feel you can no longer find yourselves in accord with what the older generation has to say to the world today. You see, as early as the 1870s, 1880s, and 1890s, people were pointing out, both in art and in philosophy, the deep gulf between the older and younger generations. But all that was said then by poets and others about this gulf, this abyss, is pale in comparison with what has to be considered today. Today, the younger and the older generations speak entirely different languages of the soul. This is so to a far greater extent than is realized. It attaches no blame to the older generation as regards the younger. To speak of blame would be to use a form of thought belonging to the older generation—one of their philistine forms of thought. We shall not speak of blame, neither shall we accuse. But we shall consider how fundamentally souls have changed over the last two to three decades, precisely in Western development. In our present time, many things clash.

A little while ago I gave a series of lectures in England, at Oxford. Oxford, with its university education, occupies a unique position in the cultural life of the West. One feels in Oxford—a town very closely connected with spiritual evolution in the West—that a relic of the Middle Ages is surviving on into the present time. It is by no means an unpleasing relic. Quite the contrary, in many respects it is worthy of admiration. We were taken around by a friend who is a graduate of Oxford University, and it is the custom there that a graduate always wears a cap and gown. After we had gone around with him, I met him again in the street. The next morning I could not help describing to the English audience the impression I had when this friend appeared in cap and gown. It seemed to me thoroughly symptomatic. This, together with other experiences, induced me to form a picture and to say why a new social structure, reaching to the depths of modern spiritual life, is necessary. When this friend met me in the street, I said to myself that if I had to write a letter now, under the immediate impression of this meeting, I would not know what date to put on the letter. I would be tempted to date it about the twelfth or thirteenth century to remain in the style in which such a thing was possible.

Something that is not of the present has been preserved there. We find nothing like it in Central Europe. But what we find in the influential cultural life in Central Europe, in influential centers of culture, is nevertheless an evolutionary product of what I have just described.

Here, in Central Europe, the gown has practically been discarded, except on festive occasions, when directors and other officials are expected to wear it, often to their great annoyance.

Our friend, who was also a barrister, said to me: "If I were taking you round the Law Courts in London, I would, as a barrister, have to wear a wig, not a cap." There you see another survival of something that has become out-of-date, and yet was still alive in the last century. So there again we have the Middle Ages in the present. In Central Europe people have outgrown a custom that belonged to the former generation and has become old. First, they discarded the costume; then, with a sudden jump, they adopted a different way of thinking, which headed straight into materialism. These contrasts between Western and Central Europe are extraordinarily great. There is a very symptomatic phenomenon in this that I prefer to describe through facts rather than by abstract words.

In Central Europe we have forgotten Goethe† and accepted Darwin, although Goethe grasped the roots of the knowledge that Darwin only indicates superficially. Many similar things might be cited. Perhaps you will say that Goethe has not been forgotten, because there exists a Goethe Society, for example. I do not believe you will say that, so I will not pursue it further. Goethe himself and what he brought to light—the Central European spiritual impulse—were, in fact, forgotten in the second half of the nineteenth century. But these things are mere symptoms. The point is that along the path taken by Central Europe and its cultural life, the leading centers of culture emancipated themselves in the thirteenth, fourteenth, and fifteenth centuries from the spirit that still remained in the West. Since that time, Central Europe has not lost the spiritual element that storms and pulses through souls, but it has lost it from consciousness. That is why one could forget Goethe.

In Western Europe this element has been preserved in traditions and in outer forms. In Central Europe, especially in the German-speaking regions, it has been pushed down, as it were, into the depths of the life of soul, and consciousness has not been filled with it. This was particularly marked in the last third of the nineteenth century.

Close study of history will reveal something strange in the last third of the nineteenth century. If we study the literature and the writings that were read by those who played a part in shaping the cultural life, we find, during the last third of the nineteenth century, up to the middle of the eighties and nineties, in German-speaking districts, quite a different style in the journals and even in the newspapers from the style that is current today. Thoughts were then finely chiseled and elaborated; importance was attached to sequence in the thoughts, and to beauty as well. In comparison with the style current in the last third of the nineteenth century, our modern style is raw and crude. We need only pick up writings—no matter what they may be—of people in the 1860s and 1870s, not deeply learned or scholarly people but people possessing an average degree of culture, and we shall find a great difference. The thought-forms have changed. Yet, what is raw and crude today arose precisely from what was often finely chiseled and brilliant, as was usual, in the scholarly culture during the last third of the nineteenth century. Those who are older chronologically, without growing old inwardly, in the sense of our contemporary world of thought, experienced that something entered quite dreadfully into every domain of thought and spiritual life at that time. I will characterize it symbolically as the "empty phrase," or the "cliché." That is the first point.

With the vogue of the cliché, the empty phrase, a lack of thought develops, a lack of principles, a lack of will. All of these are now on the increase. These characteristics were primarily the outcome of the empty phrase, the cliché, whose main development occurred during the last third of the nineteenth century. You can follow this externally. Things that crop up in a certain epoch need not necessarily appeal to you. Yet, even though you are not sympathetic to them, you can still study their significance for the whole of humanity.

Think of the rich tones of inner beauty that are to be found in German romanticism in the first third of the nineteenth century. Think of the words of a person like Jacob Grimm† when he touches on spiritual things, how his words seem to be full of the fresh, health-giving air of the woods, and you will notice that in those days the cliché did not yet dominate in Central Europe. The cliché did not make its way into Central Europe until the last third of the nineteenth century. Those who have a sense for such things are aware of how gradual the beginning of the time of the empty phrase was.

Where the empty phrase begins to dominate, the inner soul-experiencing of the truth dies away. And something else, too, goes hand-in-hand with the empty phrase. In social life, human beings cannot find their fellow human beings any longer. My dear friends, when words sound forth without soul from the mouth, as they do in the empty phrase, then we pass by other human beings and cannot understand them. This too reached its culmination in the last third of the nineteenth century, not in the soul's depths but in consciousness. People became more and more alienated from one another. When at that time the call for social impulses and reform became ever louder, that was a symptom that people had become unsocial. Because they no longer had any feeling for what is truly social, they were pressed into crying out for social reform. A hungry animal does not howl for food because it has food in its stomach, but because it has none. Similarly, the soul that cries out for social life does not do so because it is permeated with social feeling, but because this feeling is lacking. And so the human being gradually became a being whose nature is not understood today. On the whole, human beings scarcely feel any longer the soul need to draw inwardly near to other human beings. Everyone passes the other by. One's greatest interest is only in oneself.

What then entered the twentieth century from the last third of the nineteenth as the customary social feeling between person and person? Nowadays, you continually hear, "That is my standpoint." Everyone has a standpoint. As if the standpoint itself really matters! The standpoint in spiritual life is just as fleeting as it is in the physical. Yesterday I stood in Dornach, today I am standing here. These are two different standpoints in physical life. What matters is that a person should have a sound will and a sound heart in order to look at the world *from every standpoint*. But people today do not want what they can glean from different standpoints. The egoistic assertions of their own particular standpoints are more important to them. Yet, they thus shut themselves off in the most rigorous way from others. If other people say something, they do not really enter into it, because they have their own standpoint. However, people do not get closer to each other by such means. We can only come closer to each other when we know how to place our different standpoints in a world that is common to all. This common world is simply not there today. Only in the spirit is there a world that is common to all—and the spirit is lacking. That is the second point.

The third point is this. In the course of the nineteenth century Central European humanity has really become very weak-willed—weak-willed in the sense that thought no longer unfolds the power to steel the will in such a way as to make human beings, who are thought-beings, capable of shaping the world out of their thoughts.

When it is said that thoughts have become "pale," we must conclude from this that thoughts are not needed in order to live as human beings. It is just that thoughts must not be so feeble that they remain up in the head. They must be so strong that they stream down through the heart and through the whole human being, right down to the feet. Really it is better if, besides red and white blood corpuscles, thoughts, too, pulse through our blood. It is a good thing, certainly, when a person has a heart too, and not merely thoughts. But best of all is for thoughts to have a heart. And that has been lost altogether. We cannot cast off the thoughts that the last four or five centuries have brought, but these thoughts must receive a heart as well.

Now let me tell you, from an external point of view, what is living in your souls. You have grown up and have come to know the older generation. This older generation expressed itself in words; you could only hear clichés. An unsocial element presented itself to you in this older generation. People passed each other by. And in this older generation, another thing to present itself was the inability of thought to pulse through the will and the heart.

You see, people could live with the "cliché," with antisocial conventionality, with mere routine instead of warm community of life, so long as the inheritance from earlier generations was still there. But this heritage was exhausted by the close of the nineteenth century. And so, what presented itself could not speak to your own souls. At the same time, precisely here in Central Europe, you felt that in the depths below, something stood in the direst need of being rediscovered, something that once lived beyond the empty phrase, beyond convention, beyond routine. You wanted again to have a living experience of truth, a living experience of human community, of stoutheartedness in cultural life. "Where is it then?" a voice asks within you.

Often, at the dawn of the twentieth century, even if it was not clearly expressed, you could see it: a young person standing beside an old person and the old person saying, "That is my standpoint." Ah! As the nineteenth century drew to its close, everyone gradually had their own particular standpoint. One was a materialist, the second an idealist, the third a realist, the fourth a sensualist, and so on. But gradually under the domination of empty phrase, convention, and routine, the standpoint became a crust of ice. The spiritual Ice-Age had dawned. The ice-crust was thin, but as people's standpoints had lost the sense of their own weight, they did not break through it. Besides, because they were cold in heart, they did not thaw the ice. The younger people stood side by side with the old. The young had their warm hearts—not yet articulate, but warm. This warmth broke through the crust of ice. The younger person did not feel, "That is my standpoint," but felt, "I am losing the ground from under my feet. The warmth of my heart is breaking this ice that has crystallized out of empty phrase, convention, and routine." Although not clearly expressed—for today nothing is clearly expressed—this state had existed for a long time and still exists today.

It is hardest of all for those with a scholarly education who try to fit in with the times. They are confronted by thoughts that are void of heart-quality and are quite consciously striven for, precisely because of this. Now, in speaking out of the spirit it is often necessary to shape words differently from what is customary when telling people something highly logical, philosophical, or scientific. But this approach is sometimes quite improper in relation to the spiritual. For example, consider the following.

People say today that a person is not a true scientist who does not interpret an observation and experiment in a totally logical manner; who does not pass from thought to thought in strict conformity with the correct methods that have been developed. Whoever does not do this is not a genuine thinker. But what if reality happens to be an artist who scorns our elaborate dialectical and experimental methods? What if nature works according to artistic impulses? If it were so, human science, to accord with nature, would have to become an artist. Otherwise there would be no possibility of understanding nature. That, however, is certainly not the standpoint of the modern scientist. The scientists' standpoint is: nature may be an artist or a dreamer; it makes no difference to us, for we decree how science is to be cultivated. What does it matter to us if nature is an artist? It matters not at all, for that is not our standpoint!

At the outset I can only describe a few impressions to illustrate what was working in chaotic interplay with the approach of the twentieth century, the century that has placed you before such hard trials of the soul. What we have had to face in outer events, including the grim and terrible World War [WW I], are only the outward expression of what is reigning in the innermost soul in the modern civilized world. It is simply so, and we must become conscious of it. We must also become aware of the fact that, above all, we must seek something that—as your speaker truly said—the deepest soul of Germany is yearning for, but was denied precisely within Germany by human consciousness the nearer the modern age approached. We lost not only Goethe, but also a great deal of what was there in the Middle Ages and out of which Goethe grew. We must find it again. To the question of why you came here, I would answer: to find this. For you are really seeking something that is there. In his *Fairy Tale of the Green Snake and the Beautiful Lily,* Goethe answered the question, Which secret is of the highest value? His answer was: the one that is manifest. However, it can only be revealed, if one opens one's eyes to perceive it. What concerns you, if you understand yourselves rightly, are mainly longings of the inner life. Whether one becomes a teacher or adopts some other profession is not the point. What is important is that everything that those who want to become *whole* again are seeking today is to be found in the common center of true "human-ness." That is why we find ourselves together here.

It was quite a different matter when in earlier centuries—to take a radical example—people burned a Giordano Bruno.† In those times that was the customary way of refuting truths. But now—to compare the case of Bruno with the following symptom drawn from the realm of science—consider the Swabian doctor Julius Robert Maier† who, while in southern Asia on a voyage around the world, made an observation of the blood that brought him to the conception of what is known as the heat equivalent, the conservation of energy. In 1844, he wrote a treatise on the subject, which was rejected as amateurish and unsuitable by the most famous scientific periodical of the time, the *Poggendorf Annals*. And because Julius Robert Maier was so enthusiastic about his discovery—so much that whenever anyone met him in the street he began at once to talk about it—the contemporary experts decided that he was suffering from obsessions. As you know, he was declared insane and put into an asylum. Today you can go to Heilbronn and see the Robert Maier Memorial, where it is declared that the law of the conservation of energy is the most important law of physics that has been discovered in the modern age. Well, of course, such things happen! Naturally, people can make mistakes. The point I want to make is how much this can be judged out of mere phrases, out of mere convention or routine.

Think of the way this terrible tragedy, this terrible mockery, came about in the nineteenth century, and compare it with what is presented today. What has actually happened cannot be undone by abstract writings. Anyone who has a heart and reads the descriptions that are given of such a case feels as if robbed of all inner support, and a terrible impulse forms in the soul. Human beings must again become capable of feeling, not weakly, but strongly: beautiful-ugly, good-evil, true-false. They must become capable of feeling things, not weakly, but strongly, so that they live within them with their whole being, so that their very heart's blood flows into their words. Then the empty phrase will dissipate, and human beings will feel not only themselves but others within their own being; convention will dissipate, and the heart's blood will pulse through what they have in their heads; then sheer routine will dissipate, and life will become human once again.

Young people in the twentieth century feel these things. They have been seeking, but found only chaos. These things cannot be portrayed by writing up external history. At the end of the nineteenth century there was a crucial point in the inner development of humanity. Souls who were born shortly before or shortly after the turn of the century are of quite a different inner makeup from those who were born even during the last third of the nineteenth century. One can speak about this and make comparisons in a certain way if, in spite of the years piling up, one has not allowed oneself to get old.

We shall see tomorrow how the new generation has not linked up with the old, but is divided from it by an abyss. It is not a question of finding fault, but only of trying to understand. I do not want to find fault, even when I speak of the tragedy that befell Julius Robert Maier. The same kind of thing happened to many people. It is, therefore, not a matter of finding fault, but of understanding the matter. The most important thing is to understand what is deeply and inwardly experienced. For an unclear seeking cannot continue to reign for long. A certain light must come that will pour out over this unclear seeking without making it dry or cold. We must find this light, while preserving the heart's blood.

I do not wish to impose anything mystical upon you, but to point to the truth, the truth in the spirit. You know that among the many clichés which became current in the nineteenth century, it was said that the great pioneer of the nineteenth century closed his life by calling out to posterity, "More light!" As a matter of fact Goethe did not say "More light!" He lay on his couch breathing with difficulty and said, "Open the shutters!" That is the truth. The other is the cliché that has connected itself with it. The words Goethe really spoke are perhaps far more apt than the mere phrase, "More light." The state of things at the end of the nineteenth century does indeed arouse the feeling that our predecessors have closed the shutters. Then came the younger generation; they felt cramped; they felt that the shutters, which the older generation had closed so tightly, must be opened. Yes, my dear friends, I assure you that, although I am old, I shall tell you more of how we can now attempt to open the shutters again. We shall speak further about this tomorrow.

2

STUTTGART, OCTOBER 4, 1922

In speaking of a movement among the youth, a clear distinction can be made between the youth movement in the wider sense and those young people who are particularly concerned with schools, with the sphere of education in general. I do not wish to emphasize either one or the other. But our aim will be most readily attained if we consider the main difficulties pertaining to the inner life among the young at universities and colleges.

In these observations, we shall sometimes have to start from details and then quickly rise to a wider overview. Allow me then to say a few words first about the inner experiences undergone by young people at universities. Basically, this situation has been preparing for many decades, but recently it has reached a climax making it much more clearly perceptible.

Young people at the universities seek something. This is not surprising. Their purpose in going to college is precisely to seek something. They are looking for real *leaders* in those who teach them, for people who are both teachers and leaders or—as would be equally correct—teachers endowed with leadership. But they have not found them. This is the really terrible fact conveyed in all kinds of different words—one teacher spoke conservatively, another radically, one saying something very wise, another something very stupid. What is being said amounts to this: We can no longer find any teachers.

What, then, have they found when they attend universities? Well, they have met people in whom they do not find what they are looking for. They have met people who pride themselves on not being teachers any longer, but researchers. Universities have established themselves as institutes for research. They are no longer there for human beings, but only for science, which has led an existence that it defines as "objective." It has drummed into people, in every possible key, that it is to be respected as "objective" science. Sometimes such things must be expressed in an image. We may say that objective science is now going about among human beings, but it is not a human being! It is something nonhuman that is going about among people and calling itself "objective science."

This may be experienced in detail, over and over again. How often is it not said: This or that has already been discovered; it already belongs to science. And then other things are added to science, and these so-called treasures of science are an accumulation that this dreadful objective existence has gradually acquired among humankind. But human beings do not really fit in with this objective being strutting around in their midst, for true and genuine humanity has no kinship with this cold, objective, stored-up being. True, with time, libraries and research institutes have been established. However, especially young people do not look for libraries or research institutes. They look in libraries for—it is almost beyond one to say the words—for human beings, and they find librarians! They look in the scientific institutes for educators filled with enthusiasm for wisdom, for real knowledge, and they find those who are usually to be found in laboratories, scientific institutes, clinics, and the like. Those of the older generation have accustomed themselves to being so comfortable that they really do not want to be there in person at all. Only their institutes and libraries must be there. But human beings cannot do this. When they try not to be there in this way, then they are there for sure. Then they work, not through the reality that lives in them as human beings, but through the leaden heaviness within them.

One could express this in other ways too: Human beings strive toward nature. Nature—to give a radical example—is also around very young children. But in their soul and spirit, little children derive nothing from nature. Little children have to get something from nature by coming in contact with human beings with whom they can experience nature in common. In a certain respect this holds true right up to young adulthood. We must come together with other human beings with whom we can experience nature in common. This has been impossible during the last decades because no language existed in which people, young and old, could come to an understanding with one another about nature. When the older generation speaks of nature, it is as though they were darkening her, as though the names they give to the plants no longer fit them. Nothing fits! On the one side there is the riddle of "plant" and we hear the names from the old, but they do not make sense because the human being was expelled, because the objective being, "science," was wandering about on the Earth. This is a state of things that came about gradually, but it has reached a certain culmination during recent decades.

In the nineteenth century, it showed itself through a particular phenomenon in a significant way. In recent centuries, anyone with a little imagination, who cast an eye over the higher forms of culture, became acquainted at every turn with this objective creature "science," which came upon the scene in many different guises but always wanted to be the one and only genuine, objective science. But after having made its acquaintance, after having this objective science continually introduced to one, one could have the insight that another being stole bashfully away to the side, because it felt that it was no longer tolerated. And if one were spurred to speak with this being secretly in the background, it would have said: "I have a name, but it may not be spoken in the presence of objective science. I am called Philosophy, Sophia, Wisdom. Bearing this ignominious prefix 'love' [Philo-Sophia], however, something is attached to me that by its very name is connected with human inwardness and with love. I can no longer show myself. I have to go about bashfully. Objective science prides itself on having nothing of the 'philo' in its makeup. Consequently, it has also lost the real 'Sophia.' Nevertheless, I still move among you for I still bear something sublime of feeling and humanity within me."

Such an image could often present itself to the soul. It has expressed an undefined feeling in countless young people during recent decades.

People have been trying to find forms of expression—as there are forms of expression for the life of thought, so too for the life of feeling—for what they were seeking. Those who were perhaps the most zealous, who felt the greatest warmth of youth, were the most vague, because all they really knew was: we are seeking something. But when they came to express what it was that they were seeking, it was actually nothing. In reality, the nothingness was, in the words of Faust, "the All," but it presented itself as a nothingness. It was a question of crossing an abyss. Such was the feeling, and basically, it still is the feeling today. It can only be understood as historical, but historical in a new, rather than in the old, sense.

Now I want to speak of something quite different, but gradually things will link themselves together. Human beings who lived at the beginning of our era were able to feel quite differently from human beings today, because much that was old still lived in their feeling and sensing. Human beings had an inheritance in their souls. This heritage was not there only at the beginning of our era; it went far back into the Middle Ages. But now, souls enter into the world without it. The fact that souls come into the world without this heritage is very noticeable in the twentieth century. That is one aspect.

The other aspect is this. Suppose you were to ask anybody who lived at the beginning of our era if they spoke much about "education." The farther back we go, the less we find that education is spoken about. Education, of course, may be spoken about in different ways; for instance: Through education the young should gradually be brought up to be what they want to be when they are old. For after all, we must grow old in earthly life, however young we may still be.

In earlier times human beings were young and grew old in a more natural way. Today people cannot be old and young in a way that is true to nature. People do not know any longer what it means to be young and what it means to be old. Nothing is known about it, and that is why there is such endless talk about education, because there is a longing to know how to teach young people to be young in order that they may grow old respectably. But nobody knows how to direct things so that human beings should be truly young and how, in youth, they can decently assimilate what will enable them to become old in a worthy manner.

Centuries ago all this was a matter of course. A great deal is said today about education. Mostly we do not realize the absurdity of what is said. Today almost everyone is talking about education. And why?

Mostly people have only the vaguest realization of having been so badly educated, and yet, they attribute their difficulties in life to it. People talk about it because they find that they are uneducated. They admit this. But they have never experienced anything appropriate in this domain. Nonetheless, they form conclusions. People cry for programs in education, merely because they feel so insecure in themselves. One could also show that a strong will is present on all sides, but a will without any real content. And that is exactly what the young are feeling, that there is no content in this will. Why is there no content? Because only recently something genuinely new has arisen in Earth evolution.

I can indicate this only in broad outline, but if you look at my book, *Outline of Esoteric Science*, it will be brought home to you. There you will find that the Earth is shown as a heritage of other world existences. The names are immaterial. I have called them the Saturn, Sun, and Moon existences. But the first Earth existence was only a repetition of earlier world existences. On the Earth we may say that there have been three periods of repetition: a Saturn, a Sun, and a Moon period. Then came the Earth period proper. But this Earth period proper, the Atlantean epoch, was again only a repetition—at a higher level—of what was there earlier.

Then came the post-Atlantean time—a still higher stage. But this again was a repetition. The post-Atlantean epoch was a repetition of a repetition. Until the fifteenth century, humankind actually lived on nothing but repetitions, on nothing but a heritage. Up into the fifteenth century, the human soul was by no means an unwritten page. Before then, many things rose up of themselves in the soul. But from the fifteenth century onward, souls were really unwritten pages; and the Earth was new. Before that, the human beings lived on the Earth only with what they inherited. As a rule no one pays any attention to the fact that only since the fifteenth century the Earth is new. Before then human beings were fed on the past. Since the fifteenth century they have been standing face to face with nothingness. The soul is an unwritten page. And how have human beings been living since the fifteenth century? At first, children inherited from their parents through tradition what had once been inherited in a different way, so that from the fifteenth into the nineteenth century, tradition was still there. But as you can see, tradition has fared gradually worse and worse.

Think for example of the sphere of rights. It would never have occurred to someone like Scotus Erigena† to speak of rights as modern people speak, because at that time there was still something in their souls that led human beings to speak person to person. This is no longer so, because there is nothing in the soul that leads to the *human being*; people have found nothing yet that leads out of the nothingness. At one time parents could at least speak to their children. But at the end of the eighteenth century things had gone so far that a parent had really nothing to say to a child anymore. Then people began to seek, in a cramped manner to begin with, the so-called "rights of reason." Ideas and feelings on the subject of rights were supposed to be pressed out of reason. Then Savigny† and others discovered that nothing more could be pressed out of reason. People began to establish rights according to history, where it was a question of studying earlier conditions and cramming themselves with the feelings of people long since dead, because there was nothing left within them. Rights of reason were a cramped clinging to what had already been lost. Rights according to history were a confession that nothing more was to be gotten out of the human beings of the day. Such was the situation at the onset of the twentieth century. The feeling grew keener and keener that humankind was facing a nothingness, and that something must come from within the human being.

In ancient Greece, nobody would have known how to speak about objective science. Human beings expressed their relationship to the world in a different way. By referring to spiritual vision, they spoke of Melpomene, of Urania, and so on, of the liberal arts. Although these liberal arts were real, they did not go about on the Earth. Even in the age of philosophy, the Greeks experienced their connection with the spiritual world to be concrete. The Muses were genuinely loved, and they were real beings with whom human beings had a relationship. Homer's words, "Sing, O Muse, of the wrath of Peleus' son, Achilles," were not the mere phraseology they are thought to be by modern scholars. Homer felt himself to be a kind of chalice, and the Muse spoke out of him as a higher humanity that filled him.

As Klopstock† did not want to speak anymore out of the [empty] phrase, which was already prevalent in the world into which he was born, at least he still said, "Sing, immortal Soul, of that sinner's redemption." But this "immortal soul" too has disappeared little by little. It was a slow and gradual process. In the first centuries of Christendom we find that the once concrete Muses had become dreadfully withered ladies! Grammar, Dialectic, Rhetoric, Arithmetic, Geometry, Astrology, Music—they had lost all concrete reality. Already with Boethius† they had almost no more concrete physiognomy. It is actually impossible to love them any longer. But even so, they are still sturdy figures in comparison with the objective science that goes about as a being among us today. Little by little human beings have lost the connection they had in olden times with the spiritual world. They had to lose this connection, because they had to develop to full freedom, in order to shape all that is human out of themselves. To this human beings have been called since the fifteenth century, but it was not really felt until the end of the nineteenth and especially in the twentieth century. For now, not only was the inheritance lost, but the traditions were lost too. Parents had nothing to tell their children. The feeling was: We are facing a nothingness. People began to sense that the Earth has in fact become new. What I have said here can be put another way, by considering what would have become of the Earth without the Christ event. Suppose there had been no Christ event. The Earth, as it lives in the human life of soul and spirit, would gradually have withered. The Christ event could not wait until the modern age. It had to occur somewhat earlier, before the time when the old inheritance had gone, in order that the Christ event could at least be felt through the old inherited qualities of soul. Just imagine what it would have been like if the Christ event at the beginning of our era had come about at the end of the nineteenth or in the twentieth century. How our contemporaries would laugh to scorn the pretension that any event like the Christ event should be of such significance! One cannot imagine what human beings would have felt about such pretension. At the time of the Christ event, quite a different kind of feeling had to be there. The feeling of standing before a nothingness could not yet be allowed at that time. The Christ event came during the first third of the fourth post-Atlantean epoch, and with that same fourth epoch, which bears the Christ event in the first third, the old was finished.

Something new begins in the fifteenth century, with the fifth post-Atlantean epoch in which we are now living. In this epoch there are no traditions. They have gradually faded out. In this epoch, as regards the Christ event, as regards the deeper, more intimate religious questions, people clearly stand before a nothingness. It has even become impossible for theologians to understand the Christ event. Try to get from contemporary theology an intelligible conception of the Christ event. Those who argue the Christ away from out of Jesus pass as the greatest theologians today. Quite obviously, human beings are facing the nothingness, the void.

I am only describing symptoms. For these things take place in the deeper layers of human soul life. These layers of soul conjure into the souls of that humanity, which has become young in recent decades, something that makes them feel cut off from the stream of world happenings. Something has entered the evolution of the human soul which is to be likened to a terrible jerk.

Suppose my hand were capable of feeling of its own accord and were chopped off. What would it feel? It would feel cut off, dried up; it would no longer feel itself to be living. This is what the human soul has been feeling since the last third of the nineteenth century in regard to the general stream of world happenings. The soul feels cut off, chopped off, and the anxious question is: How can I once again become alive in my soul?

But then, when one strives to speak out of the impulses that can bring life again, those who want to muddle along on the lines of the old spiritual life simply do not understand at all. How little is understood of what is spoken out of life about the founding of the Waldorf school! For the most part people hear something quite different about the Waldorf School from what they ought to hear. They hear only that one speaks to them the way one spoke already decades ago. They can find the mere words that are spoken today about the Waldorf School in books. They find every single word in earlier books. But when one wants to use different words, or perhaps only different ways of putting the sentences together, then people say that it is bad style. They have not the remotest notion of what must be done now, when human beings who still have a soul in their bodies must inevitably face the nothingness.

Waldorf School education must be listened to with other ears than those with which one hears about other kinds of education or educational reform. For the Waldorf School gives no answer to the questions people want to have answered today and which are ostensibly answered by other systems of education. What is the aim of such questions? Their usual aim is much reason or intelligence, of which the present time has an incalculable amount. Intelligence, intellect, cleverness—these are widespread commodities at the present time. One can give terribly intelligent answers to questions like: What should we make out of the child? How should we inculcate this or that into this child? The ultimate result is that people answer the question for themselves: What pleases me in the child, and how can I get the child to become what I want him or her to be? But such questions have no significance in the deeper evolutionary course of humanity. And to such questions Waldorf pedagogy gives no reply at all.

To give a picture of what Waldorf education is we must say that it speaks quite differently from the way in which people speak elsewhere in the sphere of education. Waldorf education is not a pedagogical system but an art to awaken what is actually there within the human being. Fundamentally, the Waldorf school pedagogy does not want to educate, but to awaken. For today it is a matter of awakening. First of all, the teachers must be awakened, and then the teachers must awaken the children and the young people.

An awakening is needed, now that humankind has been cut off from the stream of world evolution in general. Just as a hand goes to sleep when it is blocked from the circulation of the body, so too, humanity fell asleep in soul and spirit. You object, saying that human beings have made great progress since the fifteenth century; they have developed such colossal cleverness. If World War I had not come—which, by the way, was not the experience that it might have been, although people did realize to a slight extent that they were not so very clever after all—heaven knows how often we would hear the phrase, We have made such splendid progress. It would have been unbearable!

Certainly, in the sphere of the intellect, tremendous progress has been made since the fifteenth century. But this intellect has something dreadfully deceptive about it. For people think that in their intellects they are awake. But the intellect teaches us nothing about the world. It is, in reality, nothing but a dream of the world. In the intellect, more emphatically than anywhere else, a human being dreams, and because objective science works mostly with the intellect, which it applies to observation and experiment, science basically dreams about the world. It all remains a dreaming. Through the intellect, a human being no longer has an objective relation with the world. The intellect is the automatic continuation of thinking after one has been long cut off from the world. That is why human beings of the present day, when they feel their soul within them, when they get a feeling of themselves in their soul, are again seeking a real link with the world, a return to the world. Here one makes a peculiar discovery. If, up till the fifteenth century, human beings had positive inheritances, now they are confronting a "reversed" inheritance, a negative inheritance.

Up into the fifteenth century, humanity could welcome with joy what it inherited from the evolution of the world. The world had not been completely unrolled, and human beings were not altogether cut off from it. One could greet what one received with joy. Also today, after the cutting off has occurred, one can ponder what one receives from the world without one's own effort. However, then a strange discovery is made, like someone who is left a legacy and forgets to inform himself or herself about it accurately. Then a calculation is made, and it is discovered that the debits exceed the assets. The opportunity of refusing the legacy has been missed. But this means a definite amount of debts, which have to be paid. It is a negative inheritance. There are such cases. So also humanity has a negative inheritance in its soul, even concerning the greatest event that has ever happened in humanity's evolution.

Up to the time of Golgotha it was not necessary for human beings to understand the Mystery of Golgotha, because it had not taken place. Then it happened, and with the remains of ancient inheritance it could still be dimly understood in the age that followed. Then came the fifteenth century when such remains of inheritance were no longer there, when, however, it was still possible for parent to pass on to child an understanding for the Mystery of Golgotha. None of this helps any longer today. People are dreadfully clever. Yet, even in the seventh and eighth centuries, they would have been clever enough to perceive the contradictions in the four Gospels.† The contradictions are, after all, very easy to discover. However, people began to investigate them for the first time in the nineteenth century. And so it is in every domain of life. The intellect was over-valued, and a consciousness or feeling for the event of Golgotha was lost. Religious feeling was lost in consciousness. But in its innermost depths, the soul has not lost this feeling, and the young are asking: What was the Mystery of Golgotha in reality? The elders were unable to say anything about it. I am not implying that the young are capable of this either, or that anything is known about it at the universities. What I am saying is that something ought to be known about it.

To sum up, a striving to understand the Mystery of Golgotha once again is taking place, although chaotically, in the depths of human souls. A new experience of Christ is being sought. We are standing necessarily before a new experience of the Christ event. In its first form it was experienced with the remains of the old soul inheritances, and because since the fifteenth century they were exhausted, the experience was carried on through tradition. Only in the last third of the nineteenth century was the darkness complete. There was no longer any inheritance. A light must be sought once again from out of the darkness within the human soul. The spiritual world must be experienced in a new way.

This is the significant experience that is living in the souls of profounder natures of the modern youth movement. By no means superficially but in a deeper sense, it is clear that for the first time in the historical evolution of humankind there must be an experience that comes wholly from out of the human being. As long as this is not realized it is impossible to speak of education. The fundamental question is: How does one achieve the most primal spiritual experiencing in the soul?

Original spiritual experience in the human soul is something that stands before the awakening of human beings in the new century as the all-embracing, unexpressed riddle of the human being and of the world. The question is how human beings are to awaken the deepest nature within themselves; how they can awaken themselves. Even the most zealous spirits among awakening humanity—I can only express it in a picture—are like one who only half wakes in the morning with heavy limbs, and is unable to come fully out of sleep. That is how human beings feel today—as if unable to completely emerge from the state of sleep.

This fact lies at the root of a striving that has been expressed in many different forms during recent decades and is still shining today into the souls of the young in a sympathetic manner. It expresses itself in the striving for community among young people. One seeks something. I said yesterday that the human being has lost the human being. The human being is seeking the human being again. Up into the fifteenth century, human beings had not lost one another. Naturally, evolution cannot be turned back to an earlier condition, and it would be dreadful if we wanted to attempt it. We do not wish to become reactionaries. Nevertheless, it is a fact that up into the fifteenth century, human beings could still find the human being. Since that century, through tradition and through what the parent was still able to say, one could receive dim thought-pictures that made one aware: The other person there is a human being. People sensed dimly that this form going about beside them was also a human being. In the twentieth century this has vanished. There is no more tradition that tells one anything, and yet, one still seeks for the human being. Human beings are really seeking the human being. And why? Because, in reality, they are seeking something quite different.

If things continue as they were at the turn of the century, then no one will wake up. For the others, too, are in the state where they are incapable of awakening anybody. In the end, human beings must be something for each other. Human beings must mean something to one another also in the community. It is this that has radiated through Waldorf school education from the beginning. It does not aim to be a system of principles but an impulse to awaken. It aims at being *life*, not knowing, not cleverness but art, vital action, awakening deed. That is, what matters is a question of awakening, for evolution has made human beings fall into a sleep that is filled with intellectualistic dreams. Even in the ordinary dream, people often become megalomaniacs. Yet, ordinary dreaming is a mere nothing compared with intellectualistic dreaming.

When an awakening is at stake, it will simply not do to go any further with intellectualism. This objective science, which goes about and has discarded all its old clothes because it fears that something genuinely human might be found in them, has surrounded itself with a thick fog, with the mantle of objectivity, and so nobody notices what is going about in this objectivity of science. People need something human again; human beings must be awakened.

Yes, my dear friends, if an awakening is to take place, the Mystery of Golgotha must be experienced again. In the Mystery of Golgotha, besides the earthly Jesus, yet another spiritual being came onto the Earth. In earlier times this was grasped with ancient powers of the soul. The twentieth century challenges us to understand it with new powers. Modern youth, when it understands itself rightly, demands to be awakened in its consciousness, not in the old, slumbering powers of the soul as before. And this can only happen through the spirit. It can only happen if the spirit actually sends its sparks into the communities people are seeking for today. The spirit must be the awakener. We can make progress only when we realize the tragic state of world happenings in our day; namely, that we are facing the nothingness that we necessarily have to face in earthly evolution, in order to establish human freedom. And in the face of the nothingness, we need an awakening in the spirit.

Only the spirit can open the shutters, for otherwise they will remain tightly shut. Objective science—I cast no reproaches and do not mistake its great merits—will, in spite of everything, leave these shutters tightly closed. For science is only willing to concern itself with the earthly. But since the fifteenth century, the forces that can awaken human beings no longer live in the earthly. The awakening must be sought in what is super-earthly within the human being. This is actually the deepest quest, in whatever forms it may appear. Those who speak of something new, and are inwardly earnest and sincere, should ask themselves, How can we find the unearthly, the supersensible, the spiritual, within our own being? This need not again be clothed in intellectualistic forms. Truly, it can be sought in concrete forms; indeed it must be sought in such forms. Most certainly it cannot be sought in intellectualistic forms. If you ask me why you have come here today, it is because there is living within you this question: How can we find the spirit? If you see in the right light what has impelled you to come, you will find that it is simply this question: How can we find the spirit which, out of the forces of the present time, is working in us? How can we find this spirit?

In the next few days, my dear friends, we will try to find this spirit.

3

STUTTGART, OCTOBER 5, 1922

TODAY, to lay a foundation for the next few days, I shall speak about the spirit in the most concrete way. I must call on you to try to develop a real feeling for what is meant here by spirit.

What is taken into consideration by a human being today? People attach importance only to what they experience consciously, from the time they wake up in the morning until they go to sleep at night. They reckon as part of the world only what they experience in their waking consciousness. If you were listening to the voice of the present and had accustomed yourselves to it, you might say, Yes, but was it not always so? Did human beings in earlier times include anything else in what they understood by reality than what they experienced in their waking consciousness? I certainly do not wish to create the impression that we ought to go back to the conditions in earlier epochs of civilization. That is not my intention. The thing that matters is to go forward, not backward. But in order to find our bearings we may turn back, look back rather, beyond the time of the fifteenth century, before the age I attempted to describe so energetically to you yesterday. What people of that time said about the world is looked upon today as mere fantasy, as not belonging to reality. You need only look at the literature of ancient times and you will find that when people spoke of "salt," "mercury," "phosphorus," and so on, that they included many things in what they meant that people are anxious to exclude today. People say today, Yes, in those days people added something out of their own imagination when they spoke of salt, mercury, phosphorus.

We do not want to argue about why this is so fearfully excluded today. But we must realize that human beings saw something in phosphorus, in addition to what is seen by the mere senses, in the way modern people see color. It was surrounded by a spiritual-etheric aura, just as around the whole of nature there seemed to hover a spiritual-etheric aura, even though, since the fourth or fifth century C.E., it was very colorless and pale. Even so, human beings were still able to see it. It was as little the outcome of fantasy as the red color we see today. They actually saw it.

Why were they able to see this aura? Because something streamed out to them from their experiences during sleep. In the waking consciousness of that time, people did not experience in salt, sulfur, or phosphorus any more than they do today, but when the people in those days woke up, sleep had not been unfruitful for their souls. Sleep still worked over into the day and their perception was richer; their experience of everything around them was more intense. Without this knowledge as a basis we cannot understand earlier times.

Later on the experience of the ancients in connection with sulfur, phosphorus, and so on, became a mere name, an abstraction. The spirit continued as an abstraction in tradition, until, at the end of the nineteenth century, one could not grasp the spirit in one's thinking, or at least one could not sense it. External culture, which alleges such great progress, naturally attaches the greatest importance to the fact that human beings act upon it with their waking consciousness. Naturally, with this they will build machines; but with their waking consciousness they can work very little upon their own nature. If we were obliged always to be awake, we should very soon become old—at least by the end of our twentieth year—and more repulsively old than old people are today. We cannot always be awake, because the forces we need to work inwardly upon our organism are experienced within us only during sleep. It is of course true that human beings can work on outer culture when they are awake, but only in sleeping consciousness can they work upon themselves. And in olden times, much streamed over from sleeping consciousness into the waking state.

That is the great change that took place in the middle of the fifteenth century: this trickling of sleep consciousness into waking consciousness ceased. Pictorially I would say, in the tenth and eleventh centuries of Western civilization, human beings still woke up in such a way that they felt: Divine-spiritual powers perform deeds within me between my going to sleep and waking up. They felt the influx of divine-spiritual forces, just as in waking consciousness they experienced the streaming in of the health-bringing light of the Sun. And before going to sleep there was in every human being an elemental mood of prayer, full of nature forces. People entered sleep—or, if they were people of knowledge, they at least strove to do so—by giving themselves over to divine-spiritual powers.

The education of those who were destined for the spiritual life was such that this mood was deliberately cultivated. At the end of the nineteenth century those who regarded themselves as the most spiritual had for a long time replaced this by another method of preparation. I have often witnessed how people prepare themselves for sleep: I must take my fill of beer to prepare for sleep. This sounds ludicrous. Yet we see it is historically true that vision into the spiritual world through sleep was a deliberate and conscious striving among human beings of past epochs, apart from the fact that the candidates for initiation—the students of olden days—were prepared in a sacred way for the temple-sleep in which they were made aware of the human being's participation in the spiritual world.

At the present time when people consider the development of civilization, they do not ask: How has it affected humanity educationally? The question is not asked, because people do not think of the human being as a whole, but only in part. One has a strange impression if one sees a little further than the nearest spiritual horizon. People believe they know the truth about certain things at last, whereas the people of old were altogether childish. Read any current history of physics and you will find that it is written as if everything before this age were naive; now, at last, things have been perceived in the form in which they can remain permanently. A sharp line is drawn between what has been achieved today and the ideas of nature evolved in "childish" times. No one thinks of asking: What educational effect does the science that is absorbed today have from the point of view of world-historical progress?

Let us think of some earlier book on natural science. From the modern point of view it is childish. But now let us put aside the modern point of view and ask: What educational effect had such a book at that time and what effect has a modern book? The modern book may be very clever and the older one very fantastic, but if we consider the educational value as a whole, we shall have to admit that when a book was read—and it was not so easy to read books in those days, there was something ceremonial about it—it drew something out of the depths of people's souls. The reading of a book was actually like the process of growing: productive forces were released in the organism, and human beings felt these productive forces. They felt that something real was there. Today everything is logical and formal. Everything is assimilated by means of the head, formally and intellectually, but no will-force is involved. And because it is all assimilated only by the head and is thus entirely dependent upon the physical head-organization, it remains unfruitful for the development of the true human being.

Today people struggle against materialism. It would be almost more sensible if they did not. For what does materialism affirm? It asserts that thinking is a product of the brain. Modern thinking is a product of the brain! That is precisely the secret—that modern thinking is a product of the brain. With regard to modern thinking, materialism is quite right, but it is not right about thinking, as it was before the middle of the fifteenth century. At that time people did not think only with the brain but with what was alive within the brain. People had living concepts. The concepts of that time gave the same impression as an anthill; they were all alive. Modern concepts are dead. Modern thinking is clever, but dreadfully comfortable! Human beings do not feel the thinking, and the less they feel it, the more they love it. In earlier times, they felt a tingling when they were thinking, because thinking was a reality of the soul. Now people are made to believe that thinking was always as it is today. But modern thinking is a product of the brain; earlier thinking was not.

We ought to be grateful to the materialists for drawing attention to the fact that contemporary thinking is dependent upon the brain. Such is the truth, and this matter is much more serious than is usually imagined. People believe that materialism is a false world view. That is not at all true. Materialism is a product of world evolution, but a dead product, describing life in the condition where life has already died.

This thinking which has evolved more and more since the fifteenth century and which has entrenched itself, above all, in Western cultures, has quite definite characteristics. The Eastern cultures, despite their decadence, have still, after all, preserved the old thinking. But the farther west we go, the more a way of thinking takes the upper hand that the people of the Eastern civilizations regard as inferior. It does not impress people of the East at all. They despise it. However, they themselves have nothing new, but only the old thinking that is perishing. Europeans, and more so the Americans, do not feel at ease when they have to enter into the thinking of the Vedas. That kind of thinking makes them tingle in the brain. Westerners love dead thinking, where they do not notice at all that they are thinking. Today, not only when someone is talking nonsense but also when they are talking about living things, Western people confess that a millwheel is turning in their heads. They do not want what is living. They merely want to snatch at what is dead.

Here is an example that I am giving only out of cultural interest, not polemics. I described how it is possible to see an aura of colors around stones, plants and animals. The way in which I put this in the book *How To Know Higher Worlds* was such that it made living thinking, not dead thinking, a necessity. A short time ago a proper, contemporary professor at a university, who is supposed to have something to do with philosophy, came across this description. For him it is impossible to think livingly. He cannot do it, and so, for him, it does not exist. And there is supposed to be an aura of colors around stone, plant, and animal! He has seen colors only in the solar spectrum, and so he thinks that I too can only have seen them in the solar spectrum and have transferred them to stone, plant and animal. This professor cannot in the least follow my way of describing, so he calls it just a torrent of words. For him, it is indeed a torrent of words! He cannot understand any of it. And for a great number of university professors it is the same. A millwheel is going round in their heads. So quickly, away with the head! Then, of course, nothing can possibly come out of it.

Living human beings, however, demand a living thinking, and this demand is in their very blood. You must be clear about this. You must make your head so strong again that it can stand, not only logical, abstract thinking, but also living thinking. You must not immediately get a buzzing head when you are to think living thoughts. Dead thinking was for the materialistic education of the West, for those whose characteristic was pure intellectualism. But if you look into it, you discover a very dubious perspective.

The earlier thinking could be carried over into sleep. Then one was still something in sleep. Human beings were beings among other beings. They were something—real entities—during sleep, because they had carried living thinking with them into it. They brought living thinking out of sleep when they woke up and took it back with them when they fell asleep. Modern thinking is bound to the brain, and this cannot help us during sleep. Today, therefore, in accordance with modern science, we can be the cleverest and most learned people, but only during the day. We cease to be clever during the night, when we face that world through which we might work upon our own being. For this reason, human beings have stopped working on themselves. With the concepts we evolve from the time of waking to that of sleeping, we can achieve something only between waking and sleeping. We cannot accomplish anything on the human being. People must work out of the forces with which they build up their own being. During the period when human beings must work the most to build themselves up, when they are little children, they need the greatest amount of sleep. If ever a method should be discovered for cramming into babies all that is taught to seventeen- and eighteen-year-olds, you would soon see what they would look like. It is a very good thing that babies are cared for at the mother's breast and not from the lecture podium. It is out of sleep that people must bring the forces through which they can work upon their own being.

We can carry into sleep nothing from the concepts we build through science, through external observation and experiments and the controlling of experiments. Nor can we bring anything of what is developed in sleep into the concepts of the material world. The spiritual and the intellectual do not get on well together unless united in the world of full consciousness. Formerly this union was brought about in a more subconscious way. Today it must be done with full consciousness, and humanity does not wish to turn to this today.

What happened when people of earlier times passed with their souls into sleep? They were still somebody, because they had within them what hovers around things—what we call today a "fantasy." They bore this into sleep. Human beings could still hold their own outside the physical body in the spiritual world. Formerly they were somebody in the spiritual world between going to sleep and waking up. Today people are less and less of a real entity. They are nearly absorbed by the spirituality of nature when they leave their bodies in going to sleep. In true perception of the world, this is at once evident to the soul. You just must see it, and you will be able to see it when you acquire for yourselves the necessary vision for these things. Humanity must attain this vision, for we are living in an age when it can no longer be said that it is impossible to speak of the spirit as we speak of animals or stones. With such faculties of vision you will be able to see that even though Caesar was not very portly in physical life, yet when his soul left his body in sleep it was of a considerable "size"—not in the spatial sense, but its greatness could be experienced. His soul was majestic. A person today may be one of the most portly of bankers, but when his soul steps out of his body in sleep into the spirituality of nature, you should see what a ghastly, shrunken framework it becomes. The portly banker becomes quite an insignificant figure! Since the last third of the nineteenth century humanity has really been suffering from spiritual undernourishment. The intellect does not nourish the spirit. It only distends it. That is why human beings take no spirituality with them into sleep. They are nearly sucked up, when they stretch out into the world of spiritual nature between sleeping and waking, as a thin soul-skeleton.

That is why the question of materialism is far from theoretical. Nothing is of less importance today than the theoretical strife between materialism, spiritualism, and idealism. These things are of no consequence, for the refutation of materialism achieves nothing. We may refute materialism as often as we like; nothing will come of it. For in the end, the reasons we bring in order to refute it are just as materialistic as those we bring for or against idealism. Theoretical refutations achieve nothing one way or the other. But what really matters is that we have spirit once again in our whole way of looking at the world. Then our concepts will regain the force to nourish our being. To make this clear, let me say the following.

Now, I really do not find any very great difference between those people who call themselves materialists and those who, in little sectarian circles call themselves, let us say, Theosophists. For the way in which the one makes out a case for materialism and the other for Theosophy is by no means essentially different. If people want to make a case for Theosophy with thinking entirely dependent upon the brain, then even Theosophy is materialistic. It is not a question of the words one uses, but whether spirit is in the words spoken. When I compare much of the Theosophical twaddle with Haeckel's thought, I find the spirit in Haeckel, whereas the Theosophists speak of the spirit as if it were matter, but only diluted matter. The point is not to speak about the spirit, but to speak through the spirit. One can speak spiritually about the material, that is to say, it is possible to speak about the material in mobile concepts. That is always much more spiritual than to speak un-spiritually about the spirit.

Even when many come forward today with every possible kind of logical argument in defense of the spiritual view of the world, it simply does not help us. It does not help one bit. During the night we remain just as barren if during the day we think about hydrogen, chlorine, bromine, iodine, oxygen, nitrogen, carbon, silica, potassium, sodium, and so on, and then construct our theories, as when we think about the human being consisting of physical, etheric, and astral bodies. It is all the same as far as what is living is concerned. To speak in a living way about potassium or calcium, to do living chemistry, is much more valuable than doing a dead, intellectual Theosophy. For Theosophy too can be done in a dead, intellectual way. It does not really matter whether we speak materialistically or intellectually, but what matters is that the spirit shall be in what we say. The spirit must penetrate us with its livingness. However, because human beings no longer understand this, it is most disagreeable to them when anyone gets serious with it.

I did this in one of my last Oxford lectures, and to make myself quite clear I said: It is all the same to me whether people speak of spiritualism, realism, idealism, materialism, or anything else. When I need language to describe some external phenomenon I use materialistic language. This can be done in such a way that the spirit too lives within it. If one speaks out of the realm of the spirit, what one says will be spiritual, even though the language may have materialistic form. That is the difference between what is cultivated here as Anthroposophy and what is pursued in other places under similar names. Every few weeks books against Anthroposophy are brought out. They contain statements that are supposed to be leveled against what I have said, but what they attack is always quite new to me, for as a rule, I have never said such things. They collect all sorts of rubbish and then write voluminous books about it. What they attack has usually nothing whatever to do with what I actually say. The point is not to fight materialism, but to see to it that our concepts come out of the world of the spirit, that they are really experienced, that they are concepts filled with life. What is here presented and accepted as Anthroposophy is quite different from what the world says about it.

Today people fight against Anthroposophy—and sometimes also for it—quite materialistically, un-spiritually, while what really matters is that we get down to experiencing the spirit. People then begin not to be able to get it straight in their heads. For, when one begins to speak of spiritual beings as one speaks of plants and animals in the physical world, people take one for a fool. I can understand that, because there is a little thing that is overlooked. It consists of the fact that this folly is the true reality, the actually living reality for human beings. The other kind of reality is good for machines, but not for human beings.

This is what I wanted to say quite clearly. In what I intend here and have always intended, the important thing is not merely to speak about the spirit, but to speak out of the spirit, to unfold the spirit in one's very speaking. This is then the spirit that can have an educational effect upon our dead cultural life. The spirit must be the lightning that strikes into our dead culture and kindles it to renewed life. Therefore, do not think that you will find here any plea for rigid concepts such as the concepts physical body, etheric body, astral body, which are so nicely arrayed on the walls of Theosophical groups and are pointed out just as, in a lecture room, sodium, potassium, and so on, are pointed to with their atomic weights. There is no difference between pointing at tables giving the atomic weight of potassium and pointing to the etheric body. It does not matter at all. That is not the point. In this sense, this kind of Theosophy—or even Anthroposophy—is not new, but merely the latest product of the old.

One can hear the most incredible nonsense when people suddenly feel themselves called upon to represent the spirit. I do not mention these things as criticism, but as a symptom. I will tell you two stories. The first runs as follows: I was once at a meeting somewhere in western Europe on the subject of Theosophy. After the lectures had come to an end, I came into conversation with someone about the value of these lectures. This personality, who was a good disciple of the Theosophical sectarianism that had taken place there, told me of his impression of the lectures in these words: "There are such beautiful vibrations in this hall." The feeling of well-being, you see, was expressed in terms of vibrations—in other words, materialistically.

Another time people pestered me about some discovery that had suddenly been made on the spiritual plane. It was stated that repeated earthly lives—which as a matter of fact can only be revealed to the soul by genuinely spiritual perception—must also be perceived in an earthly guise, must be clothed in terms of materialistic thinking. So these people began to speak of the "permanent atom" which goes through all earthly lives. They said: If I am now living on the Earth, and come back again after hundreds of years, the atoms will be scattered to the four winds, but one single atom goes over into the next life on Earth. It was called the "permanent atom." Quite happily the most materialistic ideas were being introduced into the truth of repeated earthly lives, into a truth that can only be grasped by the spirit. As if it could profit anyone to have a single atom, say from the fourth or fifth century, going around in one's brain! Surely it is the same as if there were a surgeon in the world beyond who had managed to equip me in this life by having preserved my stomach from a former incarnation and having inserted it in my present body. In principle, these things are exactly the same.

I am not telling you this as a joke, but as an interesting symptom of people who, wanting to speak of the spirit, talk of the pleasant sensation coming from spiritual "vibrations," or have only absorbed through thought-imitations what others know about repeated earthly lives, and then clothe this in such a way that they talk about the permanent atom. Books have been written, even by Theosophists, about this permanent atom—books with curious drawings showing the structure of hydrogen, oxygen, chlorine atoms, and so on. And when one looks at them, they are no less horrible than the sketches that materialists have made of the atoms. It does not matter whether we say that this is spiritual or that is material. What matters is to realize the necessity of entering into the living spirit. I do not say this in a polemic sense, but to make it clear to you.

In this sense, the following is extraordinarily characteristic. There lives at the present time a very gifted Benedictine Father named Mager, one of the finest minds in the order—and the Benedictines have basically the best minds. Mager has written an extremely interesting little book, *The Behavior of the Human Being in the Presence of God.* It belongs, in thought, to the time when Benedict founded his order. Had it been written then it would have been quite in accordance with the times. When someone writes a book called *The Behavior of the Human Being in the Presence of God*, one can admire it. And I do admire it. The same priest has, however, also given his opinion on Anthroposophy. And now he becomes the densest of materialists. It is really terribly difficult to characterize what he maintains when one has first to enter into such a rigid kind of thought. What he rebukes most is that the perception in imaginative knowledge, which I put first when it comes to content, is of such a nature that, for Father Mager, it amounts to mere pictures. He gets no farther. And then he says, in accordance with his scientific conscience, that Anthroposophy materializes the world. He takes terrible exception to the fact that Anthroposophy materializes the world, in other words, that Anthroposophy does not confine itself to the unreal, abstract concepts he loves—for there one loves the most abstract concepts. Just read a Catholic philosophy and you will find—Being, Becoming, Existence, Beauty, and so on—all in the greatest abstractions. Whatever you do, do not touch the world! And the Father notices that Anthroposophy contains living concepts, which can actually come down to real things, to the real world. That is an abomination to him.

One ought to answer him: If knowledge is to be anything real, it must follow the course taken by God with the world. This course started from the spiritual and always materialized. The world was first spiritual and then became more and more material, so that real knowledge must follow this course. It is not sought for in Anthroposophy, but one comes to it. The picture clicks into reality; but Father Mager criticizes this. And yet it is exactly what he must himself believe if he wants to give his faith a reasonable content. However, in our case, he calls it the materialization of knowledge.

Of course, there is no satisfying those who insist: For heaven's sake no living concepts, for they will slip into reality! Then we would have to stay far away from that with our concepts. In such cases, we can have only concepts belonging to waking consciousness and none that are capable of working upon the human being from out of the spiritual world. But that is what we need. We need a living evolution and a living education of humanity. The fully conscious human being feels the culture of the present day to be cold and arid. It must be given life and inner activity once again. It must become such that it fills human beings, fills them with life. Only this can lead us to the point where we shall no longer have to confess that we ought not to mention the spirit. It can lead us to where good will flows into us and develops within us the inclination, not for abstract speaking, but for inward action in the spirit that flows into us—not for obscure, nebulous mysticism, but for the courageous, energetic permeation of our own being with spirituality. Permeated by spirit, we can speak of matter. We shall not be led astray when talking of important material discoveries, because we are able to speak about them in a spiritual way. We shall shape what we sense darkly within us as an urge forward into a force that educates humanity. Tomorrow, we will speak further about these things.

4

STUTTGART, OCTOBER 6, 1922

TODAY, I shall begin with an assessment of ethics up to the end of the nineteenth century. I do not wish to prove that philosophical expositions can give rise to an impulse for the renewal of the moral life of human beings, but rather to show that forces that work from other sources to determine the moral life are symptomatically expressed in the philosophical expositions of ethics.

We must give up the view that systems of philosophy that start from the intellect can point the way directly. Yet the whole impulse of the age expresses itself in what the philosophers say. No one will declare that our reaction to the temperature of a room is influenced by the thermometer; what the thermometer registers is dependent upon the temperature of the room. In the same way we can gauge, from what philosophers say about morality, the condition of morals in general.

You see, I treat philosophical expositions of ethics in rather a different way, merely as a kind of thermometer for registering conditions. Just as we know the temperature of a room by reading the thermometer, so we can find out a great deal about the undercurrents of the life of humanity in a particular region or period by knowing what the philosophers express in their presentations.

Consider the following only from this point of view as I read you a passage that was printed in 1893 in the periodical *Deutsche Literatur-zeitung* [German literary newspaper] that deals with Spencer's *Principle of Ethics*.† The reviewer says, "It contains, as I think, the most complete argument, supported by a crushing weight of material, that there is absolutely no such thing as one universal morality for all of humanity, nor are there any unchangeable Moral Laws. There exists only one norm that underlies all judgments of human characteristics and actions, namely, the practical fitness or unfitness of a character or action, for the given state of the society in which the judgment is made. On this account the same things will be very differently judged according to the different cultural conditions in which they occur. The view of the present writer is that this masterpiece (Spencer's *Principles of Ethics*) must, from a scientific point of view at least, silence the recent attempts to base ethical judgments upon intuition, inborn feelings, or the most evident of axioms and the like." I read this passage to you, because it is characteristic of the attitude of most of the civilized world at the end of the nineteenth century; it has developed to the point that it could be expressed in philosophical terms.

Let us be clear about what is said here. The attempt is made in this very important work, Spencer's *Principles of Ethics,* to prove—as the reviewer rightly says—with the "crushing weight of material," that it is impossible to draw forth from the human soul moral intuitions, moral axioms— that we must stop talking about moral intuitions. We can only say with certainty that people act according to their natural endowments. These actions are judged by the social surroundings; people are forced to bring their actions into line with the judgment of this social environment. From this there arises conventional moral judgments which are modified as human society changes from age to age. And a reviewer at the beginning of the 1890s said that it is at last possible to silence, so far as science is concerned, all attempts to speak of ethics and moral views that say moral intuitions arise out of the soul. I have chosen this example because it characterizes what faced one when one thought about ethics and moral impulses at that time.

Into this mood of the age, my dear friends, I sent my *Intuitive Thinking as a Spiritual Path,*† which culminates in the view, with the end of the nineteenth century, the time has come when it is eminently necessary that human beings contemplate how they will be able to find moral impulses more and more by going back to the being of the human soul itself. Even for the moral impulses of everyday life, they must resort more and more to moral intuitions found in the soul, all other impulses will become gradually less decisive. This was the situation I faced. I was obliged to say that the future of human ethics depends upon the power of moral intuition becoming stronger with every passing day. Advances in moral education can only be made when we strengthen the force of moral intuition within the soul; when individuals become more and more aware of the moral intuitions which arise in their souls.

Over against this stood the judgment—a merely general one, for only that which is general is expressed here—that it is proven with overwhelming evidence that all moral intuitions must be silenced. It was therefore necessary for me to attempt to write a book that would represent, in an energetic way, the very point of view that, with equal vigor, science declared should be forever silenced.

I have given this example because it shows clearly the immensely significant turning point in the whole spiritual evolution of the West at the end of the nineteenth century. All of my presentations have pointed out that those who have been growing up since the end of the nineteenth century are faced with a totally new soul life situation from that of previous centuries. I already said with regard to the spiritual, that at the end of the nineteenth century, human beings stood, as soul-beings, face-to-face with the "nothingness." It was necessary to emphasize, in relation to ethics, how that which comes from the spiritual depths and which is deemed to be most necessary for the future—moral intuitions—contrasts with that which comes from the past: the nothing that is done with its development. This turning point of the nineteenth century revealed itself in German culture in a most tragic way. We need only mention the name of Friedrich Nietzsche.†

For those who lived through the transition from the nineteenth to the twentieth century consciously, Nietzsche represents an experience of real tragedy. Nietzsche was a personality who, through the successive periods of his life, poignantly experienced that he was faced with the nothingness, that nothingness which he had at first assumed to be a "something."

It will perhaps not be superfluous for what you are to take into your souls during the next few days, to say a few words about Nietzsche. In a certain respect, Nietzsche was the very human being who, through his tragic destiny, clearly pointed to what in the spiritual evolution of humankind at the end of the nineteenth century was in its twilight, making a new dawn necessary for the century just beginning. Nietzsche started from a mature scientific viewpoint; this he first met in philology in the middle of the nineteenth century. With a mind of extraordinary inner flexibility, Nietzsche assimilated the philological viewpoint of the middle of the nineteenth century and with it he absorbed the whole spirit of Greek culture. Nietzsche was not a personality to shut himself off from the general culture. The very reverse of a theoretical scholar, he accepted naturally what he found in the middle of the nineteenth century: namely, Schopenhauer's philosophical pessimism.[†] This made a profound impression upon him because he sensed more deeply than Schopenhauer the decline of the spiritual life, in the midst of which he was living. The only light that pointed towards the future for Nietzsche was in Richard Wagner's music. Wagner, as regards his worldview, was a follower of Schopenhauer at the time he made Nietzsche's acquaintance.

Thus, towards the beginning of the last third of the nineteenth century, Nietzsche developed a view that was no theory, but the very substance of life to him—namely, that already in Greek culture the age had dawned in which the full human essence was being crushed by intellectualism. Nietzsche was not correct in regard to the complete development of intellectualism, for in the form in which Nietzsche experienced intellectualism as an all-destroying spirit, it had, as I said yesterday, only since the fifteenth century come upon the scene. What Nietzsche experienced was the intellectualism of the immediate present. He dated it back to the later age of Greek culture, and held that the influence working so destructively upon what was livingly spiritual began with Socrates. And so Nietzsche became anti-Socratic in his philosophy. With the advent of Socrates in the spiritual life of Greece, he saw intellectualism and rationality driving away an old spirituality.

Not many have grasped with such innate power the contrast between the character of Greek culture as it appears in the writings of Aeschylus, of Sophocles, in the early sculpture and in the mighty philosophies of men like Heraclitus, Anaxagoras and others—this life of soul, still full of spiritual impulses—and that other life of soul which gradually began to paralyze the true spirituality. According to Nietzsche this began with Socrates who confronted all world questions with intellectual questions and who established his art of definition with regard to everything. Nietzsche felt that when that began humanity no longer looked at the immediate and living spirit in the natural way. Provided this idea is not carried too far and thus made intellectual itself, it shows that Nietzsche sensed something of great significance.

You see, real experience of the spiritual, wherever we meet it, always becomes individual. Definition, however, inevitably becomes generalization. In going through life and meeting individuals we must always have an open heart—an open mind for the individual. Towards each single individual we should be able to unfold a completely new human feeling for every individual we meet. We do justice to a human being only when we see in the person an entirely new personality. For this reason, every individual has the right to expect of us that we should develop a new feeling for that person as a human being. If we come with a general idea in our heads, saying that a human being should be like this or like that, we are being unjust to the individual. With every definition of a human being we really put up a screen to make the human being invisible.

Nietzsche felt this in regard to the spiritual life; hence his opposition to Socratic teaching. And so, during the sixties and early seventies of the nineteenth century, the idea grew in his soul that true, living Greek culture has a kind of pessimism at the root of its feeling about the world. He thought the Greeks were convinced that immediate life, in its elementary form, cannot give people satisfaction, a complete feeling of human dignity. Therefore the Greeks took refuge in what art was to them. And to the Greeks, the art they cultivated in the time of their prime was the great comforter, helping to overcome what was lacking in material existence. Thus, for Nietzsche, Greek art could be understood only out of the Greeks' tragic feeling about life, and he thought that this mission of art would again be revived by Wagner and his artistic impulse.

The 1870s approached and Nietzsche felt that this could not be, because in his time he failed to find the impulse that the Greeks had set up as the great consoler for the material life around them. And so he reflected: What was it that I wanted to find in Wagner's art as a renewal of Greek art? It was ideals! But it dawned upon him, as he let these ideals work upon his soul, that they were similar to those of his own epoch.

In the mid 1870s, there came a terribly tragic moment in Nietzsche's life, the moment when he felt his ideals belong to his own times. He was forced to admit, My ideals are no different from what this present age calls its ideals. After all, I am drawing from the same forces from which my own age draws its ideals. This was a moment of great pain for Nietzsche, for he had experienced the idealistic tendencies manifest in his day. He had experienced, for example, David Friedrich Strauss†—revered by the whole age as a great man—but whom he had unmasked as a philistine. And he realized that his own ideals, stimulated by his absorption in Wagner and in Greek art, strongly resembled those of his time. But these ideals seemed to him impotent and unable to grasp the spiritual. So he said to himself, If I am true to myself, I cannot have any ideals in common with my time. This was a tragic discovery for him, even if not expressed in these words. Any of you who have steeped yourselves in what Nietzsche lived through during the years of which I am speaking, knows that there came for Nietzsche the tragic moment when, in his own way, he said that when some people today speak of ideals and these coincide with what others call their ideals, then they are moving in the realm of empty phrases that are no longer the living body but the dead corpse of the spirit.

This brought Nietzsche to the conviction: I must resolutely put aside the ideals I have evolved hitherto. Putting aside all his ideals began in the middle of the seventies. He published his *Human All Too Human*, *The Dawn of Day* and *The Joyful Wisdom*—works in which he pays some homage to Voltaire, but which also contain a certain view of human morals.

An external inducement to forsake his former idealism and steer towards the views of his second period came from his acquaintance with the works of Paul Rée.† Paul Rée treated moral nature and its development from a purely scientific point of view, entirely in line with the natural science of the day. Paul Rée wrote the very interesting little book, *On the Genealogy of Moral Perceptions* and also a book titled *The Genesis of Conscience*. This book, which everyone should read who wants to know about the nature of thought in the last third of the nineteenth century, had a very deep influence on Nietzsche.

What is the spirit of this book? Again, I am describing it not because I think that philosophy has a direct influence upon life. I do so because I want to point to a gauge for culture by which we can read the state of the ethical impulses, views, and thinking of the time. According to Paul Rée's view, human beings originally had no more than what, in his opinion, a child has, namely, a life of instinct, impulses of unconscious, instinctive activity. Individual human beings, when they become active, come up against others. Certain of these activities unfolded toward the outer world, happen to suit other human beings to their benefit; other activities may be harmful. From this there arises the judgment that what proceeds from the instinctive activities of the human being as beneficial is gradually seen to be "good"; what proves harmful to others is branded as "evil." Life becomes more complicated all the time. People forget how they put labels on things. They speak of good and evil and have forgotten that, in the beginning, the good was simply what was beneficial and the evil what was felt to be harmful. So finally, what has arisen has become instinct, has recast itself as instinct. It is just as if someone struck out blindly with an arm—if the result is a caress, then this is called good; if it is a box on the ears, then it is evil. And so judgments pile up. The sum of such judgments becomes instinct. Just as little as we know how we raise our hand, just so little do we know how a voice comes out of the soul and utters this or that moral judgment. This voice we then call conscience. This voice of conscience is merely what has arisen out of instinctive judgments about the beneficial and the harmful. It has become instinct, and because its origin has been forgotten, it sounds from within as the voice of conscience.

Nietzsche realized fully that not everyone would agree with Paul Rée. But he was also quite clear that when views on natural science were such as they were in his day, it is impossible to think about ethics otherwise than in the way Paul Rée did. Nietzsche was thoroughly honest; he deduced the ultimate consequences as Paul Rée had done. Nietzsche bore the philosopher no grudge for having written such things. This had not much more significance for Nietzsche than what was circumscribed by the four walls of the room in which Paul Rée did his writing, just as a thermometer indicates nothing more than the temperature of the immediate environment. However, it shows something that exists in general, and Nietzsche sensed this. He felt the ethical sediment of the times in this book and with this he agreed. For him there was nothing more important than to put aside the old "empty phrase" and to say that when people talk about nebulous ideals they make nothing clear; in fact, everything is instinct.

Nietzsche often said to himself that, when people are enthusiastic about certain ideals and want to enthuse others for those ideals, it is, in the end, because they are so constituted that when they are thinking of these ideals they can work up the juices in their stomachs in the best way for the digestion of their food. I am putting this rather radically, but it is exactly what Nietzsche felt in the seventies and eighties of the nineteenth century. He said to himself: People talk about all sorts of spiritual things and call them ideals. But in reality, it amounts to no more than that people, each according to their own constitution, digest and carry out bodily functions in the best way when they feel thusly about the so-called ideal. What is known as human must be divested of the "empty phrase," for in truth, the human is all too human.

With a magnificent devotion to honesty, Nietzsche declared war on all idealism. I know that this aspect of Nietzsche has not always been emphasized. A great deal that has been said about him is pure snobbery, without anything earnest in it. So Nietzsche found himself facing the "nothingness" at the end of the first period of his spiritual development, and consciously facing the nothingness in a second period that began with *Human All Too Human* and ended with *The Joyful Wisdom*. Finally, only one mood remained, for it is impossible to reach a real spiritual content when all ideals are traced back to bodily functions. One example will show what Nietzsche's view became. He said to himself: There are people who work towards asceticism, that is to say, towards abstention from physical enjoyment. Why do they do this? They do it because they have exceedingly bad digestion and feel most comfortable when they abstain from physical enjoyment. That is why they regard asceticism as the highest aim worth striving for. But unconsciously they are seeking what makes them most comfortable. They wish to feel the greatest enjoyment in the absence of enjoyment. That absence of enjoyment is their greatest enjoyment, shows us how they are constituted.

In Nietzsche, who was thoroughly honest, this mood intensified to moments when he gave vent to words like these:

> Ich wohn' in meinem eigenen Haus,
> Hab' niemand etwas nachgemacht,
> Und lache jeden Meister aus,
> Der sich nicht selber ausgelacht.

> I dwell within my own house and
> Have imitated no one;
> And laugh at every master who
> Has not laughed at himself.

In its poetic anticipation this verse is a magnificent description of the mood that came to its climax about the turn of the nineteenth century, yet it was already there earlier in a form that made itself felt in the depths of the soul life. Nietzsche found his way out of this second period of facing the nothingness by creating what is implicit in two ideas to which he gave poetic expression. The one was the idea of the super human, because, for him, there was ultimately nothing left but to call upon something that must be born out of the human being but was not yet there. Secondly, after his grandiose experience of facing nothingness, there arose the idea of the eternal recurrence of the same, which came to him out of the idea of evolution. In his scientific period he had become familiar with the idea of evolution. But as he steeped himself in what came from these thoughts about evolution he discovered nothing that would bring evolution forward; these only gave him the idea of eternal recurrence of the same. This was his last period, which need not be described any further, although from the point of view of psychology a very great deal might be learned from it.

I do not wish to do a character study but only to indicate how Nietzsche, who was forced through illness to lay down his pen at the end of the 1880s, had experienced in advance the mood that dominated deeper souls at the turn of the nineteenth into the twentieth century. During the last third of the nineteenth century Nietzsche tried to express a mood drawn from his store of ideas, from Greek philosophy and art, from art as found in Wagner, from the philosophy of Schopenhauer, and so on. But time and again, Nietzsche himself abandoned his own views.

One of his last works is called *The Twilight of the Idols, or How to Philosophize with a Hammer*. He felt himself as a destroyer of the old ideas. It was really very remarkable, for the old ideas had already been destroyed by the spirit of cultural evolution. During Nietzsche's youth the store of ideas was already destroyed. Since the fourteenth and fifteenth centuries, ideas continued through tradition but came to an end in the last third of the nineteenth century. The old spirit was already in ruins. It was only in the empty phrase, the cliché, that these ideas lived on.

Those who thought in accordance with spiritual reality in Nietzsche's day would not have felt that they had to smash the ideals with a hammer but that they had already been smashed simply in the necessary and proper course of evolution of the human race. Humanity would not have achieved freedom if this had not happened. But Nietzsche, who found these ideals still blossoming in the empty phrase, was under the illusion that he himself was doing what had already long been done.

What had been the inner fuel of the spiritual life in the former age, the fuel whereby the spirit in humanity could be kindled and, once kindled, illuminate both nature and his own life—this had passed away. In the specific realm of the moral, this is expressed by people saying: There can be no moral intuitions any longer.

As I mentioned yesterday, theoretical refutations of materialism as world-conception are sheer nonsense, for materialism has its justification in this age. Thoughts that our age has to recognize as right are products of the brain. Therefore, a refutation of materialism is in itself an empty phrase, and no one who is honest can see the good of refuting materialism theoretically, for nothing is to be gained by it. Human beings have come to the stage of evolution where they no longer have an inner, living spirit but only a reflection of the spirit entirely dependent upon the physical brain. Here materialism is fully justified as a theoretical world-conception. The point is not that people have a false world-conception or whether they refute it, but that they have gradually come to an inner attitude of life and soul that is lacking in spirit. This rings tragically, like a cry, through Nietzsche's philosophy.

This is the situation of the spiritual life in which souls with natural feeling among the young of the twentieth century find themselves. You will not come to any clear view, to any tangible experience, of what is brewing indistinctly, subconsciously in your souls and what you call the experiences of youth, unless you look into this shift that has taken place necessarily in the spiritual life of the present period of evolution.

If you try to characterize what you experience on other bases, you will feel after a time that you can always brush it aside. You will not hit upon a truth, but only upon clichés. For unless the human being today honestly admits: I must grasp the living, the active spirit, the spirit that no longer has its reality but only its corpse in intellectualism—unless I come to this, there is no rescue from the confusion of the age. As long as one believes that one can find spirit in intellectualism, which is merely the form of the spirit in the same way as the human corpse is the form of the human being, human beings will not find themselves.

To find ourselves is only possible if we will honestly confess: Intellectualism has the same relation to the living essence of the spirit as a dead corpse to the person who has died. The form is still there, but the life of the spirit has gone out of intellectualism. Just as the human corpse can be treated with preparations that preserve its form—as indeed Egyptian mummies show—so, too, can the corpse of the spirit be preserved by padding it out with the results of experiment and observation. But thereby people get nothing of what is livingly spiritual; they get nothing that they can unite naturally with the living impulses of the soul. They get nothing but a dead thing, a dead thing that can wonderfully reflect what is dead in the world, just as one can still marvel at the human form in the mummy. However, in intellectualism we cannot get what is truly spiritual any more than a real human being can be made out of a mummy.

As long as importance is attached to preserving what the union of observation and intellect is intended to preserve, one can only say: The achievements of the modern age are great. The moment human beings have to unite in the depths of their soul with what their spirit inwardly holds up before them, there can be no link between intellectualism and the soul. Then the only thing is for them to say: We are thirsting for something, and nothing we find out of intellectuality gives us water to quench our thirst.

This is what lives in the feelings of young people today although, naturally, it is not so clear when expressed in words. Young people today say many things, annoying things when one gets to the bottom of what is said. But one soon overcomes it. The annoyance is due to the fact that bombastic words are used that express anything rather than what the speaker really feels. The empty phrase overreaches itself, and what appears as the character of the Youth Movement is, for one who lives in the spirit, like a continuous bursting of bubbles; it is really intellectualism overreaching itself. I do not want to hurt any of you personally, but if it does hurt, I cannot help it. I would be sorry, but I would still think it extraordinarily right to say it. I cannot say only pleasant things; I must sometimes say things that will not please everyone. I must say what I know to be true. So, in order to characterize what is rightly there in the souls of young people today, we need something more than a revival of old concepts overreaching themselves in empty phrases: *we need an intensively developed feeling for the truth.*

We need truth at the bottom of our souls. Truth is the alpha and the omega of what we need today, and when your chairman said yesterday that we have gotten to a point where we do not want to utter the word "spirit" any longer, that is in itself a confession of the truth. It would be much more prudent if our age, which has lost the spirit, would succeed in not talking about the spirit, because then human beings would again begin to thirst for the spirit. Instead of this, one calls everything possible "spirit," and "spiritual." What we need is truth, and if any young people today acknowledge the condition of their own souls, they can only say: This age has taken all spirit out of my soul, but my soul thirsts for the spirit, thirsts for something new, thirsts for a new conquest of the spirit.

As long as this is not felt in all honesty and truth, the Youth Movement cannot come into its own. Let me add the following to what I have said in characterization of what we must seek. In the deepest, innermost being of the soul, we must seek for light; above all else we must acquire the most profound feeling for honesty and truth. If we build upon honesty and truth, then we shall progress, and humanity must indeed progress. Then we shall again be allowed to speak of the spirit, which is most like our human nature. The soul is most of all like the spirit, therefore it can find the spirit if only it so wills. In our time the soul must strive beyond empty phrase, convention and routine; beyond the empty phrase to a grasp of truth; beyond convention to a direct, elementary warmhearted relation between one human being and another; beyond routine to the state in which the spirit lives in every single action, so that we no longer act automatically but that the spirit lives in the most ordinary, everyday actions. We must come to spirituality in action, to the immediate experience of human beings in their relations to one another and to an honest, upright experience of truth.

5

STUTTGART, OCTOBER 7, 1922

YESTERDAY, I tried to characterize the spiritual life at the end of the nineteenth and the beginning of the twentieth centuries as I experienced it, and this experience led to the writing of my *Philosophy of Freedom (Intuitive Thinking as a Spiritual Path)*.

This book was intended to point to moral intuitions as that within humanity which, in the evolution of the world, should lead to the founding of the moral life of the future. In other words, through my book, I wanted to show that the time has come in which morality can continue in the evolution of humanity in no other way than that an appeal is made to the moral impulses which each human being is able to call forth individually from his or her innermost being. I mentioned that the *Philosophy of Freedom* was published at a time when it was universally said that finally it had been recognized that moral intuitions were impossible and that any discussion about moral intuitions must once and for all be silenced. I considered it essential to establish the justification and grounds for moral intuition. Thus, there was a distinct cleft between what the age, in many of its most eminent minds, considered to be truth and what I held to be right on the basis of human evolution.

On what is this difference really based? Let us look into the depths of human soul life as it is formed today in the West. In earlier times people also spoke of moral intuitions. That is to say, it was said that, as individuals, people could call forth from within themselves, independent of external life, the impetus to action. However, in the first third of the fifteenth century and even more so in subsequent centuries, what was said about moral intuitions was less and less true. It was said that morality could not be established by the observation of external facts; people could no longer perceive of a real light when they looked into their inner being. Thus, they declared that moral intuitions were there, but that actually they knew nothing about them anymore. For centuries the thinking that existed and was justified before the fifteenth century rolled on automatically, so that the facts that people declared to be right had ceased to be so.

The traditions, of which I have spoken, persisted through the centuries and contributed to such statements. Before the fifteenth century, people did not speak in indefinite—the indefinite was already the untruthful—terms as was current later. When speaking of intuitions, also of moral intuitions, people spoke of what rose up within their inner beings, of which they had a picture as real as the picture of reality they had when they opened their eyes in the morning and looked at nature. Outside they saw nature around them, the plants and the clouds; when they looked into their inner beings, there arose the spiritual, which included the moral as a given. The further we go back in evolution, the more we find that the rising up of an inner existence in human experience was a matter of course. These facts, as I have explained them to you, which result from spiritual science, may also be studied historically by considering certain outer symptoms. In the days when speaking about an inner reality was lapsing into untruthfulness, proof for the existence of God arose.

Had anyone during the first centuries of Christianity spoken about proofs for the existence of God, as Anselm of Canterbury† did, no one would have known what was meant. In earlier times they would have known still less! For in the second or third century before Christ, to speak of proof for the existence of God would have been as if someone sitting there in the first row were to stand up and I were to say, "Mr. X stands there," and someone in the room were to assert, "No, that must first be proved!" What human beings experienced as the divine was a being of full reality standing before their souls. They were endowed with the faculty of perception for that which they called divine. The divine of that historical time appears primitive and incomplete in the eyes of modern people. They could not get beyond the point, but the people of that age would not have wanted to hear about proofs, for that would have seemed absurd. Human beings began to "prove" the existence of the divine only when they had lost it, when it was no longer perceived by inner, spiritual perception. The introduction of proofs for the existence of God shows, if one looks at the facts impartially, that direct perception of the divine had been lost. However, the moral impulses of that time were bound up with what was divine. Moral impulses of that time can no longer be regarded as moral impulses for today. When in the first third of the fifteenth century the faculty of perception of the divine-spiritual in the old sense was exhausted, perception of the moral also dried up, and all that remained was the traditional dogma of morals, which people called "conscience." The term always referred to something that was highly vague, however.

When, therefore, at the end of the nineteenth century it was said that all talk about moral intuitions must be silenced, it was the final consequence of an historical development. Until then human beings had a feeling, however dim, that such intuitions had once existed. But now they began to put themselves to the test. Intelligence had at least brought them to the point of being able to do this. They discovered that with the methods they were accustomed to use to think scientifically, they were unable to come to moral intuitions.

Let us consider the moral intuitions of olden times. History has become very threadbare in this respect. We have a history of outer events, and in the nineteenth century we endeavored to establish a history of culture. But this age has been incapable of producing a history that takes the inner life of the soul into account. There is, therefore, no knowledge of how soul life developed from the earliest times until the first third of the fifteenth century. However, if we go back in time and consider what was spoken of as moral intuition, we find that it did not arise as a result of inner human effort. For this reason the Old Testament, for instance, did not feel what figured then as moral intuition as acquired by the human soul, but as divine commandments, coming into the soul from outside. And the further back we go, the more human beings felt that what they saw when they beheld the moral was an inner gift from a living divine being outside themselves. Moral intuitions held good as divine commands—not in a figurative or symbolic sense, but in an absolutely real sense.

There is a good deal of truth in certain contemporary religious philosophies when they allude to a primal revelation preceding the historical age on Earth. External science cannot get much beyond, shall I say, a paleontology of the soul. Just as in the earth we find fossils, indicating an earlier form of life, so in fossilized moral ideas we find forms pointing back to the once living, god-given moral ideas. Thus we can come to the concept of primal revelation and say: This primal revelation dried up. Human beings lost the ability to be conscious of the primal revelation. And this loss reached its point of culmination in the first third of the fifteenth century. Human beings perceived nothing anymore when they looked within themselves. They preserved only the tradition of what they had once beheld. Religious communities gradually seized upon this tradition and turned its externalized content, this purely traditional content, into dogmas which people were expected merely to believe, whereas formerly they had living experience of their truth, as coming from outside of the human being.

The very significant situation at the end of the nineteenth century was that certain circles realized that the old, god-given intuitions, were no longer there. They realized that if someone wanted to prove, with the head, the ideas of the people of old, then he or she would have to say that there are no moral intuitions! Science has silenced them. Human beings, even when receptive, are no longer capable of receiving moral intuitions. To be consistent, one would have had to become a kind of Spengler, and say that there are no moral intuitions and that in future humanity will have no alternative but gradually to wither up. One would perhaps, at best, ask one's grandfather, "Have you heard that there were once moral intuitions, moral influences?" And the grandfather would answer: "One would have to search the libraries; at second- or third-hand, one might still glean some knowledge of moral intuitions, but no longer from actual experience." One would then have to say that there is no alternative but to wither up and become senile, not to have youth any more. That would have been consistent. But people did not dare, for consistency was not an outstanding quality of the dawning age of the intellect.

Indeed, there were many things that one did not dare! If a judgment were pronounced it was only half given, as in the case of Du Bois-Reymond,† who delivered a speech about the boundaries of the knowledge of nature. He said that supernaturalism could not be mentioned in connection with natural science, for supernaturalism was faith and not knowledge. Science stops short of the supernatural—and nothing further was said by him on the subject. If mentioned, people got excited and said it was no longer science. Consistency was not a characteristic of the century then ending.

So, on one hand, there was the alternative of withering. The spiritual passes over gradually into the life of soul, the life of soul into the physical. As a result, after some decades, souls would have been able only to ferret out antiquated moral impulses. After some years, not only the thirty-year-olds but also the twenty-year- olds would be going about with bald heads, and the fifteen-year-olds with grey hair! This is a figurative way of speaking, but that would have been Spenglerism as a practical life impulse. That was one alternative.

The other was to become fully conscious that with the loss of the old intuitions, we are facing nothingness. What are we to do? In this nothingness, seek the "All"! Out of this very nothingness seek something that is not given, but which we ourselves must strenuously work for. This was no longer possible with passive powers of the past, but only with the strongest powers of cognition of this age: with the cognitional powers of pure thinking. For with pure thinking, this thinking goes straight over into the will. You can observe and think, without exerting your will. You can carry out experiments and think, but it does not pass over into the will. Pure thinking, that is, the unfolding of primary, original activity, requires energy. There the lightning-flash of will must strike directly into the thinking itself. But the lightning-flash of will must come from each single individual. Courage was needed to call upon this pure thinking that becomes pure will and arises as a new faculty—the faculty of drawing out of the human individuality moral impulses that have to be worked for and are no longer given in the form of the old impulses. Intuitions must be called up that are strenuously worked for. Today, what we work for in our inner being is called "imagination." In this present age—which has, apart from this, silenced inner work—moral impulses for the future must be produced out of moral imagination. The human being must be shown the way from the merely poetical, artistic imagination, to a productive moral imagination.

The old intuitions were always given to groups. There is a mysterious connection between primal revelation and human groups. It was always to groups of human beings in association that the old intuitions were given. The new intuitions must be produced within each single, individual human soul. In other words, each single human being must be made the source of morality. This must be brought forth through intuitions out of the nothingness which humanity is facing.

That was the only possibility left if, as an honest person, one was not willing to turn to a kind of Spenglerism.† And to work in the Spengler way is far from alive. It was a question of finding a living reality out of the nothingness that confronted human beings, and it goes without saying that at first one could only make a beginning. For a creative power in the human being had to be called upon, the creation, as it were, of an inner person within the outer person. In earlier times the outer person received moral impulses from outside. Now the human being had to create an inner person and with this inner person there came, or will come, the new moral intuition. So, out of the times themselves there had to be born a kind of "philosophy of freedom"—something that must inevitably stand in sharp opposition to the times.

Let us complete this survey of the condition of the soul of modern humanity by considering another aspect. You see, as a preparation for intellectualism in Western civilization, the consciousness of the human being's pre-earthly existence had already been wiped out for a long time. It was taken from Western civilization in very early times. So, in the West there was not this consciousness: "When I issue from the embryonic state of physical development, something unites itself with me, something that descends from the heights of spirit and soul and permeates this physical earthly being."

Now, in this connection, the following presents itself quite clearly to our vision. I have already given you a picture to elucidate it. I said that when we look at a corpse we know that it cannot have its form through the forces of nature, but must be the remains of a living human being. It would be foolish to speak about the form of the human body as if it were itself something living. We must go back to what was the living human being. In the same way, looked at impartially, intellectual thinking presents itself as dead. People naturally will say, Prove this for us. It proves itself in the very beholding, and the kind of proofs necessary, which are actual only for the side issues, are indeed available. But to demonstrate it, I would have to go into a good deal of philosophy, and this lies outside the scope of our present task. To anyone looking at it without prejudice, intellectual thinking, out of which our whole modern civilization flows, bears the same relation to living thinking as the corpse does to the living human being. Just as the corpse is derived from the living human being, so the thinking we have today is derived from the living thinking of an earlier time. But upon sound reflection I must say to myself: This dead thinking must have originated in a living thinking that was there before birth. The physical organism is the tomb of the living thinking, and the receptacle of dead thinking.

But the strange fact is that during the first two periods of human life, up to the sixth, seventh or eighth years, to the end of the change of teeth, and then further, up to the thirteenth, fourteenth, fifteenth years—that is to say, to the age of puberty—the human being's thinking is not completely dead, but it is in the process of dying. It was only living thinking in pre-earthly existence. During the first two periods of life it comes to the point of dying, and for modern humanity, since the first third of the fifteenth century, thinking is quite dead by the time of puberty. It is then the corpse of living thinking. It was not always so in the evolution of humanity. If we go back before the fifteenth century, it becomes evident that thinking still was something living. There existed the kind of living thinking that human beings today do not like because they feel as if ants were swarming in their brain. They do not like it when something is really alive within them. They want their head to behave in a quiet and comfortable way. And the thinking in it, too, should take a peaceful course so that all one needs is to help things along with the laws of logic. But *pure thinking*—that is just as if an ant hill were in one's head, and that, people say, is not healthy.

At the beginning of the fifteenth century the human being was still able to endure living thinking. I am not saying this in order to criticize; that would be out-of-place, just as out-of-place as to criticize a cow because she is no longer a calf. It would have been the greatest disaster for humanity if this had not happened. There had to be human beings who could not endure having an ant hill in their head! For what was dead had to be brought to life again in a different way.

And so it came about after the middle of the fifteenth century that human beings inwardly experienced a dead thinking once puberty was passed. They were filled out with the corpse of thinking. Go really deeply and seriously into this idea and you will understand that it is only since that time that an inorganic natural science could arise, because the human being began to grasp purely inorganic laws only as of that time. Now for the first time humanity could grasp what is dead in the way striven for since Galileo and Copernicus. The living had first to die inwardly. When people were still inwardly alive in their thinking, they could not grasp the dead in an external way, for the living kind of knowledge imparted itself to what was external. Natural science became increasingly pure science and nothing more, and this continued until, at the end of the nineteenth century, it was almost only mathematics. That was the ideal towards which it strove; it strove to be a kind of system of pure mechanics.

So, in the modern age, people began more and more to make what is dead into the actual object of knowledge. That was the whole aim. This lasted for some centuries, but evolution took this direction. People of genius like de Lamettrie, for example, said, as if prophetically, that human beings were really just machines. Yes, human beings who only want to grasp what is dead, avail themselves of what is merely a machine within themselves, of what is dead within themselves. And this makes the development of natural science easy for modern human beings. Their thinking is dead by the time of puberty, whereas in earlier days, they had God-given intuitions, because thinking preserved the forces of growth within itself far beyond puberty. Today, human beings lose this living thinking after puberty. Thus, in later life, they learn nothing more; they simply repeat mechanically what they had acquired in earlier youth.

You see, this suited the old, who held the control of culture in their hands, to comprehend a dead world with dead thinking. With this dead thinking, science can be founded marvelously. However, one can never teach or educate the young with it. And why? Because up to puberty the young preserve the livingness of thinking, if even in an unconscious way. And so, in spite of all the thought given today to principles of education, if rigidified objective science, which comprehends only what is dead, becomes the teacher of the living, of the youthful, the young feel it like a thorn in the flesh. One thrusts this thorn, the death, into their heart, and they are supposed to tear out from their heart what is living. Many still overlook what has had to come about out of the depths of human evolution: a definite cleft between the young and the old. And this cleft is due to the fact that the young cannot allow the dead thorn to be thrust into their living heart—the thorn that the head produces out of intellectualism. The young demand the livingness that can only come out of the spirit as the result of strenuous effort by the individual. We are making a beginning in the sphere of moral intuitions.

If a beginning has been made in what I have tried to present in my *Philosophy of Freedom* in regard to what is purely spiritual—for such moral intuitions, striven for by human individuality are purely spiritual—and if one has dared to open one's mouth while others were saying that nothing should be said, the powers that ordained that one should be stopped from speaking of moral intuitions, will themselves be silenced. And so I called upon the living, the purely spiritual. Science is dead. Science cannot make what is living flow from the mouth. And without this, one cannot build on it. One must appeal to an inner livingness, and so one must really begin to seek. The divine lies precisely in the appeal to the original, moral, spiritual intuitions. But if one has once grasped the spiritual, then one can unfold the forces that enable one to grasp the spirit in wider spheres of cosmic existence. And that is the straight path from moral intuitions to other spiritual contents.

In my book *How to Know Higher Worlds*, I have tried to show that knowledge of the supersensible worlds is built up gradually out of imaginative, inspired and intuitive experience. If we look at outer nature, we reach first Imagination, then Inspiration, and lastly Intuition. In the moral world it is different. If in that world we reach picture-consciousness, imaginations as such, then with the imaginations we have at the same time developed the faculty for moral intuitions. Already here at the first stage, we acquire what is not attained until the third stage in the other. In the moral world, intuition follows immediately upon outer perception. In the world of nature, however, there are two intermediate stages. So that if, in the moral world one speaks of intuitions not in mere phrases but honestly, truthfully, one simply cannot do otherwise than recognize these intuitions as being purely spiritual. But then one must work further to discover the other realms of the spirit. For what one has grasped qualitatively in moral intuition is the same as what one fills with content for natural evolution, with esoteric science, if you will.

We must proceed as follows. On the one hand, we must acknowledge that outer science by its very nature can only comprehend what is material; hence, the view of the material must be not only materialism, but also phenomenalism. On the other, we must work to bring life back into what has been made into dead thinking by natural science. Thus certain scriptural words become alive on a higher level. I do not want to intersperse what I say in a sentimental way with words from the Bible, but only to elucidate some things. Why is it that today we no longer have any real philosophies? It is because thinking, as I have described it, has died. When based merely upon dead thinking, philosophies are dead from the very outset. They are not alive. And if people, like Bergson,† seek something living in philosophy, nothing comes of it, because, although they struggle for it, they cannot lay hold of the living. To grasp the living means first to attain vision. What we need to reach the living is what can be added out of what worked within us before our fifteenth year. This, from before our fifteenth year, is not disturbed by our intellect. We must carry what works within us, as spontaneous, living wisdom, over into the dead thinking. Dead thinking must be permeated with forces of growth and with reality. For this reason, and not out of sentimentality, I want to refer to the words from the Bible, "Except ye become as little children, ye cannot enter the Kingdom of Heaven."

For it is always the Kingdom of Heaven that one is seeking. But if one does not become like the child before puberty, one cannot enter the Kingdom of Heaven. Childlikeness, youthfulness, must be brought into dead thinking. Thereby it becomes alive; it comes once more to intuitions. Thus we learn to speak out of the primal wisdom of the child. Out of a science of language such as Fritz Mauthner has written, not only are moral intuitions silenced, but also actually all talk about the world. People ought to stop talking about the world, because Mauthner proves that all talk about the world consists only of words, and words are incapable of expressing reality!

Such thinking has made its appearance only since the first third of the nineteenth century. People do not consider what it would be like, if our words and concepts not only meant something but had real existence. Then indeed they would not be transparent; then, like clouded lenses before our eyes, they would conceal what is sense-perceptible; because they are realities they would hide the world from us. Something splendid would be made of human beings, if they had concepts and words that have meaning in and of themselves! They would have been held fast by them. Concepts and words must be transparent, so that we may reach the things through them. It is imperative, when the desire is almost universal to silence all talk about reality, that we learn to speak a new language.

In this sense, we must return to childhood and learn a new language. The language we learn in the first years of childhood gradually becomes dead, because it becomes permeated by dead intellectual concepts. We must quicken it to new life. We must find something that strikes into what we are thinking, just as when we learned to speak, an impulse arose in us out of the unconscious. We must seek a science that is alive. We should consider it a matter of course that the thinking that reached its apex in the last third of the nineteenth century silences our moral intuitions. We must learn to open our mouth by letting our lips be moved by the spirit. Then we shall become children again, that is to say, we shall carry childhood on into our later years. And that is what we must do. If a youth movement wants to have truth and not only phraseology, then such a movement is imbued of necessity with the longing for the human mouth to be opened by the spirit, a longing for the quickening of human speech by the spirit which wells forth from the individual. As a first step, individual moral intuitions must be brought out of the human individuality; we shall then see how, as a result, the true Science of the Spirit, which makes all anthropology into Anthroposophy, is born.

6

STUTTGART, OCTOBER 8, 1922

In the ways you want to be active during your stay here, many of you are thinking, above all, about the question of education. It is not so much, perhaps, about education in the sense of ordinary school pedagogy, but the pedagogy that results when we consider that we are living in an age when many new impulses must come into the evolution of humanity and that the attitude of the older towards the younger generation must assume a different character. One reads the fundamental character of the age as something pedagogical.

In saying this, I want to describe an impression that I believe may be noticed in many of you. It seems to me important that when people look at their epoch, they should not only bear in mind the generation now young, entering the century in full youth, and its relation to the older generation that has, in the way I have described, carried over something from the last third of the nineteenth century; but they must also consider: What will be the attitude of this young generation towards the coming generation, to the generation which cannot, as the first, after the last third of the nineteenth century, maintain the same attitude to the nothingness that I have described? For the coming generation will not have what the present age has given to the younger generation through opposition towards their elders, namely enthusiasm—more or less indefinite, but nevertheless enthusiasm. What will further evolve will have much more the character of a longing, of an undefined yearning, than was the case among those who derived their enthusiasm from a mood of opposition against the traditional.

And here we must look still more deeply into the human soul than I have done up to now. I have already shown that in the evolution in the West, consciousness of the pre-earthly existence of the soul has been lost. If we take the religious conceptions that are closest to the development of the human heart in the West during the past centuries, we can only say: For a long time, existence before the descent into a physical earthly body has been lost to human sight. Form a feeling for a moment of how utterly different it is when one is permeated with the consciousness that something has come down from divine-spiritual worlds into the physical human body, has united itself with the physical human body. If nothing of this consciousness exists, there is quite a different feeling, especially about the growing child.

The growing child, when looked at with this consciousness, reveals from its very first breath, or even before, what is being manifested by the spiritual world. Something is revealed from day to day, from week to week, from year to year. Observed in this way, the child becomes a riddle, which one approaches in quite a different way from what is possible when one thinks one is confronting a being whose existence begins with birth or conception, and who, as is said today, develops from this starting point, from this point of germination.

We shall understand one another still better if I call your attention to the fact that the fundamental feeling for the riddle of the world is connected with this. You know that in former days this fundamental feeling about the world riddle was expressed in the paradigm, "Man, know thyself!" This saying, "Man, know thyself!" is about the only saying that can hold its own against the objections always arising when a solution of the world riddle is broached. Now I will say something rather paradoxical. Suppose someone found what one might call the solution of the world riddle. What would there remain to do after the moment when this world riddle was solved? Humanity would lose all freshness of spontaneous striving; all livingness in striving would cease. It would indeed be comfortless to have to admit that the world riddle has been solved with cognition. All that is necessary is to look in some book or other; there the solution is given.

A great many people think thus about the solution of the world riddle. They consider the world riddle to be a question, or a system of questions, that must be answered by explanations, characteristics, or something of the kind. Just feel the deadening effect of such a view! One feels oneself really frozen at the thought that somewhere a solution for the world riddle could be given in this way, that the solution could actually be studied! It is a terrible, a horrible thought, in the face of which all life freezes.

But what lies in the words "Man, know thyself!" expresses something quite different. It really says: Human, look around you at the world; the world is full of riddles, full of mystery, and the human being's slightest movement is a hint or pointer, in the widest sense, for the cosmic mysteries. Now one can indicate precisely where all these riddles are solved. There is quite a short formula for the indication. We can say: All the riddles of the world are solved in *the human being*—again in the very widest sense. The human being himself or herself, moving as a living being in the world, is the solution to the world riddle! Let us gaze at the Sun and experience one of the cosmic mysteries. Let us look into our own being and know that within myself lies the solution of this cosmic mystery. "Human, know thyself and thou knowest the world!"

Yet, this way of expressing the formula is an intimation that no answer is final. The human being is indeed the solution of the world riddle, but to know the human being, we have what is infinite before us and so imbued with life that we will never be done. We know that we bear the solution of the world riddle within ourselves, but we also know that we shall never come to an end of what there is to search for in ourselves. From such a formula, we know only that we are not given abstract questions out of the universe that are to be answered in just as abstract a way, but that the whole universe is a question, and the human being is an answer. We know that the question of the nature of the universe has resounded from times primeval until today, that the answer to these world questions has resounded from human hearts, but that the questioning will go on resounding endlessly. Human beings must learn again living answers on into the unending, distant future. We are not directed in a pedantic way to what might be found in a book, but to the human being. Yet in the sentence, "Man, know thyself!" there sounds to us from ancient times, when school, church, and centers of art were all united in the Mysteries, something that points not to what has been learned from formulas, but to that book about the world that can be deciphered, but deciphered only through endless activity. And the name of this book about the world is the human being.

If the full import of what I put before you yesterday is grasped, through such a change in the experiencing of knowledge, through the attitude we have to knowledge, the spark of life will strike into the whole cognitional nature of the human being. And that is what is needed.

If we picture the moral evolution of humanity up to the time when it became problematic, up to the first third of the fifteenth century, we find that the most diverse impulses were necessary to follow what I characterized yesterday as God-given commandments. When we imagine the driving forces prevalent among various peoples in different epochs, we find a great range of inner impulses arising like instincts, depending on particular conditions of life. We could make an interesting study of how these impulses to obey the old moral intuitions originate: how they grow out of the family, out of the tribe, out of the inclination towards the opposite sex, out of the necessity to live together in communities, out of people's pursuit of their own advantage, and so on.

But in the same way as the old moral intuitions have lived themselves out in historical evolution, to which we were obliged to call attention yesterday, so, too, the impulses mentioned no longer contain an impelling force for the human being that they once had. They cannot contain it if the self-acquired moral intuitions, of which I spoke yesterday, appear in human beings; if, in the world evolution, single individuals are challenged, on the one hand, to find moral intuitions for themselves by dint of the labor of their own souls, and, on the other, to awaken the inner strength, the inner impulses to live according to these moral intuitions. And then it dawns upon us that the old moral impulses will increasingly change, taking a different course.

We see emerging in the depths of the soul, although misjudged and misunderstood today by the majority of civilized humanity, two moral impulses of supreme importance. If attempts are made to interpret them, confused ideas usually result. If people want to put them into practice, they do not know, as a rule, what to do with them. Nonetheless they are arising: as regards the inner life of the human being, the impulse of *moral love*; and outwardly, regarding the interaction between human beings, the moral impulse of *trust* or *confidence* in the other.

Now the degree of strength of and kind of moral love that will be needed in the immediate future for all moral life, was not necessary in the past. Certainly, also for former times, the saying held true: Joy and love are the pinions which bear humankind to great deeds. Yet, if we would speak truly and not in mere phrases, we must say: That joy and that love, which fired human beings to do this or that, were only a metamorphosis of the impulses described before. In the future, pure love, working from within outwards, will have to give human beings wings to fulfill their moral intuitions. Those human beings will feel themselves weak and lacking in will, in the face of moral intuitions, who do not kindle the fire of love for what is moral from out of the depths of their souls when, through their moral intuitions, they confront the deed that should be accomplished.

There you see how in our times we have a parting of the ways! It becomes evident by contrasting the atavistic elements of the older age, which play over in many ways into the present, with what is living within us like the early flush of dawn. You will often have heard those fine words Kant wrote about duty: "Duty! Sublime and mighty name, you embrace nothing that charms and require only submission," and so forth. These were the sternest terms in which to characterize duty! Here the content of duty stands as a moral intuition imparted from outside, and human beings confront this moral intuition in such a way that they have to submit to it. It is felt as moral when no inner satisfaction is gained from obedience to duty; only the cold statement remains: I must perform my duty.

You know Schiller's answer to Kant's definition of duty:

> Gerne dien' ich den Freunden,
> doch tu' ich es leider mit Neigung,
> Und so wurmt es mich oft,
> dass ich nicht tugendhaft bin.

I serve my friends gladly,
but unfortunately I do it with inclination,
and so it often worries me
that I am not virtuous.

Thus Schiller retorts ironically to this categorical imperative.

You see, over against the so-called categorical imperative, as it comes down from former times out of old moral impulses, there stands the summons to humanity to unfold more and more, out of the depths of the soul, the love for what is to become action and deed. For however often in future there may resound, "Submit to duty, to what brings you nothing that will please," it will be of no avail. Just as a person of sixty years cannot behave like a little baby, so can we not live at a later age in a way that was suitable in an earlier epoch. Perhaps that would please people better. But that is of no account. The important thing is what is necessary and possible for the evolution of humanity. We simply cannot debate whether what Kant has said, as a descendant of very ancient times, should be carried on into the future or not. It cannot be carried on, because humanity has developed beyond it, developed in such a way that action out of love must give humankind the impulse for the future.

On the one hand we are led to the conception of ethical individualism;† on the other, to the necessity of knowing that this ethical individualism must be borne on the love arising from perception of the deed to be accomplished. Thus it is, from the human being's subjective viewpoint.

From the aspect of the social life, the matter presents itself differently. There are people today in whom something rumbles—now no longer through a progressive evolution, but through all kinds of opinions taken from outside. They say: Yes, but if you try to found morality on the individuality of the human being, you will ruin the social life. But such a statement is meaningless. It is just as sensible as if someone were to say: If it rains in Stuttgart a certain number of times in three months, nature will ruin some particular crop in the field. If one is conscious of a certain responsibility towards knowledge, one cannot imagine anything more empty. As humanity is developing in the direction of individualism, there is no sense in saying that ethical individualism destroys the community. It is rather a question of seeking those forces by which human evolution can progress; this is necessary for human evolution in the sense of ethical individualism, which can hold the community together and fill it with real life.

Such a force is confidence—confidence between one human being and another. Just as in our inner being we must call upon *love* for an ethical future, so we must call upon *confidence* in the relationship of human beings with each other. We must meet the human being in such a way that we feel each to be a world riddle, a walking world riddle. Then we shall learn in the presence of every human being to unfold feelings that draw forth confidence from the depths of our soul. Confidence in an absolutely real sense, individual, unique confidence, is the hardest to wring from the human soul. But without a system of education, a cultural pedagogy, which is directed towards confidence, civilization can progress no further. In the future, humanity will have to realize the necessity to build up social life on the basis of confidence. Human beings will also have to experience the tragedy when this confidence cannot develop in the proper way in the human soul.

Oh my dear friends, what people have ever felt in the depths of their souls when they have been disappointed by a human being on whom they had relied, all such feelings will in future be as nothing compared with the tragedy when, with an infinitely deepened feeling of trust, human beings will tragically experience disillusionment in their fellow beings. It will be the bitterest thing, not because people have never been disappointed, but because the feeling of confidence and disillusionment will be infinitely deepened in the future; because one will build to such a degree in the soul upon the joy of confidence and the pain of the inevitable mistrust. Ethical impulses will penetrate to the depths of the soul where they will spring directly from the confidence between person and person.

Just as love will fire the human hand, the human arm, so that it draws the strength from within to do a deed, so there will flow the mood of confidence from outside, in order that the deed may find its way from the one human being to the other. The morality of the future will have to be grounded on the free moral love arising from the depths of the human soul; future social action will have to be steeped in confidence. For if one individuality is to meet another in a moral way, above all an atmosphere of confidence will be necessary.

So we anticipate an ethics, a conception of morality that will speak little of the ethical intuitions of old, but will emphasize how human beings must develop from childhood so that there may be awakened in them the power of moral love. Much will have to be given in the pedagogy of the future by teachers and educators through what educates effectively without words. In education and teaching there will have to be imparted much of that knowledge which is not an abstract indication of how humanity consists of this or that, but which leads us over to the other human being in such a way that we can have the proper confidence in that person.

Knowledge of the human being, but not a knowledge that makes us cold towards our fellow human beings, but that fills us with confidence—this must become the very fiber of pedagogy for the future. For we have to give weight again, but in a new way, to what once was taken seriously but is so no longer in the age of intellectualism.

If you go back to Greece, you will find that the doctor in his medical art, for example, felt extraordinarily related to the priest, and priests felt themselves related to the doctor. Such an attitude can be seen dimly, and somewhat chaotically, in the personality of Paracelsus[†] who was, and still is, so little understood. Today we relegate to the sphere of religion the abstract instruction that leads away from real life. For in religious instruction we are told what a person is without the body, and so on—in a way that is singularly foreign to life. Over against this, stands the opposite pole in civilization, where everything brought forth by our own time is kept far from the realm of religion.

Who today sees in healing, for instance, any trace of a religious act, an act in which permeation by the spirit plays a part? Paracelsus still had a feeling for this. For him, the religious life continued on into the science of healing. It was a branch of the religious life. This was so in olden times. The human being was a totality, for what a person had to perform in the service of humanity was permeated by religious impulses. We must strive to permeate life again with this religious character, however, in quite a different way; not through God-given moral intuitions but those we have developed ourselves. This must be made evident first in the sphere of education and teaching. Confidence between one human being and another—the great demand of the future—must permeate social life.

If we ask ourselves what one needs the most in order to be a moral human being in the future, we can only answer: You must have confidence in the human being. Now when children come into the world, that is to say, when human beings come out of pre-earthly existence and unite with their physical bodies in order to use them as instruments on Earth between birth and death—when human beings confront us as children and reveal their souls to us—what must we bring to them in the way of confidence? Just as surely as children, from their first movement on Earth, are human beings, just as surely is the confidence we bring them different from the confidence we bring to adults. When we meet children as teachers or as a member of the older generation, this confidence is transformed in a certain respect. The children come into earthly existence from a pre-earthly world of soul and spirit. What we observe when we look at what reveals itself in them in a wonderful way from day to day, permeating the physical out of the world of soul and spirit, may be called—in the modern sense of the word—the divine.

We need again the divine, which leads human beings out of pre-earthly into the present, just as through their bodily nature they are led onwards in earthly existence. When we speak of confidence between human beings in the moral sphere, and apply it to education, we must specialize and say: We confront the child who has been sent down to us by the divine-spiritual powers, and for whom we should be the solvers of all riddles, with confidence in God. Yes, in face of the child, confidence in the human being becomes confidence in God. In the future what works in a more neutralized way from person to person, will, of itself, assume a religious nuance in relation to the child, or to young people generally, who have to be guided into their development in the world.

There we see how through actual life, morality is transformed back into religiousness that expresses itself in everyday life. In olden times all moral life was a special part of the religious life, for in the religious commandments, moral commandments were given at the same time.

With such things humanity has passed through the epoch of abstraction; now, however, we must again enter the epoch of the concrete. We must feel once again how the moral becomes the religious. And in future the moral deeds of education and instruction will have to shape themselves in a modern sense into what is religious. For pedagogy, my dear friends, is not merely a technical art. Pedagogy is essentially a special chapter in the moral actions of human beings. Only the person who finds education within the realm of morality, within the sphere of ethics, discovers it in the right way. What I have described here as a specifically religious nuance of morality, receives its right coloring if we say: Life stands before us as a riddle. The solution of the riddle lies in the nature of the human being. Indeed it does lie there. But anyone who teaches has to work unceasingly, in a living way, on the solution of this riddle. When we learn to feel how, in education, we are working unceasingly on the solution of the world riddle, we stand quite differently in the world from what would have been the case had we sought for solutions merely by means of head knowledge.

In regard to the feeling about education with which you may have come here, the important thing is to carry away with you into the world this special aspect of pedagogy. This feeling will enable you to stand in the world in such a way that will lead you not only to ask: What tragedy has resulted for the young who had to follow the old? You will also ask, looking into the future: What living forces must I release in myself to look rightly upon those who are coming after me? For they, in turn, will look back to those who were once there. A youth movement, in whatever form, if it considers life in a fully responsible way, must have a Janus head; it must not only look at the demands the young make on the old, but also be able to look at the still undefined demands raging toward us with tremendous power, demands that the coming youth will make upon us.

Not only opposition against the old, but a creative looking forward, is the right guiding thought for a true youth movement. Opposition may, to begin with, have acted as a stimulus to enthusiasm. The power of deed will only be bestowed by the will to work, the will for creative forming within the present evolution of humanity.

7

STUTTGART, OCTOBER 9, 1922

YESTERDAY I pointed out how the longing that can permeate the young today must have something like a Janus-head. At first, this appears to be permeated by enthusiasm that comes from opposition. But however strongly, at the beginning of the twentieth century, this feeling breathed the present, we can say already today that whoever has a sense for the yearning characterized, no longer finds the opposition in its full measure. Many do not yet admit this impartially, particularly among the young themselves. Yet it indicates something very significant.

The generation, which at the beginning of the twentieth century confronted world evolution in such a way that "facing nothingness" was a most profound experience, was actually something quite new in human evolution. Today, the situation is such that this feeling must reckon with many disappointments prepared out of its own depths.

The full spread of the sails as it was some twenty years ago is no longer there. Not only the terrible event of the World War [I] has deflated these sails, but certain experiences working outward from within have arisen in young people and modified their original feeling. One such experience became evident at the beginning of the twentieth century in the feelings of those who had grown older in years but were not inwardly old. It was not clearly expressed in words, but in other than the literal words there was in the young something that pointed to a responsive tiredness.

I am placing a concept before you here that wants to describe something that is difficult to describe precisely. It is difficult, because what I really mean is only fully intelligible to those who have experienced the Youth Movement with a certain wakefulness, whereas a great part of humanity has been asleep to this youth movement. When one speaks to people in the way I have during the past days, it is as if one were talking of something quite foreign to them, something they have slept through, and towards which even today, they act in an extraordinarily sleepy manner.

Responsive tiredness, I call it. In ordinary life organic existence requires not only activity but also the accompanying state of tiredness after the accomplished work. We must not only be able to get tired, we must also from time to time be able to carry tiredness around within us. To pass our days in such a way that we go to sleep at night simply because it is customary to do so, is not healthy; it is certainly less healthy than to have the due amount of tiredness in the evening and for this to lead in the normal way into sleep. So too, the capacity to become tired-out by the phenomena meeting us in life is something that must be.

When education, for example, has been discussed, I have often heard it said that there must be a pedagogy that makes learning into a game for children; school must be all joy for the child. Yes, those who speak like this should just try making school all joy for children, so that the children laugh all the time, so that learning is play, and at the same time, they are learning something. This is the very best possible educational principle for ensuring that nothing at all is learned.

The right thing is for teachers to be able to handle what does not give the child joy, but perhaps a good deal of toil and woe, in such a way that the child, as a matter of course, submits to it. It is very easy to say what should be taught to the child. But childhood can be ruined by learning being made into a game. For it is essential that we should also be made tired in our soul by certain things; that they should cause toil and exertion. One must express it thus, even if it sounds pedantic. Tiredness existed among the young in earlier times, too, when they had to strive towards something living, a certain knowledge, a certain kind of insight. I mean times when those possessing a certain amount of knowledge were still able to stand before the young who wanted to acquire it, as an embodied ideal. Tiredness certainly existed even then.

My dear friends, there may be some here who take the above statement with mild skepticism. There are many people today who would take it with skepticism, for when it is claimed that those who knew something stood as a kind of ideal for those anxious to learn, this idea appears to many as unrealizable. For, at the present time, it is almost incredible that anybody should be regarded as a kind of embodied insight or knowledge, which we strive for like a personal ideal.

Yet, disregarding ancient times, this feeling was still present to a high degree even in the later Middle Ages. Those wonderful and inspiring feelings of reverence, permeating life with real re-creative forces for the soul still in the later Middle Ages, have to a great extent been lost. And because the yearning that once fired people up for science was no longer there, the young could no longer get tired from their studies. To give this concrete expression I should have to say: Science became something that did not live in human heads, but was stored in the libraries. Science gradually became something that was not really wanted any more. Hence, one did not tire from it anymore. Because one did not feel oneself pervaded by the yearning for it, it no longer made one tired. There was no possibility of getting tired from the knowledge that was to be achieved.

And from this, what permeated the young, at the turn of the nineteenth century and the twentieth century, derived a quite special character—the character of the life force in human beings who go to bed at night, who are not tired and keep turning and twisting about without knowing why. I do not want to imply anything derogatory, for I am not of the opinion that these forces, which are there at night in human beings when they turn and twist about in bed because they are not tired, are unhealthy forces. I am not calling them unhealthy. They are quite healthy life forces, but they are not in their proper place; and so it was, in a certain sense, with those forces that worked in the young at the turn of the nineteenth century. They were thoroughly healthy forces, but there was nothing to give them direction. The young had no longer the desire to apply these forces to what was told them by their elders. Yet, forces cannot be present in the world without being active, and so, at the time referred to, innumerable forces yearned for activity and had no guiding line. These forces appeared, for example, in the young students.

Since the first third of the fifteenth century, all human striving for knowledge out of intellectuality has taken on a quite particular character.

Human beings are supposed to devote themselves to something that one called science, but which hardly touches or has anything to do with the human being at all. People can no longer feel what humanity holds sway in writings of the twelfth or thirteenth century. This does not imply that we have to return to the twelfth or thirteenth century, to implicit belief in all we find there. We certainly do not want to comply with the demands of certain churches in this direction.

It is not possible to go deeply into what, for instance, Albertus Magnus† wrote with the same indifference with which people today study biology or some other work. In that way we cannot get to know what he wrote at all. We must take the book and sit down with it as if we were sitting down in front of another human being, with whom we do not take what he or she says with indifference—or objectively as one says—but with whom the inner being of our soul is engaged; it rises and falls, and is quickened to movement. The soul is at work when we read even the driest chapter written at that time, by an Albertus Magnus, for instance. Quite apart from the fact that in these writings there is still the power of pictorial expression for what appear abstract things, there is always something in the general ideas that gives us a feeling of movement as if we might be working with spade and shovel—I mean in the soul. Quite aside from this splendid human activity, through the pictures, care is taken that those who possess this knowledge have full confidence in what they are imparting.

For such people it was not a matter of indifference whether they felt that what they discovered in their seeking pleased God or not. To those who realize the difference between the picture that an Albertus Magnus gives, as the great scholar of the Middle Ages, and that of one of the eminent minds of the nineteenth century, for example, Herbart†—one could name others but Herbart had a great influence on education up into the last third of the nineteenth century—Albertus Magnus appears like a fiery, luminous cloud. When Albertus Magnus devotes himself to knowledge—something that lights up in him or becomes dim—we feel him as it were in a fiery, luminous cloud, and if we are gradually able to enter into such a soul, we come into this fire ourselves. Even if for the modern soul it is antiquated, we feel that it is not a matter of indifference, when we steep ourselves in what is moral, write it down, speak about it, or even just study it, whether or not one is sympathetic or antipathetic toward a divine-spiritual being. This feeling of sympathy or antipathy always plays a part.

On the other hand, if we steep ourselves in the way Herbart objectively and scientifically discusses the five moral ideas: goodwill, perfection, benevolence, rights, and retribution, we do not have a cloud that encircles us with warmth or cold, but something that gradually freezes us; it is objective to the point of iciness. And that is the mood that has crept into the whole nature of knowledge and reached its climax at the end of the nineteenth century.

And so knowledge gradually became something to which people devoted themselves in a way that even outwardly was quite remarkable. It was only at the lecture podium that one got to know those represented as men of knowledge. I do not know if others as old as I am have had similar experiences, but in the 1890s I had cause for annoyance again and again. At that time I had been mixing in all kinds of learned circles. I often needed to enjoy such society and was eager to discuss this or that question. I looked forward to speak once again about the difference between epigenesis and evolution, for instance. However, when one began with this, one soon heard: No, there is to be no shop talk. Anything that savored of talking shop was taboo. The knowledgeable were only experienced at the lecture podium. When they left it, they were no longer the same as they had been; they became someone else. They spoke about everything under the sun, except their own special subject. In short, life in science became so objective that those with a special subject treated this, too, very objectively, and wanted to be ordinary people when not obliged to deal with their subject. One can connect still other feelings with this. I have said this only for the sake of elucidation. But I will tell you the real point in another way.

Teachers can bring what they have only half learned in this way or that to the young. We find, for example, those who teach, standing before their classes with notebooks, or even books written by someone else—for all I know, their notebooks, too, may contain things written by other people, but I will not assume that—and boldly setting to work to give their lessons out of these books. By such a procedure they are presupposing that there is no supersensible world at all.

How is it that one says that those who give their lessons from a notebook, or some other book, are presupposing that no supersensible world exists? Here, too, Nietzsche had one of his many interesting flashes of insight. He called attention to the fact that within every human being another is hidden. This is taken to be a poetic way of speaking, but it is no such thing. In every human being another is hidden! This hidden being is often much more intelligent than the one who is visible. In the child, for example, this hidden being is infinitely wiser. This being is a supersensible reality and is within the human being. And if teachers sit in front of a class of say, thirty pupils, and teach with the help of a book or a notebook, they may perhaps be able to train these thirty pupils to regard this, in their visible selves, as something natural, but—of this we can be quite certain—all of the thirty invisible human beings sitting there are judging differently. They say of those teachers: "They are wanting to teach me something that they first have to read. I should like to know why I am expected to know what they are reading. There is no reason for me to know what they are only now reading for themselves. They do not know it themselves, otherwise they would not need to stand there with the book in hand. I am still very young and am expected to learn what they, who are so much older, do not know even yet and read to me out of a book!"

These things must be taken concretely. To speak of a supersensible world does not mean merely to lose oneself in fantastic mysticism and to talk of things that are—I say this with quotation marks—"hidden" from one. To speak of supersensible worlds means, with regard to life, to speak about actual realities. We are speaking of actual realities when we speak as the thirty invisible children spoke about the teacher of the thirty visible ones who, perhaps only out of obedience, were too timid to say this aloud. If we think it through, it does not seem so stupid; the statements of these thirty invisible, supersensible beings are, in fact, quite reasonable.

Thus, we must realize that in the young individuality sitting before the teacher or educator, much goes on that is entirely hidden from outer perception. And that was how there arose deep aversion to what came in this way. For naturally students could not have a great deal of confidence in a teacher who faced their hidden being out of the objective, scientific approach generally common at the end of the nineteenth century. So a deep antipathy was felt; one simply did not try to take up what should have carried one through life, and consequently could not get tired from it. There was no longer the desire to have what would have made one tired. And nobody knew what to do with the forces that could have led to the tiredness.

Now one could also meet such people, like those who were in the Youth Movement at the turn of the nineteenth century, elsewhere. Often they were not young physically, but rather very old. They could be met in movements like the Theosophical Movement. There were many in that movement who were no longer young, yet had a feeling towards what contemporary knowledge gave them that was similar to the young. They did not want this knowledge, because it could no longer make them tired. Whereas the young, as the result of this incapacity to get tired, raged,—forgive the expression—many Theosophists were looking in their Theosophy for a kind of sleeping potion or opiate. For what is contained in Theosophical literature is to a great extent a sleeping potion for the soul. People were actually lulling themselves to sleep. They kept the spirit busy, but look at the way in which they did so. By inventing the maddest allegories! It was enough to drive a sensitive soul out of its body to listen to the explanations given to old myths and sagas. What allegories and symbols were thought up! Looked at from the biology of the life of soul, it was all sleeping potion. It would really be quite good to draw a parallel between the turning and twisting in bed after spending a day that has not been tiring and the taking of a sleeping draught in order to cripple the real activity of the spirit.

What I describe are not theories but moods of the age, and it is imperative to become familiar with these moods by looking from every angle at what was there. This incapacity to get tired at the turn of the nineteenth century is extraordinarily significant. Yes, but this led to the impossibility of finding anything right, for human evolution had arrived at a point where people said with great enthusiasm, "We shall allow nothing to come to us from outside; we want to develop everything from within our own being. We want to wander through the world and wait until there comes out of our own inner being what neither parents, nor teachers, nor even the old traditions can give us any longer. We want to wait for the new to approach us."

My dear friends, ask those who have spoken in such a way whether this new thing has come to them, whether it has dropped ready-made into the laps of those who have had this great longing. Indeed the intoxication of those times is beginning in some degree to be followed by the "morning-after" headache. My only aim, however, is to characterize, not to criticize. The first thing that arose was a great rejection, a rejection of something that was there, which human beings could not use for their innermost being. And behind this great rejection there was hidden the positive—the genuine longing for something new.

This genuine longing for what is new can be fulfilled in no other way than by human beings permeating themselves with something not of this Earth. When people only let soul and body function as they do, nothing can come that really has the power to satisfy. The human being who is unwilling to take in anything is like a lung that finds no air to breathe. Certainly a lung that finds no air to breathe may first, before it dies, even if only for a moment, experience the greatest thirst for air. But the lung cannot, out of itself, quench this thirst for air; it has to allow for the air to come to it. In reality, the young who honestly feel the thirst of which we have been speaking, cannot help but long for something with which to be in harmony, that does not come only out of the self like the science that has grown old and is no longer a wholesome air for the soul to breathe.

That was felt in the first place, but far too little, that a new, young science must be there, a new spiritual life that is able once again to unite with the soul. Now what belongs to present and future ages must link itself with older phenomena of human evolution. The difference is that these old phenomena of human evolution arose from a life of soul that was full of pictures and dreamlike, whereas the life of soul we bear within us, and towards which we are still striving, must become fully conscious. But we must in many respects go back to older contents of the soul.

Now I should like to turn your mind's eye to a disposition of the spirit prevailing in old Brahmanism in the ancient East. The old

Brahmin schools spoke of four means to knowledge on the path of life. It is difficult to give ancient thoughts in a suitable form, because we are living, not only centuries, but thousands of years later. However, in order to get somewhere near the mark, I will depict these four means to knowledge.

The first means was what hovered, as it were, midway between tradition and remembrance, something connected with the Sanskrit root s-mr-ti, of which today one has only an idea. Yet, it can be characterized. Everyone knows what remembrance, personal memory is. These people did not connect the idea I have here in mind with personal remembrance as closely as we connect certain concepts with memory today. It was much more so that what they remembered out of their own childhood flowed together and became one with what was passed on to them by others. They did not distinguish between what they themselves remembered and what they received through tradition. If you were to practice a more subtle psychology, you would notice that actually these things flow together in the soul of the child, because the child takes in a great deal that is based on tradition. Modern human beings see only that they acquired these things in childhood. Ancient Indians did not see this. They paid much more heed to its content, which did not lead them into their own childhood, but to their parent, grandparent, and great-grandparent. Thus, tradition and personal remembrance flowed into each other indistinguishably. That was the first means of acquiring knowledge.

The second means for acquiring knowledge was what we might describe as "being introduced," (not an introduction in the sense of conventional social interactions today in which one says the name, but literally, an "appearing before the eyes") what we call "perception" today. The third means to knowledge was what we might call thinking that synthesizes. Thus we could also say: remembrance with tradition, observation, and the thinking that synthesizes.

A fourth means for acquiring knowledge was also taught with all clarity in ancient Brahmanism. This can be described as having something communicated by other human beings. So I ask you to notice that in ancient Brahmanism, tradition was not identified with having something communicated by other human beings. This was a fourth means for the attainment of knowledge. Perhaps this will be clearer if we link it up with what is tradition and, at the same time, what the nature of remembrance is. Where tradition is concerned, human beings did not become conscious of the way in which it came to them; they were conscious only of the content. However, with the fourth means to knowledge, the way and manner in which it came to one was the important thing. In human remembrance, a person had in mind that it had been communicated to him or her by someone else. The fact of having received something from others was an awakening force in knowledge itself.

I think that today many of those who are true children of the nineteenth century would shake their heads, if we counted this "what-is-told-us-by-others" as one of the means of acquiring knowledge. Philosophers, who dabble in thinking that synthesizes and regard what they are told by others as a means to knowledge, will never succeed with their thesis, nor be accepted as university lecturers. At most they might succeed in joining a theological faculty, for theology is judged in a different way. What is at the bottom of all this? In olden times people understood the experience of having something kindled within them in mutual interaction with another human being. They counted somebody else's telling them what they themselves did not know as among the things they needed in order to be able to live. It was reckoned so emphatically as one of the factors necessary for life that it was considered equal to perception through the eyes and the ears.

More often today people will naturally have a different feeling: that it is splendid for human beings to tell another what the other does not know, and the world calls for this. But it has nothing to do with the essence of things. What is essential is for observations and experiments to be made and for the results to be clearly expressed. The other has nothing to do with the essential nature of knowledge. It is natural to feel this today, but from the human standpoint, it is not correct. It is part of life that humans should be permeated in soul and spirit by what I described yesterday as a necessary vehicle of the social life, namely, by confidence. In this particular domain, confidence consists of what one human being tells another, thus becoming for the other a source of soul-spiritual experience.

Confidence must above all things be evoked in the young. That for which the young are thirsting must be found out of confidence. Our whole modern spiritual development has moved in the opposite direction. Even in theoretical pedagogy no value is attached any longer to the fact that a human being might have something he or she would like to tell another which the latter did not know. Theoretical pedagogy was thought out in such a way that, as far as possible, there was presented to the young only what could be proved in front of them. But that could not be a comprehensive proof. In this regard, people have therefore remained at a very infantile stage. Pedagogy thought to a certain extent: How can I give the children something, even under the assumption that they do not believe me? How can I introduce a method which proves perceptibly? No wonder there came the corresponding echo, and it was henceforth demanded of teachers: Yes, now prove that to me! And now what I am going to say may sound antiquated, my dear friends, but I do not feel it to be old but really quite young, even as part of the Youth Movement.

Today when someone stands there before a number of young people who are to be taught, it is as if there sounds out of the young souls even before this teacher has approached them: Prove that to me! You have no right to ask us to believe you. I feel it as tragic—and this is no criticism—that the young should suffer from having been educated by the old in such a way that they no longer have the ability to receive what is necessary for life. And so, there arises a tremendous question, which we shall be considering in the next few days. I should like to give you a somewhat radical description of it.

Let us imagine the Youth Movement progressing and taking hold of younger and younger human beings and finally mere infants. We would then get an infant Youth Movement, and just as the later Youth Movement rejects the knowledge that can be given to it, so will the infants who ought still to be at their mothers' breasts, say: We refuse it; we refuse to receive anything from outside. We don't want our mothers' milk any longer; we want to get everything out of ourselves!

What I have here presented as a picture is a burning question for the Youth Movement. For the young are really asking: Where are we to obtain spiritual nourishment? And the way in which they have asked hitherto has been very suggestive of this picture of the infants. And so, in the coming days, we shall consider the question of "the source of life," after which Faust was striving. The question I have put before you as a picture is intended to stimulate us to contribute towards a solution, but a solution which may mean something for your perception, for your feeling, even for your whole life.

8

STUTTGART, OCTOBER 10, 1922

Up to now we have given an outer description of what was experienced by those growing up around the turn of the nineteenth century, by considering the trend of human spiritual culture. Today, in order to find the transition to a true self-knowledge, we will study the human being from within.

When we consider spiritual evolution outwardly, especially in the West, we are led back to the first third of the fifteenth century; for an inward study we must go back to the fourth century B.C.E. A date indicating an important moment would be the year 333 C.E. Yet, this date is, of course, only approximate. It is not a date from which to make calculations, but serves as an approximation in pointing to weighty matters affecting a large proportion of European humanity.

Let us look into the soul of a person who before this date lived into the culture of southern Europe, or in certain districts of northern Africa. These districts are the prominent ones to be considered when we try to gain an idea of the definitive cultural life of the time. The souls of these human beings still were conscious that human thought was not simply worked out in the head, but that it was revealed, either directly to the individual, or, where the human being was not able to receive such revelation directly, through the confident communication of other human beings. The prevalent feeling among the educated and uneducated today, that their thoughts are worked out in their own head, did not exist then. It was a period of actual transition. In the Middle East outstanding spiritual personalities were concerned with how thoughts came to humanity from spiritual realms. In southern

Europe and in northern Africa, doubts began to creep in as to whether the human being possessed the faculty to receive thoughts by revelation. These doubts were only faint at first. There was still an overwhelming feeling: When I have a thought, this thought has been put into me by a god either indirectly or transmitted by way of human heredity, that is, through tradition, not natural heredity. Thought can enter earthly evolution only as revelation.

The first westerners to feel strong doubts in this direction were those who had come from the northern peoples and entered the civilization of the south. They were of Germanic-Celtic blood and had moved with the various migrations from the north to the south. These people probably would have reached the point, out of their own nature, of saying: Thoughts are something we work out for ourselves. This feeling, however, was dulled down by what they found as the Greco-Latin culture, as the culture of the east. These cultures were extraordinarily intermixed up to the fourth century; every possible trend was working within them. Yet, in the migrations southward, one felt strongly that thoughts were grasped only by drawing them into the world of the senses from a supersensible world.

We have only an external history. We have no history of feeling, no history of thought, no history of the soul. Hence, we were not made aware how the whole disposition of the soul changed from one century to another. There was a tremendous change in inner human perception precisely in the fourth century C.E. We find then something that for the very first time caused people to reflect upon the origin of thought: what previously had been accepted without question, namely the fact that thoughts were revealed, gradually came to a point where a theory was needed, in order for people to understand it. But these people were by no means convinced that human beings could create their thought world out of themselves.

Consider the great difference in this connection between souls of the present day and souls of that time. I am speaking of some souls only. What I am describing to you was naturally present in the most varied nuances. For one part of humanity, matters were as I have described them; for another, there was still an invincibly strong, intense belief that soul-spiritual beings descended into the human organism and communicated thoughts. It was, to an extent, an "elite" of humanity who at that time grasped thought in such a way that the question could arise: Where do thoughts come from? For the others, it was quite evident that thoughts were given.

Now take the souls born after the year 333 approximately. These souls were no longer able, out of a natural feeling, to give a matter-of-course explanation of the origin of thought. Thus a period followed in which theorists, philosophers and philosophical theologians wrestled with the question of the significance of thoughts in the world. Then arose the struggle between Nominalism and Realism. The Nominalists were those in the Middle Ages who said: Thoughts live only in the human individuality; they are only a summary of what exists outside in the world and within separate individuals. The Realists still had a vivid recollection of those ancient times when people regarded thoughts as having substance, as something substantial that was revealed. They conceived thoughts in such a way that they said: It is not I who think the thought; it is not I who, for instance, sum up all dogs into the general concept dog; but there exists one general thought "dog" and this is revealed out of the spiritual world, just as a color or tone is revealed to the senses. It was a struggle to understand rightly the nature of thought that had, as it were, alighted as an independent possession in the human soul. It is of extraordinary interest to steep oneself, from this point of view, in the spiritual history of the Middle Ages.

The closer we come to the fifteenth century, the more we see with what intensity human beings struggled to come to terms with what is revealed through thought in human nature. Whereas, human beings before the year 333 really had the idea: There is a divine weaving streaming around the Earth just as in the physical world the atmosphere streams round it; and in this streaming, beings, the thoughts, remain behind and reveal themselves to human beings. They are, so to speak, the footprints of the divine world surrounding the Earth, which are buried in human beings as thoughts. Whereas, those souls who before the year 333 considered that in the thought world a feeling of their connection with the spiritual world existed, we find the Middle Ages permeated by the tragedy of still seeking to connect thought in some way with the divine-spiritual.

Why did those souls, who up into the fifteenth century thought about thoughts—if I may put it so—strive so vigorously to connect thoughts with what is divine-spiritual in the cosmos? It was because they felt an inner impulse, which they were unable to express in clear concepts, but which was present in them as a definite soul experience. This originated from all the souls who were born as the leading souls of humanity from the fourth to the fourteenth century; who were reincarnated from the time long before the year 333 and who argued energetically over the reality or merely nominal character of concepts, having lived previously at the time of the Mystery of Golgotha.

The Mystery of Golgotha took place in comparative isolation in the Middle East. But that was only the external manifestation of a spiritual event that took place in the physical world. Something happened in the souls who had reached a certain degree of maturity. When we consider those actually fighting over the reality or unreality of thoughts, we find souls whose previous incarnation had taken place during the first three centuries B.C.E. Essentially however, civilized humanity was made up of souls reincarnated from the time before the Mystery of Golgotha. Out of the real connection between the human soul and the divine spiritual world, which expressed itself in the acceptance of thought being received through revelation—out of this experience, which souls living in the Middle Ages had had in an earlier earthly life many centuries before, arose the impulse to dispute about the reality or unreality of the thought world.

For what is it that is known as scholasticism at the beginning of the new era in the thirteenth, fourteenth, fifteenth centuries? What actually filled the souls of the scholastics? It is the fact that a decisive moment had arrived in the evolution of humanity; it was not given utterance but was felt by outstanding souls of that time. For them, it was as if the gods had forsaken the sphere of human thought, as if humans only had thoughts that were wrung dry.

When we observe the souls who lived from the fifteenth century on into later times, we find them to be those who in their previous incarnation had lived not long after the year 333. Up to the eighth, ninth centuries C.E., at least those who were teachers still had the feeling that human thought was a gift of the gods. And the people who in their previous earthly life had already felt the world of thought to be forsaken by the gods were—naturally I am speaking only of a part of humanity—destined to be born again about the turn of the nineteenth and twentieth century.

When, therefore, we observe not only external destiny, but the inner destiny of the human soul, we must pay no heed to what wells up out of our childhood from the depths of the soul. We must look to the time in which souls were incarnated who could no longer hear from their teachers that thoughts were beings permeated, imbued by the divine. Thereby the inner feeling arose to flee from thought and that something warmer, more saturated with substance should be found. This arose because already in a previous incarnation the divine character of thought had become subject to the gravest doubts, or had indeed been entirely lost. What thus shines through now out of the previous earthly life was experienced with the greatest intensity as tragedy at the turn of the nineteenth century.

Since the first third of the fifteenth century, the receiving of thought from the divine-spiritual world was already lost to humanity. Because human beings could no longer receive thoughts out of the divine-spiritual world, they took them from outer observation. External observation and the art of experimenting reached such a height, because the inner conceiving of thoughts was replaced by gleaning them from the external sense world.

In the development of world history, however, what is not dependent on outer circumstances does not immediately become apparent. For even if since the fifteenth century human beings had lost the ability to conceive thought from within outward, to receive thoughts from the divine-spiritual world, those souls were not yet there who could have sensed the full tragedy of being forsaken by revealed thought. In those souls who had lived their former life on Earth before the sixth or seventh century, namely, before the fourth century after Christ, there lived in their feeling: We must admit that we receive our thoughts from the external world, but in spite of this, our soul tells us that even the thoughts received from the external world are God-given. We no longer know how one experiences them as God-given, but our inner being tells us that this is so.

A truly brilliant spirit who had such a mood of soul was Johannes Kepler.† Johannes Kepler was as much a natural scientist of an earlier time as of the later one. He drew his thoughts from external observation, but in his inner experience he had absolutely the feeling that divine beings are there when human beings receive thoughts from nature. Kepler felt himself to be partly an initiate, and for him it was a matter of course that he experienced his abstract building up of the universe artistically.

It is extraordinarily valuable, from a scientific point of view, to immerse oneself in the progress human thought has made through Kepler. Yet, one is more deeply stirred when one steeps oneself in Kepler's life of soul. A soul life of such intensity and inwardness did not exist in any other natural scientist in later times, and certainly not in any authoritative teacher of the majority of humanity. Between the fifteenth and the nineteenth centuries, the feeling was entirely lost that through thought the human soul is brought into connection with the divine-spiritual.

Those who do not merely study the course of time in an unimaginative fashion by just taking in the content, but are able to sense something in the course of events, have something peculiar revealed to them. I do not wish here to talk of how Goethe's special way of thinking about nature has become an impossibility for later science. I mean for the external science of the times following his; for this science did not realize where the difference lay between external science and that of Goethe. I do not want to speak about this. You need only look at scientific books of the first third of the nineteenth century that set the tone for the later mode of thought, such as, for instance, the physiological works of Henle or Burdach†—the latter of which belonged absolutely to the first third of the nineteenth century, even though his work was written somewhat later—and you will note in all of them a different style. There is still something of the spirit which wells up directly out of the soul when, let us say, they speak of the embryo or of the structure of the human brain; there is still something of what has been entirely lost with later scientists.

In this connection it is significant to bring to mind a personality still actively working during the last third of the nineteenth century.

He was already subject to the forces driving out the spirit from science; nevertheless he still had the spiritual life in his own soul. I am referring to the anatomist Hyrtl,† who belongs to only the smallest part of the last third of the nineteenth century, to the last two-thirds. Try to let the anatomy books of Hyrtl work upon you. These books are written in the style of later anatomists, but one can see that it was difficult for Hyrtl. He writes chapter after chapter, always restraining the impulse to allow anything of the soul to flow into his sentences. Occasionally, it peeps through in the style and sometimes even a little in the content. It is as though the iron necessity existed to extinguish the soul-spiritual welling up from out of the human being's inner being whenever they wrote about some natural process. Today we can barely imagine what can be experienced when, let us say, we go back from a contemporary anatomical book to Hyrtl or Burdach. One feels as if something were charged with a certain amount of warmth in comparison to the limited degree of warmth in the scientific feeling of the first third, but particularly to the second third, of the nineteenth century. Certainly, at that time science was not at its zenith. That is only of secondary importance and need not be considered further. I am speaking of what was experienced in science. And about that one can say: We can see from the path taken by the scientist that which spiritual science shows, namely, that at the end of the nineteenth century more and more souls came, in whom there no longer lived, from their previous earthly life, the impulse that thought is god-given. There was no longer even an echo of this. The sense for the individual past earthly life had been lost, yet its echo still lived on long afterwards.

Thus there were those, who had a really living warmth within them, who had not become dried up by the prejudice that in science one must be objective. What we strive for in spiritual science is the truly objective, but not in the scientists' meaning of the word. These souls not dried up through striving after objectivity asked: What is in us that is still bound up with the divine-spiritual from which we were torn in our previous earthly incarnation? They did not ask this consciously but subconsciously. Rising to the surface of consciousness was the feeling that human beings had lost their connection with the divine-spiritual world. On the other hand, it is a feeling that humanity dare not lose this connection, for without this consciousness, even if so dim, the soul cannot live. Hence, the strong inclination arose toward an indeterminate yearning for the spirit, and at the same time, the incapacity to reach it.

It is precisely the characteristic of the generation growing up about the turn of the nineteenth century and at the beginning of the twentieth that it would ask the older generations: Is there even any possibility to discover the spiritual in our earthly surroundings? And the leaders, who were asked unconsciously by the youth how they could find the spiritual in nature, how they could find it within human life itself, rejected as unscientific this bringing of the spirit into the consideration of nature and even of human life.

Thus in the second half of the nineteenth century a dreadful thing happened—the slogan "psychology, science of the soul without a soul" arose. I do not attach great importance to the fact that individual philosophers said that we need a science of the soul without soul. What the philosophers say has no great influence, but it is symptomatic of what figures very widely as feeling and of how one deals with the younger generation. True, only a few philosophers actually said: We need a psychology without soul. But the whole age says: We older people wish to teach you mineralogy, zoology, botany, biology, anthropology, even history, in a way to make it appear as if, at the most, there are experiences of the soul, but not a human soul as such. Thus, the whole world, in so far as it is observed scientifically, had to be experienced as having no soul. Those who were first to bring with them out of their previous earthly life this tragedy of experiencing soullessness were compelled to ask with the utmost insistence: Where can we look to fill the soul with spirit? And from what their age considered of greatest value—in other respects rightly so—they gleaned the least information.

Those who, in the last third of the nineteenth century, wrote books in such a way that one can gather something of the nature of their soul life from them were, naturally, even in the nineteenth century, a vanishing minority. I can assure you that, in general, the people who wrote these books were not the most brilliant. Among those who do not write books there are people who are distinctly more intelligent than among those who do write them. In the last third of the nineteenth century profounder natures were living in the midst of the superficial ones content with a science bereft of spirit. And when one looks into the more profound natures of that time, which is possible through spiritual science, one finds a certain wrestling with deep problems. However those who had this inner life were no longer listened to. They no longer found the opportunity to become leaders.

Many people foresaw clearly what the microscope was bringing in its wake in the second half of the nineteenth century. There were souls among them who participated in the cultural life, but did not really penetrate it, because they could not handle a culture devoid of spirit. Therefore they became silent, even in their thoughts, in face of the scientific views. Yet they felt the question in their depths: How can the microscopic evolution be brought into relation with macrocosmic evolution? They faced this problem increasingly in their feeling life.

There were also people who, as a result of their education, followed the scientific tradition and hoped for ever more scientific results from the further development of the microscope. However, others of a deeper nature looked with disturbed feelings upon the further development of the microscope, particularly upon the views that arose as a result. The highest hope of one group was, by examining ever smaller and smaller objects, to penetrate into the nature of what is living. But others felt that this whole business would make the world go under. Yes, there were those who felt the use of the microscope to be a sucking dry of the soul.

I trust you will not think that I am indulging in satire in a mystical, fantastic fashion on the use of the microscope. That would never occur to me. I am, naturally, fully aware of the services rendered by the microscope, and I would never wish to turn the wheels of science back. I am, however, stating facts about the life of the soul.

The number of these solitary spirits steadily decreased. Fortlage, who lived as Professor in Jena at the end of the nineteenth century, was one of them. He spoke somewhat as follows: One can look more and more thoroughly into the microscope and go on discovering ever smaller things, but in this minuteness, one loses what is substantially true. If you want to see what is being sought with the aid of the microscope, then turn your gaze out into the infinite space of the universe. From the stars, there speaks what you are seeking within the microcosm. You talk of the secrets of life, and seek for them in what is ever more and more minute. But there one loses life, not for reality, but for knowledge. You can find it again when you understand how to read the stars.

Some have said: Life is brought down from the cosmos.† But they sought for a material means, possibly in the meteor showers flying through cosmic space and bringing the germs and seeds of life out of other worlds down to the Earth. But when one gazes from the Earth out into limitless space, it is not limitless at all. For the mechanistic mathematical way of perception, the firmament was done away with by Giordano Bruno; but for the inner contemplation, it is again there, in the sense that one cannot simply draw a radius from the Earth and prolong it into infinity. This radius has in fact an end, and at this end, there is everywhere at the inner periphery, life to be found and not death. From this world-periphery life radiates in from everywhere.

I only wish to indicate to you by these examples the nature of those inner problems of feeling that confronted the soul at the turn of the nineteenth century. Out of the soul's dullest feeling, the question really was put: Where can we rediscover the spiritual?

You see, this question must set the mood if any phase of the Youth Movement is to find a right content: Where can I find the spiritual? How does one experience the spiritual? The really important thing is that, side by side with all yearning expectation, there shall also be found among the young, single ideals striving towards an inner activity of the soul. I should like to preface what I have to say tomorrow by the following.

In what I have named Anthroposophy, in fact in the foreword to my *Intuitive Thinking as a Spiritual Path*, you will meet with something that you will not be able to comprehend if you give yourself up only to the passive thinking so specially loved today, to that popular godforsaken thinking that was already godforsaken in the previous incarnation. You will only understand it if you develop, in freedom, the inner impulse to bring activity into your thinking. You will never get on with spiritual science if that spark, that lightning, through which activity in thinking is awakened, does not flash up. Through this activity, we must re-conquer the divine nature of thinking.

Anthroposophical literature demands that one shall think actively. Most people are only able to think passively and believe that active thinking is impossible. But active thinking does not allow sleeping nor intellectual dreaming. One must keep in step with it and get one's thinking on the move. The moment thinking is set in motion, one keeps up with it. Then what I should like to call modern clairvoyance ceases to be anything miraculous. That this clairvoyance should still appear as something particularly miraculous comes from people not wishing to develop the energy to bring activity into their thinking. It often drives one to despair. One often feels when demanding active thinking of human beings that their mood is like the following: A man was lying in a ditch without moving hand or foot, not even opening his eyes. He was asked by a passerby, "Why are you so sad?" The man answered, "Because I don't want to do anything." The questioner was astonished at this, for the man lying there was doing nothing and had apparently done nothing for a long time. But he wanted to do even more "doing nothing!" Then the questioner said, "Well, you certainly are doing nothing," and got the answer, "I have to revolve with the Earth and even that I don't want to do!"

This is how people appear who do not wish to bring activity into thinking, the power that alone can bring back, out of the human being, a connection between the human soul and the divine-spiritual content of the world again. Many of you have learned to despise thinking because it has met you only in its passive form. This, however, is only head-thinking in which the heart plays no part. But try for once really to think actively, and you will see how the heart is then engaged. Human beings of our age enter with the greatest intensity into the spiritual world if they succeed in developing active thinking. For through active thinking we are able to bring hearty, courageous forces into our thinking again.

If you do not seek the spirit on the path of thought that, although difficult to tread, must be trodden with courage, if you do not seek through the path of thinking, the spiritual life that has flowed through humanity from the very beginning, then you are like infants who believe themselves able to draw nourishment out of themselves and not from the mother's breast. You only come to a movement with real content when you find the secret of developing within yourselves an activity which enables you to draw again, out of cosmic life, true spiritual nourishment, true spiritual drink.

But that is preeminently a problem of the will, a problem of the will experienced through feeling. Infinitely much depends today upon good will, upon an energetic willing, and no theories can solve what we are seeking today. Courageous, strong will alone can bring the solution.

Let us devote the next few days to the question of how to find this good will, this strong will.

9

STUTTGART, OCTOBER 11, 1922

FROM what I said yesterday about the course of the human soul in historical evolution, you will have gathered that the way human beings confront their fellow human beings today is different from what it was before the year 333 C.E.

I assume that you are familiar with the members or sheaths of the human being, according to Anthroposophical knowledge. You know that we must differentiate in the soul between what was active in human nature up to the fifteenth century—the so-called intellectual or mind soul—and the consciousness soul, which since that time has been principally active in those who have developed to the level of culture to which humanity has advanced so far.

In describing a particular activity of the soul, such as that of the intellectual or mind soul, it does not indicate that the intellect, as we understand it today, is a special characteristic of the intellectual or mind soul. The intellectual or mind soul was developed particularly by the Greeks and among them, the intellect was certainly not what it is today. What is meant by the intellect today you will have been able to gather from yesterday's lecture.

Among the Greeks, concepts, ideas, were bestowed by the spirit. Because of this, their intellect was not so cold, so lifeless and dry as ours is today, which is the result of being worked out by ourselves. Intellectualism has first arisen through the special development of the consciousness soul. You can only get the right conception of the intellectual or mind soul by transporting yourselves into the mind of a Greek. Then you will certainly discover the difference between the relation of the Greek towards the world, and our own. This will be made somewhat clearer by our lecture today.

These introductory words serve as a basis to understand that in the centuries preceding the modern age, that is, up to the fifteenth century, human beings met and spoke to one another out of the intellectual or mind soul. Today we face the consciousness soul. However, human beings really could sense it only around the turn of the nineteenth to the twentieth century because of all the circumstances already described. Because of this, life questions appeared in an entirely new way. Certain life questions must be regarded in a new way today, otherwise the connecting bridge between consciousness soul and consciousness soul, which means for modern humanity the bridge between one person and another, cannot be found. We are suffering from this in our time, that we cannot find the bridge from human being to human being.

We must ask many of our questions in such a new way that it may at first seem strange. It is not meant to be so, however. Now let us suppose that a three-year-old child were to decide not to wait until the seventh year of life for the second teeth to come in, but that this child were to say: It would be boring to go through four more years until I get my second teeth; I want to get them at once. (I could use other comparisons which would appear still more strange, but this one will suffice.) Such a thing is impossible, isn't it? For there are certain conditions of natural development.

And so, too, it is a condition of natural development, for which today only few people have any sense, that only from a certain age onwards human beings can know something about the connections in life, of which they must know, but which cannot be exhausted by information about external things. Naturally, already at the age of nine we may know, for example, that the human being has ten fingers. But matters, in which a judgment formed by active thinking is necessary, cannot be known before we reach a certain time in life between about the eighteenth and nineteenth years approximately. Just as it is impossible to get the second teeth before the seventh year, so it is impossible before the eighteenth year, really to know about those things that are not just under our nose, things for which active judgment is necessary.

Before this, one could hear something and believe it on authority, but one could not know anything about it. Before the eighteenth year, we cannot unfold that inner activity of soul necessary to be able to say: I know something about this or that which does not lie in a region accessible merely to the eyes or ears. Such things are hardly mentioned today. They are, however, exceedingly important for life. If culture is to find roots again, one must speak about such things and treat them in a knowledgeable way.

What then follows from the fact that before their eighteenth year human beings cannot know anything of the kind? It follows that human beings before they are eighteen must depend upon those who are older, just as infants are dependent upon their mother's breast; it is in no way different. From this, however, there is something of the greatest significance for the interaction between teachers, educators, and the younger generation. If this is not heeded, the interaction is simply false.

People are not conscious today that this is so, and do many things backwards in the sphere of education. It was not always so. If we look back before the first third of the fifteenth century, something like today's Youth Movement would not have been possible. At that time, it would never have been justified to have a youth movement in the present form; it could not be. Why could there have been no such thing? To answer this question we must turn to the especially significant conditions that were encountered among those preparing for life in the monastic schools. We could also take the conditions for the young who were being prepared for trades. We would not find much difference; it is actually just the same. In the earliest of those times, it was quite definitely realized that none could be brought before their eighteenth year to the point of real knowledge. It would have seemed absurd had one maintained that it was possible to give anyone real knowledge before the eighteenth year. At that time it was known among older people, especially if they wanted to teach or educate: The young cannot be brought to the point of actual knowledge. We must be capable of bringing up the young to believe in what we, according to our knowledge, hold to be true. And to lead the young to such a belief was considered a sacred task.

Today this is all upside down, because what in earlier times was demanded only of the young, namely, belief, is now demanded in connection with the supersensible of those who are grown up. At that time the concept of belief was only there for those who were young, but it was regarded as something sacred. Teachers and educators would have reproached themselves for having violated their most sacred duty if they had failed to make the young believe in them out of the freshness and lively conviction of their individual human nature, so that they thus received the truth. This shade of feeling lay in all education, in all instruction. In other respects the education and teaching of that time may today arouse a sense of antipathy because of its division into all kinds of classes and distinctions. But putting that aside, the education was such that the young could believe in the teacher.

Something else was connected with this: that teachers felt that it was first of all necessary to earn the right that the young should believe in them. I shall explain this by means of an example in the monastery schools, which were the only educational institutions in the time preceding the fifteenth century. One had first to earn the right to be taken seriously, for this was the prerequisite upon which the belief of the young was to be founded. Human beings did not think that, just because they were adults or because some authority had granted them a diploma or had hired them, the young had to believe in them. It is true that diplomas, and the like, played a certain outer role even in those days. The right to be taken seriously was not earned by giving them knowledge. It is difficult for us today to make any sense of the remark: We do not wish to impart knowledge to the young. Yet, at that time, it was a matter of course that, before any knowledge was imparted, the young should be made to see and to feel that one was capable of something. It was only when the young people had reached a certain age that the teachers told them what they knew. The first step was to show what one could do, and for this reason the substance of the teaching was the trinity of grammar, dialectic and rhetoric. These were not sciences. For it is only in the course of time that grammar has become the present pseudoscientific monstrosity. In those times, grammar was not at all what it is today; it was the art of combining and separating thoughts and words. Instruction in grammar was the teaching of an art, and all the more so in the case of dialectic and rhetoric. Everything given was so arranged that the pupils should feel the ability of their teachers; that they should feel their teachers capable of speaking and thinking and of letting beauty hold sway in their speaking. Grammar, dialectic and rhetoric—this was instruction in ability, in an ability closely connected with the human activity and quickness of the teacher and educator.

Today when we speak of visual or object teaching, we keep the teaching quite apart from the personality of the teacher. We drag in every possible kind of gadget, even those dreadful calculating machines, in order that the teaching may be as impersonal as possible. We try to separate it entirely from the personal. Such a separation is not really possible. The endeavor to keep the teaching entirely apart from the personal only leads to the worst sides of teachers coming into play, and their good sides are quite unable to unfold when so much objectivity is dragged in.

Thus, it was a natural demand on teachers that they should first let the young feel what they were capable of in the very highest sense as human beings. They had to show their mastery of speech, their mastery of thought, and how beauty was part of their speech. Only by letting the young witness for a time what they could do, was the right acquired to lead their students gradually to what can be known, to arithmetic, geometry, astronomy and music; to music as it was conceived of at that time, as a permeation of the whole world order by harmony and melody. Because the teachers started with grammar, dialectic and rhetoric, they were able later to pour into arithmetic, geometry, astronomy, and music as much of the artistic as is possible, when having had an artistic point of departure.

Now all this has evaporated and vanished into thin air with the first dawning of intellectualism. Of the old artistic element that appeared then, we have but the scantiest remains. Here and there, in certain universities, the doctor's degree still bears with it the title: "Doctor of Philosophy and of the Seven Liberal Arts." But you know the real state of affairs where the Seven Liberal Arts are concerned! Historically, we can recall that the famous Curtius who taught in Berlin and was an extraordinary personality, held a diploma that was very different from his field. If you ask for what subject he actually received the *venia legendi*, you would expect it to have been for history of art. But that is not correct. His teaching certificate was for Eloquentia—fluency of speech. However, already by his time this branch of knowledge was out of date. He was professor of eloquence, but in order to teach he took up history of art—and dealt with it most excellently. Even at the time when Curtius was teaching, it would have been strange had eloquence been a field of instruction. Eloquence, or rhetoric, however, was one of the fundamental branches of instruction given to the young of earlier times, with the result that something thoroughly artistic came into education. But the introduction of the artistic into education was still in keeping with the old order, in which intellectual or mind soul encountered intellectual or mind soul. And today people are still not able to put the question from the new point of view: How must things be in human affairs if consciousness soul is to meet consciousness soul? As soon as education is considered in the wider sense this question arises of itself. The question has been put for a long time, for decades, but human beings have not yet developed an active enough thinking to formulate and feel it clearly. And where do we find an answer?

An answer to this question is found by learning to understand—for it is a matter of the unfolding of will and not of a theoretical solution—that when children enter earthly existence, they bring with them the power of imitation; up to the time of the change of teeth, children just imitate. Out of this power of imitation, speech is learned. Speech is, so to speak, poured into children just as their blood circulation is poured into them when they come into earthly existence. But they should not come to a more and more conscious education by giving them, out of the consciousness soul, knowledge in the form of so-called truth. In earlier times it was said: Before the eighteenth year children cannot know anything, so they must be led through [the teacher's] ability to knowledge, which they accept first as belief. Through the belief the children have developed in their younger years, the forces of knowledge will be awakened in them between the eighteenth and nineteenth years. For it is out of the inner being that the forces of knowledge must be awakened. To help the young wait until their eighteenth year, adults behaved in relation to youth in such a way as to show what they were capable of, afterwards educating them to experience together with the teacher, in a provisional way, up to the eighteenth year, what they would be expected to know later. Up to the eighteenth or nineteenth year, the "acquisition of knowledge" was provisional, because before the eighteenth or nineteenth year, it is not possible really to know anything. However, no teacher can convey knowledge to any child if in that child's feeling the conviction has not ripened: This teacher is capable! It would be an irresponsible beginning in regard to humanity if teachers wanted to set to work without the young believing, as a matter of course, that they are capable.

Before the students came to arithmetic—arithmetic as it was understood in those days, and not the dry, abstract stuff of today—they were clear that those who were to guide them into arithmetic, knew how to speak and think, and had the gift of eloquence as well. When the young knew this out of their own feeling, it was a good reason for looking up to those who were older. When they know only that the teacher has a diploma, it sometimes happens that, when the child is not more than ten, everything goes to pieces. The question that was living in those days must again be given life. Because today consciousness soul encounters consciousness soul in human affairs, this question cannot be solved in the same way as formerly when human beings confronted each other with their mind souls. Today a different solution must be found.

Naturally, we cannot return to the liberal arts, although it would be preferable to what is being done today. We must reckon with modern conditions—not the external conditions, but those dealing with the evolution of the human race. Here we must find the transition from imitation, which up to the change of teeth is natural in children, to the stage when we can bring knowledge to human beings, reckoning first upon trust and belief and later upon their own judgment.

However, there is an intermediate period, and this period is a very critical one for the young today. For this intermediate time, we must find the solution of the most significant world problem, upon which the future progress or backward steps in human evolution, or even its total fall, depends. The question is: How must adults handle children between the years of imitation and the years when knowledge can be given? Today this is one of the most important cultural questions of all.

And what was the Youth Movement in so far as it is to be taken seriously? It was a languishing for an answer to the cultural question about the intermediate time. And it became clear to the young that no such answer was to be found in the schools, so they drifted out into grove and meadow and into the fields. They preferred, instead of being school boys and girls, to become birds—birds of passage (Wandervögel).

We must look at life, not at theories, if we want to master the great questions of world culture. If one really looks into life today, one will find that the period between the age of imitation and the age at which the human being can receive knowledge in the form of truth must be filled so that humanity does not become stunted. This must be done by giving human beings, with artistic beauty, what they need for head, heart and will. The seven-fold nature, consisting of grammar, dialectic, rhetoric, arithmetic, geometry, astronomy and music, grew out of an old cultural order as something artistic. Today, too, we need the artistic but, in accordance with the demands of the consciousness soul, it must not be specialized in the way of the seven liberal arts. During the primary school age and far beyond it, for as long as education is involved, the whole teaching must be warmed through and fired by the artistic element. During the primary school years, everything must be steeped in beauty, and in later years beauty must rule as the interpreter of the truth.

Those human beings who have not learned to walk in the ways of beauty, and through beauty to capture truth, will never come to the full humanity needed to meet the challenges of life. The great German writers divined this even if its full importance was not emphasized. They were not understood, however. How clearly we see this search for truth through beauty in Goethe. Listen how he says: "Art is a manifestation of secret forces of nature," which simply means that only through an artistic grasp of the world do human beings reach the living truth—otherwise it is dead. And Schiller's beautiful words: "Only through the dawn of beauty do you penetrate to the land of knowledge." Unless we first permeate ourselves with the meaning of the path, that we can penetrate into the realm of truth only through the artistic, there can be no question of acquiring a real understanding of the supersensible world in accordance with the age of the consciousness soul.

For you see, with the help of today's recognized sciences, knowledge of the human being is limited to the physical body alone. With modern science there is no possibility of knowing anything about the human being beyond the physical body. That is why science can speak conclusively—even grandly—about physiology or biology only so long as it is a question of the physical body. True, people talk about psychology. It is only known as experimental psychology; phenomena of the life of soul are observed, are connected with the physical body. They cannot form the slightest conception of pure manifestations of the soul. Hence they have hit upon the idea of psychophysical parallelism. Parallel lines, however, can meet only at infinity. So, too, the connection between the physical body and the soul can be understood only at infinity. Thus, psychophysical parallelism was set up.

All this is symptomatic of the incapacity of the age to understand the human being. For, firstly, if one seeks to understand the human being, the power of intellectualism ceases. The human being cannot be understood out of the intellect. One may choose to adhere firmly and rigidly to intellectualism, but then one must do without knowledge of the human being. However, for that one would have to tear out one's mind and heart, and that is impossible. If we tear it out, it withers away. The head can indeed renounce knowledge of the human being, but the mind and heart become stunted. All of our present culture is expressed out of a withered life of mind and heart. And secondly, understanding of the human being is not to be achieved with concepts that direct us in the domain of outer nature. However much we may achieve outwardly with these concepts, they cannot lead us even to the second member of the human being, namely, to the etheric body, or body of formative forces.

Just imagine that with the methods of modern science human beings could know as much, let us say, as they will know at the end of Earth evolution—quite a formidible amount! I will assume the existence of a very finished and very clever scientist. I am not saying that there are not among us scientists already near this stage, for I do not think that in the future we will make much more progress in intellectualism. A different path will be taken. I have the very highest respect for the intellectualism of our learned people. Do not for a moment think that I am saying this out of a lack of respect. I mean this in all seriousness. Without a doubt, there are vast numbers of very clever scientists. Yet, even were I to assume that science had reached its highest peak, it would still only be able to understand the physical body of the human being and nothing at all of the etheric body. It is not that the knowledge of the etheric body is based upon fantasy. That is not the case. It is a real perception. However, the stimulus to acquire the faculty for perceiving this most subordinate of the supersensible members of human nature can arise only out of an artistic experience of the soul. Art must become the life blood of the soul.

The more people wish in our objective science to carefully avoid everything of the nature of art, the more are they led away from knowledge of the human being. Through the microscope and other instruments we have come to know a great deal. Yet it never leads us nearer to the etheric body, but rather farther from it. In the end, we lose entirely the path to what is a prime necessity for understanding the human being. In the case of plants we can still use the instruments, for the plants do not concern us so intimately. The plant does not care that it is not the product of the laboratory that modern science makes it out to be. It still goes on growing under the influence of the etheric force of the cosmos and does not limit itself to the forces presumed to exist by physics and chemistry. But when we confront people, things are different. Then our feeling, our confidence, our reverence, in short all that is in our mind, which in the age of the consciousness soul naturally rises above instinct—with the consciousness soul everything rises above instinct—depends upon our having an education that allows us to perceive something more than merely the human physical body.

When teachers deprive us of insight into what the human being really is, we cannot expect those forces to flourish that help the human being face another human being in the right way. Everything depends upon the human being's ability to free the self from the shackles of mere observation and experiment. Indeed we can value observation and experiment properly only when we have become free of them, and the simplest way of breaking free is through the artistic.

Yes, when teachers stand in front of the children again as in an earlier epoch—suited for grammar dialectic, rhetoric—that is to say, when teachers stand before the young so that their way of teaching is again artistic and all instruction is permeated by art, there will arise a different youth movement that will crowd around the teachers who are artists, because there they will draw nourishment and receive what the young must expect from those who are older. It may appear unattractive to you, but nevertheless it will arise. The Youth Movement cannot be a mere opposition, a mere revolt against the older generation, for then it becomes like the infant who can do nothing because it cannot receive milk from its mother. What is to be learned must be learned. But it will be learned when there is as natural an urge towards those who are older as the infant has towards its mother's breast, or as the small child feels when, by imitating, it learns to speak. This urge will be stimulated when the young find the artistic coming from the older generation, when truth first appears in the garb of beauty. In this way all that is best will be kindled in the young, not the intellect that always remains passive, but the will that stirs thinking into activity. Artistic education will be an education of the will, and it is upon the education of the will that everything else depends.

Tomorrow, then, we shall continue.

10

STUTTGART, OCTOBER 12, 1922

Yesterday I wanted to show how we must come to an education, steeped in artistic form. I drew attention to how in earlier times teachers took their start from the artistic in higher education by treating as arts what today has become entirely abstract and scientific, namely, grammar, dialectic and rhetoric. This was done in such a way that young people first recognized in their teacher: This human being can do something that I cannot do. And through this alone, the right relationship was established between the younger and the older generations, for this relationship, my dear friends, can never develop along the path of intellectuality. As soon as, one works with the intellect, ideas are no longer inwardly revealed in the intellectual or mind soul, and there is no possibility of differentiating between human beings. For human nature is so constituted that when it is a matter of making something clear through the consciousness soul, when people come only to concepts, they believe they can discuss them with anyone. Thus it is with the intellect. For the intellect, neither human maturity nor experience comes into consideration. Maturity and experience only do so when it is a question of ability. The ability of an older person will be recognized and accepted by the young quite as a matter of course.

Now, in order to understand these things thoroughly we must consider from a different point of view the course taken by humankind's evolution with regard to the interaction between human beings.

External documentary history can go back only a few thousand years before the Mystery of Golgotha, and what is to be found can never be estimated rightly because even the spiritual achievements of ancient Greece cannot be grasped by modern concepts. Even for the old Grecian times, completely different concepts must be used. Nietzsche, among others, felt this. Hence the charm of his brief, unfinished essay on "Die Philosophie im tragischen Zeitalter der Griechen" [Philosophy in the tragic age of the Greeks], where he deals with philosophy in connection with the general development of Greek culture up to the time of Socrates. In Socrates he saw the first flicker of pure intellectuality, while everything philosophical in the tragic age of Greek development proceeded from comprehensive human foundations or depths. When these are expressed in concepts, we must note that concepts are a language through which only what is experienced can be conveyed. In the earliest times philosophy was quite different from what it later became. But I only want to point this out.

What I really want to speak about is that with spiritual Imagination, and especially with Inspiration, we can look back much further into human evolution and, above all, into human souls. When we go very far back, some seven or eight thousand years before the Mystery of Golgotha, we find that the young had a natural veneration for old age. Why was this a matter of course? It is because what exists today only in earliest youth existed then for the whole evolution of humanity.

If we look at the human being with less superficiality than is often done today, we find that the whole evolution of the human soul changes at about the time of the change of teeth, during the sixth, seventh, or eighth year. Human souls become different, and they change again at the time of puberty. I discussed this fully in my book *The Education of the Child.* Briefly, it is noticed that souls become different in the seventh year and again in the fourteenth or fifteenth. But what people no longer notice is that changes still take place at the beginning of the twenties, at the end of the twenties, in the middle of the thirties, and so on.

Whoever is able to observe the life of soul in a more intimate way knows that such transitions take place in human beings, that human life runs its course in rhythms. Try to perceive this, let us say, in Goethe. Goethe records how he was cured of certain childlike religious ideas by the Lisbon earthquake, thus about the time of the change of his teeth, and how puzzling everything was for him. He tells how, as a small child, he began to reflect: Is there a good god ruling the world, when one sees that countless people have been swept away through these terrible fiery forces in the Earth? Especially during such transitional moments of his life, Goethe was susceptible to the influences of external events working upon his soul, such as to be conscious of the transformation of his soul. And he says, concerning this period of his life, that he became a strange kind of pantheist and that he could no longer believe in the ideas imparted by the older people in his home and by his parents. He tells how he took his father's music stand on which he set out minerals, placing on top a little candle that he lit by holding a burning-glass to catch the first rays of the morning sun. In later life he explained that he had wanted to bring an offering to the great god of nature by lighting a sacrificial fire, kindled on nature herself.

Take the first period of Goethe's life, then the following one, and so on, until you piece together his whole life out of segments of about the length of his first period of childhood, and you will find that with Goethe something always happened in each of these periods to change his soul thoroughly. It is extraordinarily interesting to see that the fact of Schiller's urging Goethe to continue *Faust* only found fruitful soil in Goethe because at the end of the eighteenth century, he happened to be at a transitional period of this kind. It is interesting, too, that Goethe rewrote *Faust* at the beginning of a following life-period. Goethe wrote the beginning of *Faust* in his youth in such a way that he makes Faust open the book of Nostradamus. There we have the great scene:

> "What powers celestial, lo! ascend, descend
> Each unto each the golden vessels giving!"

Then turn the page, and there we find:

> "Thou, Spirit of the Earth, to me art nearer."

Goethe rejects the great tableau of the macrocosm and allows only the Earth-spirit to approach Faust. When, at the beginning of the nineteenth century, he was persuaded by Schiller to revise *Faust*, he wrote the

"Prologue in Heaven." Anyone who observes his own life inwardly will discover that these changes hold good. Nowadays we only notice them when we deliberately train ourselves to look deeply into our own life.

In ancient times, six thousand, seven thousand, eight thousand years before the Mystery of Golgotha, these changes were so noticeable that they were experienced in the life of soul like the change of teeth or puberty is today. And, indeed, approximately up to the middle of life, up to the thirty-fifth or thirty-sixth year, life was experienced as ascending. But then it began to decline. Human beings experienced the drying up of life. Yet, while they felt certain products of metabolism become deposited through sluggishness in the organism and the physical organism become increasingly heavy and lethargic, they became aware that at the same time, up to the greatest age, precisely the soul and spirit were on the ascent. They felt how the soul is set free with the drying up of the body. And people in olden days would not have spoken with such ardor of the patriarchs—the word itself only arose later—had they not noticed externally in people: True, they are getting physically old, but they have to thank their physical aging for lighting up the spirit. They are no longer dependent on the body. The body withers, but the soul becomes free.

In this modern age it is most unusual that such a thing happens, for instance, as occurred at the Berlin University. Two philosophers were there. The one was Zeller†—the famous Greek scholar—and the other Michelet.† Zeller was seventy years old and wanted to retire. Michelet was ninety and lectured with tremendous vivacity. Eduard von Hartmann† told me that Michelet is supposed to have said, "I do not understand why that young man does not want to lecture any more."

Today people seldom keep their freshness to such a degree. However in those times, it was so, especially among those who devoted themselves to true spiritual life. What did the young say when they looked at the Patriarchs? They said: It is beautiful to get old. For then one learns something through one's own development that one cannot know before. It was perfectly natural to speak in this way. Just as a little boy with a toy horse wants to be big and get a real horse, so, at that time there was the desire to get old because it was felt that something is then revealed from within.

Then came the following millennia. It was still experienced up to a considerable age, but not anymore as long as was the case in the old Indian epoch—according to the terminology of my *Esoteric Science*. At the zenith of Greek culture, human beings still had a vivid experience of the change occurring in life in the middle of the thirties. People still knew how to distinguish between body and spirit, and said: At the age of thirty, the physical begins to decline, but then the spiritual begins to sprout. They experienced this in the soul and spirit in the immediate presence of human beings. The original feeling of the Greeks was based upon this, not upon that fantasy of which modern science speaks. To understand the fullness of Greek culture, we should bear in mind that the Greeks could still be conscious of becoming thirty, thirty-five, thirty-six years old, whereas a more ancient humanity was conscious of their aging up to a far greater age. Herein consists the evolution of humanity. Then humanity had, by nature, to experience aging more and more unconsciously. Now the call arises to experience it consciously, for it must again be experienced consciously.

Whoever observes their own lives can recognize the seven-year changes. The length of these periods is not pedantically exact, but approximate. Those who look back to the period of their forty-ninth, forty-second, thirty-fifth years, can recognize quite well: at that time something happened in me through which I learned something that I could not have attained before out of my own nature, just as I would not have been able to bite with my second teeth before I had them. The ability to experience life as something concrete has been lost in the course of human evolution. And if people today do not inwardly train themselves to observe these things in themselves, these epochs from the thirtieth year onwards will become completely blurred. An inner transformation can still be noticed at the beginning of the twenties—even up to the end of the twenties, though it is then rather less noticeable. However, today with the present human organization, human beings are carried by their natural evolution actually only up to their twenty-sixth or twenty-seventh year, and this age-limit will become lower and lower. In earlier times people were not free in their organization, destined as they were to have these experiences out of their own nature. Freedom has become possible only by the withdrawal of the determining by nature. To the extent that nature ceases to determine us, freedom becomes possible. Through their own striving human beings must find the spiritual, whereas formerly, the older human beings became from year to year, the more the spiritual sprouted forth naturally.

Today emphasis is no longer placed on what the old become merely by growing older. Human beings stopped in their development with that intellectualism, which is developed between the eighteenth and nineteenth years to the point that, from then onwards, one can know with the intellect. But as far as intellectuality is concerned, one can at most reach a greater degree of proficiency but can make no qualitative progress. If one has fallen victim to the desire to prove or to refute everything intellectually, one cannot progress. That is why if someone puts forward what is the result of decades of experience but wants to prove it intellectually, an eighteen-year-old can refute it intellectually. For whatever is possible intellectually at sixty years of age is equally possible at nineteen. Intellectuality is a stage reached during the consciousness soul that brings no further progress in the sense of deepening, but only in proficiency. The young may say: "We are not yet as clever as you are; you can still take us in." But they will not believe the other to be their superior in the sphere of intellect.

These things must be expressed radically to make them clear. I do not wish to criticize, but am only showing what a natural evolution of humanity is. We must be clear about the following characteristic of our age, namely, that if human beings today do not strive out of inner activity for development and maintain it consciously, they will rust with mere intellectualism from their twentieth year on. They will keep themselves going only through stimuli from outside. Do you think that if things were not like that people would flock to the cinema so much? This longing for the cinema, this longing to see everything externally, is caused by the human beings becoming inwardly inactive, by their no longer wanting inner activity.

The only way spiritual scientific lectures, as they are meant here, can be heard is for those present to work continually along with the speaker. But today that is not to people's liking. They flock to meetings or lectures with slides so that they can sit and do as little thinking as possible. Everything just passes before them. They can remain perfectly passive.

But our system of teaching is ultimately of this character too, and anyone who, on educational grounds, objects to the triviality of the modern object lesson is said to be behind the times. But one has to oppose it, for humanity is not a mere apparatus for observing, an apparatus that wants simply to look at things. Humans can live only by inner activity. To bring or express something out of spiritual science means to invite human beings to work along with you with their souls. People do not want this today. Spiritual science must become such an invitation to inner activity, that is to say, it must lead all studies to the point where there is no more support in external sense-perception and the inner play of forces must move freely. Imagination cannot be reached before thinking moves freely in this inner play of forces. Thus the basis for all Anthroposophy is inner activity, the challenge to inner activity, the appeal to what can be active when all the senses are silent and only the activity of thinking is astir.

Here is something of extraordinary significance. Just suppose you were capable of this. I will not flatter you by saying that you are. Assume that you are capable of it, that you can think in such a way that your thoughts are only an inner flow of thoughts. What I called "pure thinking" in my *Intuitive Thinking as a Spiritual Path* was certainly not well named when judged by outer cultural conditions. For Eduard von Hartmann† said to me, "There is no such thing; one can only think with the aid of external observation." And all I could say in reply was; "One only has to try it, and one will learn and finally be able really to do it." Thus take it as a hypothesis that you could have thoughts in a flow of pure thought. Then there begins for you the moment when you have led thinking to a point where it need not be called thinking any longer, because in a twinkling—in the twinkling of a thought—it has become something different. This rightly-named pure thinking has become pure will, for it is willing through and through. If you have advanced so far in your life of soul that you have freed thinking from outer perception, it has become at the same time pure will. You hover with your soul, so to speak, in a pure course of thought. But this pure course of thought is a course of will. The pure thinking or the striving for the practicing of pure thought begins to be not only a thought exercise but also a will exercise, and indeed such a will exercise that works right into the center of the human being. For you will make the following remarkable observation. It is only now, for the first time, that you can speak of thinking, as it is in ordinary life, as an activity of the head. Before this, you really have no right to speak of thinking as an activity of the head, for you know this only as external fact from physiology, anatomy, and so on. But now you feel inwardly that you are no longer thinking so high up, you begin for the first time to think with the heart. You actually interweave your thought with the breathing process. You actually set going what the yoga exercises have striven for artificially. You notice that, as thinking becomes more and more an activity of the will, it wrenches itself free first from the breast and then from the whole human body. It is as though you were to draw forth this thinking from the last fiber of your big toe! And if with inner participation you study what has appeared with many imperfections—for I make no claims about my *Intuitive Thinking as a Spiritual Path*—if you let it work upon you and feel what this pure thinking is, you will experience that a new person is born within you who can bring out of the spirit an unfolding of the will.

How do humans know that they have a will otherwise? They do not *have* will, for they are given up to instincts connected with their organic development. They often dream that they do this or that out of an impulse of the soul, but they really do it because of the good or bad condition of their stomachs. But now you know that you have permeated the physical organism with what fills it with consciousness. You do not need to be a clairvoyant for this. All you need do is to be interested in *Intuitive Thinking as a Spiritual Path* and let it work upon you. For *Intuitive Thinking as a Spiritual Path* cannot be read as other books are today. It must really be read so that once you get into *Intuitive Thinking as a Spiritual Path* you have the feeling that it is an organism, with one member developing out of another, and that you feel that you have found your way into something living. When such a thing is asked of people, their skin begins immediately to crawl, and they say: Something is going to get into me which will take away my freedom. Something will enter me that I do not want to have.

That is no different than if one were to maintain that we would be unfree if we had to accustom ourselves to speaking a certain language in two or three years. Human beings ought to be warned against language for they will no longer be free when brought into this chance association of ideas. They ought to be able to speak at will: now Chinese, now French, now German. No one says this, because it would be too absurd, and life itself refutes such nonsense. On the other hand there are people who either hear or see something of eurythmy and say that it is based on the chance association of the ideas of individuals. But one should be able to expect that philosophers would say: One must look into this eurythmy and see if, in evoking gestures, we may not have the foundations of a higher freedom and find that it is only an unfolding of speech at a higher level.

So one need not be surprised—for really nothing that goes beyond intellectualism can be regarded without prejudice today—that people get gooseflesh when one tells them that a certain book must be read quite differently from other books, that it must be read in such a way that one really experiences something from it. What is it that must be experienced? It is the awakening of the will out of the spiritual. In this respect my book was intended as a means of education or training. The intention was not merely to communicate content, but to make it work educationally. Hence you find in my *Intuitive Thinking as a Spiritual Path* an exposition on the art of forming concepts, a description of what takes place in the soul when one does not keep to the impressions from outside with one's concepts, but lives within the free flow of thoughts.

This, my dear friends, is an activity that aims at knowledge in a far deeper sense than the external knowledge of nature, but it is at the same time artistic, wholly identical with artistic activity. In that moment when pure thinking is experienced as will, human disposition becomes artistic.

And this artistic disposition is what teachers need today to guide and lead the young from the time of the change of teeth to puberty, or even beyond puberty. The mood of soul should be so that out of the inner life of soul one comes to a second human being, who cannot be known in the same way as is the outer physical body, which can be studied physiologically or anatomically, but who must be livingly experienced and may rightly be called, in accordance with the real meaning of the terms, life body or ether body. This ether body cannot be known through external perception but must be experienced inwardly. To know this second human being, a kind of artistic activity must be developed. Hence there is this mood in *Intuitive Thinking as a Spiritual Path* that most people never discover; everywhere it touches the artistic element. Most people do not notice this, because they look for the artistic in the trivial, in the naturalistic, and not in free activity. Only out of this free activity can education really be experienced as art, and teachers can become artists in education when they find their way into this mood. Then, in our epoch of the consciousness soul, all teaching will be so arranged as to create an artistic atmosphere between teacher and pupil. And within this artistic atmosphere there can develop a relationship between those being led and the leaders that is an inclining towards the leader, because they can do something and are able to show it forth artistically, and one feels that what they can do, one would also like to be able to do. Thus no opposition is aroused because it is felt that one would destroy oneself by opposing.

The way writing is taught today, it often happens that, even as a child—for in the child there is always a being who is cleverer than the teacher—one asks: Why should I be bothered to write? I have no relationship to writing. Something similar is really what the Native Americans felt when they saw European script. They felt the black signs to be magic. The feeling of the child is often similar. But let us awaken in the child what it means to look at black, red, green, yellow, white. Let us call up in the child what it is when we surround a point by a circle. Let us call up the great experience contained in the difference there is when we draw two green circles and in each of them three red circles, then two red and in each of them three green, two yellow with three blue ones in them, then two blue containing three yellow circles. We let the children experience in the colors what the colors as such are saying to the human being, for in the colors there lives a whole world. But we also let the children experience what the colors have to say to one another: what green says to red, what blue says to yellow, blue to green and red to blue—here we have the most wonderful relation between the colors. We do not show the child symbols or allegories, but we do something artistically. Then we shall see how out of this artistic feeling the child gradually puts down figures out of which the letters then develop, just as writing once developed from picture-script. How foreign to the child today are *B*, *G*, or any other sign that has developed through inner necessity to its present form. What is a *G*, *K*, or *U* to a seven-year-old today? The child really has not the slightest kinship with it. It has taken the human being thousands of years to acquire this relationship. The child must acquire a relation to it in an aesthetic way. Everything is exterminated in the child because the written characters are not human; and the child wants to remain human.

In order to understand youth in its relation to the older generation we must go right into the art of education. The cleft between age and youth must be bridged, not by hollow phrases, but by education that is an art, education that is not afraid to find its support in real spiritual scientific knowledge. That is why I said a few days ago: Where does this art lead? It leads to the experience of the real spiritual. And where does it lead that the age has gradually developed in such a way that it believes it must be given as a matter of course to the young? It does not lead to the spirit, but to what is devoid of spirit. It is regarded as a sin to bring the spirit into what one calls knowledge and science.

Science does not leave the human being alone even in earliest childhood. It cannot very well be otherwise. For the teachers are so drilled in systematized botany (and many books are entirely given over to systematized botany) that they believe they are committing a sin if they speak to the children about botany in a way that is not scientific. But what is found in a botanical textbook is not appropriate for a child before the age of ten, and it is not until at least eighteen or nineteen that one can develop any real relationship to it.

What I have said should not bring about another intellectual theory about education. The aim is to create an artistic atmosphere between the older and the younger people. Only when this comes about, does something happen that must occur if young people are to grow into the world in a healthy way. What the human being of today grows into can be described quite concretely. Between the ninth and tenth years an undefined feeling lives in the soul of every human being who is not a psychopath. There need not necessarily exist either a clear or unclear concept of this. But it begins to live within the human being from the ninth or tenth year. Up until then, the astral body alone took care of the life of the soul. However, from that time onwards, the force of the "I"-nature first begins to stir in the human being. It is not formulated in concepts. But in the life of feeling, deep within the soul, there lives unconsciously a question in the heart of the growing human being. This question takes different forms in different people. But a question arises that, put in the form of a concept, might be expressed as follows: Up to now the astral body has believed in other human beings; now I need something that somebody says to me so that I may believe in this person or in others in my surroundings. Those who as children have resisted this the most are those who need it most. Between the ninth and tenth years, human beings begin to be dependent on an older person in whom they can believe, in order to strengthen their "I." They must be able to believe in this human being without this trust needing to be drummed in, but rather through the artistic atmosphere that has been created. And what great sorrow when nothing happens from the side of an older person to answer rightly this question, which may still remain for many children up to their sixteenth or seventeenth year and, for some, even to the eighteenth or nineteenth year, so that the young say: I am grateful that I have learned from the old what I can learn only from the old. What this person can tell me, he or she alone can tell me, for it will be different if I learn it when I am old.

Through this something can be created in an educational way which, applied in the right way, can be of the greatest significance for the epoch of the consciousness soul, something which, in fact, was already alive between young and old in the earliest times of the Patriarchs. At that time all young people said to themselves: The old people with their snow-white hair have experiences that can only come when one is as old as they are. Before then one does not have the necessary organs for it. Therefore, the old must tell their experiences to us. We are dependent on what they relate because they alone can relate it. Certainly I shall one day be as old as they are. But I shall only experience what they can tell in thirty-five or forty years. The times will have progressed by then, and I shall experience something different.

In the foundations of the spirit life of the world there is, so to speak, a chain that reaches from the past over into the future, and which each generation must take up and carry onwards, forge, and perfect. This chain has been broken in the age of intellectualism. This was generally felt among those growing up about the turn of the nineteenth century to the twentieth. Try to feel that you did experience something of the kind, even if at the time you were not able to express it. Try to sense that, with feeling this, you were feeling about it in the right way. And if you sense this, you will realize the true significance of the Youth Movement today, the Youth Movement, which has, and must have, a Janus-head, because it is directed towards experience of the spiritual—an experience of the spiritual that carries thought so far it becomes will, it becomes the innermost human impulse.

We have been seeking now for will at its abstract pole where it is thought. In the days to follow, we will seek it in the deeper spheres of the human being.

11

STUTTGART, OCTOBER 13, 1922

DURING the epoch of the consciousness soul the most abstract elements come consciously to life in the inner human being, yet also in the subconscious, in what human beings desire of life, the most concrete is seeking to work its way into existence.

The human being who is growing into the epoch of the consciousness soul is held fast today in the abstract ideas of the head. However, there lives outside of the head, if I may so express myself, the desire to experience more than the head is able to. To begin with, people's only connection with nature is formed between nature and the head. Everything they absorb in science, so far as they regard it as valid, is acquired from nature through the head. Between the human being and nature today there always stands the person's head. It is as though everything that comes to the human being from the world were to pour itself into the head, as though the head were entirely stopped up so that it lets nothing through its dense layers that could bring about a relation with the world. Everything remains stuck fast in the head. People think everything through only with their heads. But the human being cannot, after all, live merely as head, for joined to the head is the rest of the organism. The life of the rest of the organism remains dull, unconscious, because everything is directed towards the head. Everything stops short there. The rest of the human being receives nothing from the world, because the head allows nothing to reach it. The head has gradually become an insatiable glutton. It wants to have everything that comes from the world outside, and one is obliged to live, where the heart and the rest of the organism is concerned, as if one had nothing whatever to do with the surrounding world.

But these other parts of the organism develop wish, will, capacity for desire and feel themselves isolated. For instance, the eyes catch colors and allow only scanty remains to be experienced in the head, and so, the colors cannot work down: they cannot reach the blood or the nervous system in the rest of the body. It is only in the head that human beings still know something about the world. But they have all the more capacity for intensely desiring with the rest of their organism to come together with the outside world in some way. In the young human being who is growing up lives this desire to find some kind of connection with the world, not only with the head, but with the rest of the organism; to learn to think and come to experience the world, not only with the head but with the whole person.

Human beings today still have the capacity of learning to experience the world with the whole person only at an early age. For what I have just been saying refers to the adult. Before the change of teeth children still have the faculty of grasping the world with their whole being. It would be a mistake to suppose that the baby's experience when nursing is as abstract as an adult's. When we drink milk we taste it on our tongue, and perhaps around our tongue. But we lose the experience of taste when the milk passes through our throat. People ought to ask why their stomach should be less capable of tasting than the palate. The stomach is not less, but equally, capable of tasting, but the head is a glutton, and in the grown person, the head claims all taste for itself. The child, however, tastes with its entire organism and, therefore, with its stomach. The infant is all sense organ. There is nothing in the infant that is not sense organ. The infant tastes with its whole being. Later this is forgotten, and this tasting is impaired when the child learns to speak. For then the head, which has to take part in learning to speak, begins to stir and develops the first stage of insatiability. The head, in return for giving itself up to learning to speak, reserves for itself the pleasures of tasting. Even as regards "tasting the world," the connection with the world is very soon lost. Now this "tasting the world" is of no particular importance, but, in another connection, the relation of the whole human being with the world is of extraordinary importance.

You see, we can get to know an important philosopher, such as Johann Gottlieb Fichte,† in various ways. Every way is right. I do not wish to stress any one of the following in particular. It is wonderful to go deeply into the philosophy of Fichte—which not many people do today, because they find it too difficult—and much is gained from it, yet they would have gained far more, if with their whole feeling, they had followed behind Fichte and had seen him walk, planting the whole sole of his foot, and especially his heels, firmly on the ground. In Johann Gottlieb Fichte's walk, in the curious way he set his heel on the ground, is a tremendous power. For those able to experience each step with the whole being, this would have been a more intensive philosophy than all Fichte was able to say from the platform. It may seem preposterous, but perhaps you will feel what I am trying to say.

Today such things have been entirely lost. Those who were little, not twenty but fifty years ago, can still remember that such a philosophy still existed among those living in the country. In the country, people still got to know each other in this way, and many expressions out of the dialect, with their wonderful sculptural quality, reveal how what is seen today only in the head was seen then in the whole person. It was said, for instance, of some woman in the country: She goes around *schneuzen*. (An idiom in Austria.) Among us "head" people, "schneuzen" means to blow one's nose, in a perhaps not-so-appropriate manner. That is not what it meant back then. At that time, the whole human being "schneuzte"—"blew the nose." The manner in which a person walked, the posture, the way he or she set one foot in front of the other, the whole behavior and affectation could be a "schneuzen." It was felt that there was something in the whole being of such a person that was like a blowing of one's nose in a not-so-appropriate manner.

As I have said, these things have been lost. Human beings have reduced themselves to their head and have forced themselves to believe that the head is their most valuable part. But this has not made them overly happy, because the rest of human nature asserts its claims in the subconscious. Experiencing through something other than the head is lost today in early childhood with the change of teeth. If you have an eye for these things you can see the walk of the father or the mother in the son or daughter two or three decades later. So exactly have the children lived into the adults around them that what they have sensed there becomes part of their own nature. But this living into others no longer spells culture today. Culture is what the head observes and what can be worked out by means of the head. Sometimes people even dispense with the head, and then they write everything down and put it in the archives! Then it goes out of the head into the hair where it cannot be retained, because at thirty, they no longer have any hair!

But really I am not saying this as a joke, nor for the sake of being critical, for this is all part of the necessary development of humanity. People had to become like this to find, through inner effort, through inner activity, what they can no longer find in a natural way: the possibility to experience freedom.

And so today, after the change of teeth, we must simply pass over to a different way of experiencing the surrounding world from that of experiencing with the whole human being, which still exists among children. Therefore, primary school education in future must proceed by the roundabout way of the artistic that I described yesterday, so that, through the outer human being, the soul-nature of the other person is experienced. If you educate human beings through what is abstract and scientific, they experience nothing of your soul. They only experience your soul if you approach them through art. For in the realm of the artistic, everyone is individual, each one is a different person. It is the ideal of science that everyone should be alike. It would be quite a thing—so say people today—were everyone to teach a different science. But that could not be, for science confines itself to what is the same for all human beings. In the realm of the artistic, each human being is an individuality. Through the artistic element, therefore, there can come about an individual, personal relation of the child to the person who is alive and active, and this is necessary. True, one does not come to the feeling for the whole person as outer physical being as in the first years of childhood, but to a feeling for the soul of the one who is to lead.

Education must have soul, but as a scientist, one cannot have soul. We can have soul only through what we are artistically. We can have soul, if we give science an artistic form through the way it is presented, but not through the content of science as science is understood today. Science is not an individual, personal affair. Hence, during the elementary school age, it establishes no relation between teacher and pupil. All instruction must therefore be permeated by art, by human individuality, for the individuality of the teacher and educator is of more value than any curriculum is that is thought out. It is the individuality of the teacher that must work in the school.

What grows between teacher and pupil from the change of teeth to puberty and creates the link between them? What binds them together is solely what human beings bring with them into their earthly existence from supersensible, spiritual worlds, from their pre-earthly existence. My dear friends, the head never recognizes what people bring with them out of their pre-earthly life. The head is made for the purpose of grasping what is on the Earth. And on the Earth, there is only the physical human being. The head understands nothing of what in the other human being comes from pre-earthly existence. In the particular coloring the artistic impulse gives to the human soul, there lives and weaves what the human being has brought down from pre-earthly existence; and between the period of the change of teeth and puberty, children are particularly disposed to feel in their hearts what meets them in the teacher as coming out of pre-earthly existence. Just as young children have the tendency to feel the outer human form in its earthly shape; so from their seventh to their fourteenth or fifteenth year they seek, through living together with human beings, something that does not lend itself to be grasped in concepts but is manifested in the teacher. If we wanted to find a concept for this "something," it would resist conceptual form. Concepts have contours, that is to say, external boundaries. But human individuality, in the sense described, has no external boundaries, only intensity and quality and is experienced as intensity, as quality, very particularly in the period of life referred to. It is experienced, however, through no other atmosphere than that of the artistic.

But we are now living in the epoch of the consciousness soul. The first treasures we acquire for the soul in this epoch consist of intellectual concepts, of abstractions. Today even the farmer loves abstractions. How could it be otherwise, for the farmer indulges in the most abstract reading matter, the village newspaper, and much else besides! Our riches consist really in abstractions. And therefore we must free ourselves from this kind of thinking, through developing what I spoke of yesterday. We must purify our thinking and mold it, into will. To this end we must struggle to make our individuality stronger and stronger, and this happens only when we work our way through to pure thinking. I do not say this out of idle vanity, but because that is how I see it. Whoever works their way through to pure thinking, as I have described in my *Intuitive Thinking as a Spiritual Path*, will find that this does not bring them simply to the possession of a few concepts that make up a philosophic system, but that it lays hold of their own individuality, of their pre-earthly existence.

Human beings do not need to become clairvoyant immediately. That will happen only when they are able to behold pre-earthly existence. Yet, they can confirm what is said by gaining the strength of will that is acquired in the flow of pure thoughts. Then the individuality comes forth. Then one does not feel happy with a philosophic system in which one concept proceeds from another and everything has rigid outlines. One feels compelled to have one's being in a living and weaving world. We acquire a special kind of life of soul when we experience in the right way what is meant by the "philosophy of freedom."

It is really a bringing in of pre-earthly existence into the life of the human being that is brought about, and this is the preparation for the vocation of teacher, of educator. We cannot become teachers through study. We cannot drill others into being teachers, because each one of us is already a teacher. All human beings are teachers, but the teacher within is slumbering and must be awakened, and art is the awakener. When this is developed, it brings the teachers, as human beings, nearer to those whom they would educate. And as human beings the pupils must get close to the teachers. Those who are to be educated must get something from the educators as human beings. It would be terrible if people were to believe it possible to teach just because they know a great deal. This leads to absolute absurdity. This absurdity will be apparent to you if you think about the following picture.

Now take a class in a school that has perhaps thirty pupils. Among these pupils there are, let us say, two geniuses, or only one, for that is enough. If we have to organize a school we cannot always give the post of teacher to a genius just for a future genius to be able to learn all he or she must be able to learn. You will say that this would not matter in the elementary school and that the child will go on to a higher school and will certainly find geniuses as teachers there. You would not say this, because experience does not bear it out, but you must admit, the case may arise that the teacher is faced with a class in which there are children predestined to become more brilliant than the teacher is. Now our task, as teachers, consists in bringing the children not merely to our degree of aptitude, but to the full development of their own potential.

As teachers, therefore, we may come into the position of having to educate somebody who will be greater than we. It is impossible to provide schools with enough teachers, unless one holds to the principle that it does not matter if the teacher is not as brilliant as the pupil will be some day. Nevertheless, this person will still be a good teacher, because the giving out of knowledge is not what is important, but the individuality and making the pre-earthly existence come to life. Then it is really the children who educate themselves through us. And that is the truth, for in reality, we do not educate at all. We only disturb the process of education when we intervene too energetically. We only educate when we behave in such a way that, through our own behavior, the children can educate themselves. We send children to primary school in order to rid them of troublesome elements. The teacher should see to it that the troublesome elements are eliminated so that the children escape conditions under which they cannot develop. So we must be quite clear that we cannot cram anything into human beings through teaching and education. What we can do is to see to it that human beings, as they grow up, should succeed in developing their potential. That we can do, not through what we know, but through what stirs inwardly within us in an artistic way. And even if the rare thing should happen that as teachers we are not particularly endowed with genius—one should not say this, but in spite of your youth movement, you are old enough for me to say it—and we have only a kind of instinctive artistic sense, we will offer less hindrance to the growth of the child's soul than the teacher who is tremendously learned but inartistic. To be tremendously learned is not difficult.

These things must be said most emphatically for once, for even when spoken clearly, our age does not hear them. Our age is terribly unreceptive toward such things. And regarding those who assure one that they have understood everything, it is often apparent, after thirty years, that they have understood nothing. Thus the configuration of soul in the human being is what is essential in practical pedagogy, in instruction and education, during the child's life between the change of teeth and puberty. And after this the human being enters a period of life in which, in this age of the consciousness soul, still deeper forces must work up out of human nature, if humans are to give anything to one another.

You see, the manner of feeling with which one person meets another is tremendously complicated. If you wanted to describe the whole round of sympathies and antipathies, and the interworking of sympathies and antipathies with which you meet another person, you would never come to an actual definition. In fifty years you would not succeed in defining what you can experience in five minutes as the relations of life between person and person. Before puberty it is preeminently an experience of the pre-earthly. The pre-earthly sheds its light through every movement of the hands, every look, through the very stressing of words. Actually, it is the quality of the gesture, the word, the thought of the teacher that works through to the child and which the child is seeking.

And when as grownup people—so grownup that we have reached the age of fifteen or sixteen or even beyond—we meet other human beings, then the matter is still more complicated. Then, what attracts or repels others in a human being actually veils itself in a darkness impenetrable to the world of abstract concepts. But if, with the help of Anthroposophy, we investigate what one can really experience in five minutes but cannot describe in fifty years, we find that it is what rises up from the previous earthly life or series of earthly lives into the present life of the soul, and what is exchanged in the souls. This indefinite, indefinable element that comes upon us when we meet as adults is what shines through from earlier lives on Earth into the present; not only the pre-earthly existence, but everything we have passed through in the way of destiny in our successive earthly lives.

And if we study what is working upon the human being we find how today, in the epoch of the consciousness soul—because everything is pushed into the head and what we take in from the outer world cannot get through to the whole human being—our head culture sets itself against what alone can work from person to person. Human beings pass one another by because they stare at each other only with the head, with the eyes—I will not say, because they knock their heads together! Human beings pass one another by, because only what plays over from repeated earthly lives can work between person and person, and modern culture does nothing to develop a sense for this. This must also be brought into our education: that we be able to sense and feel what is in the depths of the human being that plays over from previous earthly lives. This will not be achieved unless we include in our education the whole human life as it takes place on Earth.

Today there is only a feeling for the immediate present. Therefore all that is asked of education is that it shall benefit the children. But if this is the only thing that is asked, very little service is rendered to life. Firstly, because the question is put one-sidedly, one gets a one-sided answer; and secondly, children should be educated for the whole of life, not only for the schoolroom or the short period after school so that they do not disgrace us. We need an understanding for the imponderable things in life, an understanding for the unity in human life as a whole as it unfolds on Earth.

There are human beings whose very presence, at a certain age, is felt by those around them as a blessing. There are such human beings. If we were to look for the reason why such people have become a blessing to those around them, not through their acts but through their beings, we would find that as children they were fortunate to have been able, in a natural way, to look up to someone in authority whom they could revere. They had this experience at the right time of life. And because they were able to revere, after many years they become a blessing to the world around them. It can be expressed concisely by saying that there are human beings who can bless. There are not many, but there are human beings who attain the power to bless at a later age. They acquire it in later life, because in their childhood they learned to pray. Two human gestures are causally connected: praying and blessing. No one learns to bless who does not learn it from prayer. This must not be understood sentimentally or with the slightest tinge of mysticism, but rather as a phenomenon of nature is observed, except that this phenomenon is nearer to us in a human way.

Children must be able to grow according to their nature. If you were to devise an apparatus for children that would keep them a certain size so that they could not grow, so that they would remain as they are all their lives, this would be terrible. Human beings must be able to grow. Yet, in school we supply the children with concepts and have as our ideal that they should remain unchanged for the whole of their lives. Children are supposed to preserve these concepts in memory, and in fifty years these concepts are to be the same as they are today. Our school textbooks work on the children in such a way that they must remain little. The right way is to educate children so that all their concepts can grow, that their concepts and will impulses are really alive. This is not easy, but the artistic way of education succeeds in doing it. And the children have a different feeling when we offer them living concepts instead of dead ones, for unconsciously they know that what they are given grows with them just as their arms grow with their bodies.

It is heartbreaking to witness children being educated to define a concept, so that they have the concept as a definition only. It is just the same as if we wanted to confine a limb in an apparatus. Children must be given pictures capable of growth, pictures which become something quite different in ten or twenty years. If we give them pictures that are capable of growth, we stimulate in them the faculty through feeling to find their way into what is often hidden in the depths of another human individuality. And so we see how complicated are the connections. We learn to come to a deeper relation to human beings through the possibility being given us in our youth for growth in our life of soul.

For what does it mean to experience another human being? We cannot experience other people through dead concepts. We can comprehend them only if we meet them in such a way that they become for us an experience that takes hold of us inwardly. For this, however, inner activity is needed. Otherwise, our culture will already reach the point that it is fast approaching. People go out to luncheons, dinners and teas, without knowing much about one another. It is about themselves that modern people know the most. And what do they instinctively make of their experiences? How do they judge the people they meet at lunch or dinner. At most they think: are they like me or are they different? And if we believe them to be like ourselves, we consider them to be quite fine. If they are not like ourselves, then they are not fine people, and we do not trouble ourselves about them any longer. And as most people are not the same as we are, the most we can do is sometimes to believe—because really it would be too boring to find no fine person anywhere—that we have found someone like ourselves. However, in this way, we do not really find another human being but always only ourselves. We see ourselves in other people. For many people this is relatively good. For if they were to meet somebody who in their opinion was not altogether, but yet to a certain extent, a fine person, and were really to comprehend this person, it would be so overwhelming an experience that it would quite drown out their own humanity. By a second encounter, their "I" would be drowned out still more deeply. In the case of a third or fourth, there would be no approaching the person at all, for by that time, they would certainly have lost themselves! There is too little inner strength and activity, too little kernel, too little inner individuality developed, so people, for fear of losing themselves, dare not experience the other human being. Thus people pass one another by.

The most important thing is to establish an education through which human beings learn once again how to live with one another. This cannot be done through hollow phrases. It can be done only through an art of education founded upon a true knowledge of the human being, that art of education referred to here. But our intellectualistic age has plunged the whole of life into intellectuality. In our institutions we actually live very much as if we are no longer among human beings at all; we live in an embodied intellect in which we are entangled, not like a spider in its own web, but like countless flies that have got themselves caught in a spider's web.

When we meet anyone, do we feel, in any sense, what this human being can be for us? Do we judge today as humanly as this? No, for the most part we do not. We ask if perhaps on the door of a certain person's house there will be a little plate with an inscription, "Counselor at Law," conveying a concept of some kind. In another case the inscription is "Medical Practitioner." Now we know that this person can cure us. In another case the inscription is "Professor of English." And now we know something about this person. If we want to know something about chemistry, we have no other choice than to enquire if somewhere there is a person who is a qualified chemist. What this person can tell us then is chemistry. And so it goes. We are really caught up in this spider's web of concepts. We do not live among human beings. We only concern ourselves with what is on paper. For many people that is their only essential fact. How else should they know what kind of human being I am unless it is written down somewhere on paper!

This, of course, is all said somewhat radically, and yet, it does characterize our epoch. Intellectuality is no longer merely in our heads but it is woven around us everywhere. We are guided by concepts and not by human impulses.

When I was still fairly young, when at Baden near Vienna, I got to know the Austrian poet Hermann Rollett, long since dead. He was convinced that the right thing was development towards intellectualism. At the same time, however, he had an incurable dread of this, for he felt that intellectualism only takes hold of a person's head. And once when I visited him with Schröer, he began to speak in poetical fashion about his incurable fear in regard to culture. He said: When one looks at human beings today, they cannot use their fingers properly. Many of them cannot write; they get writer's cramp. Their fingers atrophy. When it is a question of sewing on trouser buttons, they cannot do it. Only tailors can do that! The fingers and the limbs will not only become less skillful, but will also become smaller. They will wither away, and heads will get larger and larger. That is how he described his poet's dream. He said he thought the time would come when only heads, like balls, would be rolling about over the surface of the Earth.

That was the cultural dread I met with in this man in the last third of the nineteenth century. He was a child of his age, that is to say, a materialist, and that was why he had so great a dread that, at some point in the future, such heads would be rolling about on the Earth. Physical heads will not do this, but to a serious extent, the etheric and astral heads do it already today. A healthy education of the young must protect human beings from this, must set human beings upon their legs again, and lead them to the point where, if they are pondering something, they will feel the beating of their heart again and not merely add something to their knowledge. These are the things we must take into account, if in preparation for humanity's future, we wish to live into what must be decisive for the pedagogical art, for the art of education. I shall try to develop what is yet to be said about this for you tomorrow.

12

STUTTGART, OCTOBER 14, 1922

FROM what has been said during the last few days it will be clear that today one human being meets another in a different way from what was the case in the past, and this is of quite recent date—in fact, it entered human evolution with the beginning of the twentieth century.

In poetic language no longer capable of doing so today, former ages foretold what has come for the whole of humanity in this century. Former ages spoke of how, at the end of the nineteenth century, the so-called Dark Age would have run its course and that, in a new age, quite new conditions must enter into human evolution. These conditions will be difficult to attain, because at first humanity is not accustomed to them. In spite of the fact that we have now entered an epoch of light, much will seem more chaotic than what was brought by the long, gloomy Age of Darkness.

We must not merely translate into our language what was formerly presented in a picture derived from ancient clairvoyant vision. Then we would understand only the old again. We must learn to perceive it anew with the spiritual means of today. We must permeate ourselves deeply with the consciousness that in this epoch for the first time human "I" meets human "I" in an interaction of souls that is free of all veils.

Were we to go back to the first epoch after the great Atlantean flood, to the seventh or eighth millennium before Christ, we would find that adult human beings actually encountered one another in the way that today only the child encounters adults, with comprehension of the complete human being, as I characterized it yesterday; a comprehension where soul and spirit are not found separated from the body, but where the physical body is perceived as being of the nature of soul and spirit. In the epoch I have called the ancient Indian, which followed immediately upon the Atlantean catastrophe, the human being did not speak of the soul and spirit as separate in the abstract way that we do today, with a certain justification.

It is precisely expressions used in this most ancient epoch, which seem to us entirely spiritual, that are misunderstood today. We misunderstand them, because we believe that in the first post-Atlantean epoch of culture, people overlooked all they saw in the outer world and were only willing to point to what existed beyond the world of the senses. This was by no means the case. They had a much fuller perception of, let us say, a human movement, or of the play of expression on a countenance, or of the way young people grow in five years, or of the formative development of new leaves and blossoms in a plant, or in an animal of the way the whole of its forces pour into the hoof and other parts of its leg. These human beings directed their gaze into what we call the world of the senses, but in the material processes, they saw the spiritual. For them, what presented itself to their senses in the material world was at the same time spiritual. Naturally, such perception was only possible because over and above what we see in the sense world, they actually perceived, in their way, the spiritual. For instance, they saw not only the meadow carpeted with flowers, but over the flowers they saw, in a vibrating, active existence, the cosmic forces that draw the plants forth from the Earth. In a certain way, they saw—it seems peculiar to modern human beings, but I am telling you facts—how human beings bear on their heads a kind of etheric-astral cap. In this etheric-astral cap they experienced the forces underlying the growth of the hair. People today are prone to believe that the hair grows out of the head simply by being pushed out from inside, whereas, the truth is that outer nature draws it forth. In olden times, people saw the reality of things which later shone through the culture as an artistic impression. Consider the helmet of Pallas Athene. We do not rightly experience this helmet if we think of it as having been put on. It is not put on. It is bestowed by a concentration of raying cosmic forces that are working around the head of Pallas Athene and densifying, so that in olden times it would have seemed impossible to the Greek to form the head of Pallas Athene without this covering. They would have experienced it just as we today would experience a scalped head. I am not saying that this was the case among Greeks of later times.

In ancient times people were able to experience the sense world as something soul-spiritual, because they were to experience something of an etheric and soul-spiritual nature. But these people did not ascribe any special importance to the soul and spirit. People readily believe that in the oldest Mysteries the pupils were principally taught that the sense world is semblance and the spiritual world the only reality, but this is not true. The strivings of the Mysteries were directed to making the material world comprehensible to the human soul by the roundabout way of comprehending what is of the nature of soul and spirit.

Already in the epoch of the first post-Atlantean culture, the Mysteries were striving to understand the human being soul-spiritually in the form he or she has on Earth—not theoretically—and, namely, to feel inwardly and to interpret what any manifestation of the physical human being means spiritually. For example, it would have been impossible for them to have given a mechanistic explanation of walking, because they knew that when human beings walk they have an experience with every step. Today this experience lies deep beneath the threshold of consciousness. Why do we walk? When we stretch our leg forward and put down our foot, we come into a different relation to the Earth and to the heavens, and in the perception of this change—that we place one foot, for instance, into a different degree of warmth (as in a bath) from that in which the other foot has remained—there lies something that is not only mechanical but distinctly super-dynamic.

This was the perception in more ancient times. The gaze of the human being then was directed to the human's external form, to the external movements. And it would never have occurred to the people of that time to imagine that what they saw as a play of the features in nature—the growth and configuration of plants, the growth and configuration of animals—was to be interpreted in the way that we do scientifically today. There was something altogether different in the human heart and mind when a person belonging to the old Indian civilization, to which I referred yesterday, felt it as entirely natural that during a certain period of the year the Earth breathes in the being of the heavens, and during another period of the year it does not breathe in the being of the heavens, but works within itself by shutting it out. Naturally, it was different in ancient India, because the climatic conditions were different. But were we in imagination to describe our own climatic conditions we would have to say: During the summer the Earth sleeps, gives herself up to the heavenly forces, and receives the power of the Sun in such a way that this power of the Sun pours into the Earth's unconsciousness. Summer is the sleep of the Earth. Winter is its waking. During the winter, the Earth thinks, through its own forces, what it thought in relation with the heavens while sleeping and dreaming during the summer. In the winter, the Earth works over, in her own being, what has come to her through the influence of the forces and powers of the cosmos during the summer.

Today little more is known of these things in practical knowledge than that the farmer puts potatoes into the ground and leaves them there through the winter. But nobody thinks about the fate of these potatoes, because people have lost the ability to understand the being of nature. It would never have occurred to human beings who felt, as the ancient Indians did, to look out into nature at animals, plants, and minerals shining and sparkling in their most varied colors and to imagine that in this there is one single reality, a dance of atoms. That would have seemed utterly unreal. Certainly, many will object that people need this dance of atoms in order to make calculations about nature. Yes, that is just it; people believe they need the dance of atoms to be able to make calculations about nature. Calculations in those days meant being able to live in numbers and magnitudes themselves and not having to attach these numbers and magnitudes to what is only densified materiality. I do not want to raise objections against the good service that densified materiality renders today, yet one must state how different the configuration of souls was in that more ancient age.

Then another age came. In my book *Outline of Esoteric Science*, I have called it the old Persian. In this age everything was built upon the principle of authority. People preserved during the whole of their life what is today experienced in a dull, repressed form between the seventh and fourteenth years. They took it with them into later life. It was more intimate but at the same time more intense. In a certain sense, human beings looked through the external movement, through the human being's external physiognomy, or through a flower. They looked at something that was less concrete outwardly. What they saw gradually became only a manifestation of true reality. For the first post-Atlantean epoch of civilization the whole external world was reality, but spiritual reality. Human beings were spirit. They had a head, two arms and a body, and that was human spirit. There was nothing to deter the ancient Indians from addressing the human beings they saw standing on two legs, with arms and a head, as spirit. In the next epoch people already saw through things more. What they saw was more in the nature of a surface behind which something more etheric was perceived, a human being who was more a light-form. People had the faculty of perceiving this light-form, because atavistic clairvoyance was still present.

And then came the epoch of the third post-Atlantean culture. One felt the need for penetrating still further into the inner being of the human being or of nature. The outer had become clearly sense-perceptible and people were beginning to look through the outer perceptible to the spirit and soul within. The Egyptians, who belong to this epoch of the third post-Atlantean culture, mummified the human body. In the epoch of the old Indian culture, mummification would have made no sense, for it would have been a fettering of the spirit. One had to distinguish between body and spirit when one became inclined to practice mummification. Otherwise, people would have felt they were imprisoning the human spirit if the body had been mummified, because no distinction had yet been made between body and spirit.

Among the Greeks—and actually into our own time—there was already a clearly established separation between the body and the spirit and soul. Today we can do nothing other than keep these two apart: the bodily and the soul-spiritual. Thus, in earlier epochs, human beings really saw the "I" through the sheaths.

Imagine the ancient Indians. They did not look at a person's "I." Their language was such that it really only expressed outwardly visible gestures and outwardly visible surfaces. The whole character of Sanskrit, if studied according to its spirit and not only according to its content, is of the nature of gesture and of surface. It expresses itself above all in movement and contour. The "I" was therefore seen through the sheath of the physical body in the ancient epoch, in the next epoch through the sheath of the etheric, in the third epoch through the sheath of the astral. And the human "I" still remained indefinite, until in our epoch, it cast off its veil as it entered into human interaction.

One does not adequately describe the decisive point that entered modern evolution, unless one points out that in the relationship of "I" to "I," free from the sheaths, something totally new entered human development, albeit slowly. I shall certainly not speak in the usual sense of our age being an age of transition. For which age is not? Every age is an age of transition from the preceding one to the one that follows. And as long as one simply says that our age is an age of transition, it is just a hollow phrase. It will make sense only when one describes *what* makes a transition. In our age we are going over from experiencing the other person through sheaths, to a real experience of the other person's "I." And this is the difficulty in our life of soul, that we have to live into this quite new relation between person and person. Do not think that we must learn all the teachings about the "I." It is not a question of learning theories about the "I." No matter whether you are a farmer, a handworker, or a scholar, it holds good for all of you that at the present time, in as much as we have to do with civilized people, the "I" of each meets the other "I" without sheaths. But that gives the whole cultural development its special coloring.

Try to develop a feeling for how in the Middle Ages there was still much that was elementary in the way in which one human being experienced another. Let us imagine ourselves in a medieval town. Let us say, a locksmith meets a town councilor in the street. Now, what was experienced was not just that the locksmith knew the other to be a town councilor. The experience was not exhausted by the locksmith knowing that the people have elected this person. It is true, there existed links that gave people a certain stamp. One belonged to the tailors' guild, one to the locksmiths' guild, but this was experienced in a more instinctive way. And when locksmiths met town councilors, they knew from other sources than from the directory: They are town councilors. For they walked differently; their look was different; and they carried their head differently. People knew that they were town councilors from things other than documents or the newspaper. Human beings experienced the other, but through his or her sheaths.

In the sense of modern evolution we must experience human beings from now on without sheaths. This has gradually come about. But in a certain sense humanity is afraid of it. If we had a cultural psychology then it would describe, in connection with recent centuries, people's fear of being obliged to consort with another human being whose "I" is unsheathed. When we picture this, we might say that those people, who in the last century really experienced their own times, had frightened eyes. These frightened eyes, which you would not have been able to find either among the Greeks or the Romans, make their appearance in the middle of the sixteenth century. We can follow these frightened eyes in literature. For instance, one can form a clear mental picture on reading the writings of Bacon of Verulam. We can glean from his writings with what eyes he looked out at the world. And still more so with Shakespeare. They can be pictured quite clearly. One need only supplement the words by the descriptions which circulated of Shakespeare's appearance. And so we must picture the people of recent centuries, who lived most deeply in their own times, as having frightened eyes, an unconsciously frightened look. At least once in their lives they had this frightened look. Goethe had it; Lessing had it; Herder had it. Jean Paul never got rid of it to the day of his death. We must have an organ for perceiving these subtleties, if we want to develop any understanding of historical evolution.

The humanity that wants to find its way livingly into the twentieth century must realize that those representatives of the nineteenth century can no longer represent the twentieth. If one reads books about Goethe written in the nineteenth century by the philistine Lewes, or the pedant, Richard M. Meyer, one does not come to a real conception of Goethe. The only literary work of the last third of the nineteenth century that can still give an idea of Goethe is *Goethe* by Herman Grimm. But that is a nightmare to those suffering from the great cultural disease of modern times, philistinism. For in this vast volume on Goethe you find the sentence: "*Faust* is a work that has come down from heaven." Just imagine what the commentators who pull everything to pieces have said, and imagine that someone comes along and says this should not be pulled to pieces. This may not seem important, yet we must notice such things in speaking about cultural phenomena. Read the first chapter of Grimm's *Raphael*, and you will have the feeling that it must be an abomination to every orthodox professor. Nevertheless, something of it can be taken over into the twentieth century, for the very reason that for the orthodox professor nothing in it is right.

Thus one saw human beings within sheaths. Now we must learn to see them as "I"-beings without sheaths. This alarms people, because they are no longer capable of sensing what I have described as the sheaths in which, for instance, one could have seen our town councilor. It is no longer possible, at any rate not in Middle Europe, to give people outer representations of the sheaths. For the outer representations of the sheaths still had a connection with the spiritual content existing in medieval councilors. Today—I must confess—it would be difficult for me to distinguish, by their outer sheaths, between a civil-service councilor and a private councilor. In the days when the military was at its height, one could still discern the difference. But one had to study it; to learn it through careful study. It was no longer connected with elemental human experience.

So there existed a kind of terror, and people made themselves indifferent to it by means of what I described yesterday as the web of intellectualism that spreads itself around us, and within which all are caught. In the cultural centers which have retained something of the East, the inner is still brought into a relation with the outer, the elemental with the intellectualistic. Those of you who come from Vienna will know that in the last century, this could be felt strongly. For in Vienna, for instance, a man who wore spectacles was known as "doctor." People did not bother about the diploma, but rather about the exterior. And anyone who could afford to take a cab was a baron. It was the exterior. There was still a feeling of wanting to live within what can be described in words.

The great transition to this newer age consists in human being meeting human being free of the sheaths—according to each person's inner dispositions, to what the soul demands—but the capacities for this encounter without sheaths have not yet been acquired. Above all, we have not yet acquired the possibility for a relation between "I" and "I." But this must be prepared for through education. That is why the question of education is of such burning importance.

And now let me tell you quite frankly when the great step forward can first be made in the way of educating the individual "I"-humans of the new age. But I beg you not to use what I am going to say to impress other people who are of an opposite opinion, for if you do so the only result will be a terrible scolding and cursing of Anthroposophy. We shall work rightly in education only when we have learned to feel a certain bashfulness about speaking about it at all, when we feel abashed at the idea of talking about education. This is astonishing but it is true. The way in which education is being talked about will be regarded as shameless in future. Today everyone talks about it and about what one considers to be right. But education does not allow itself to be tied down to formal concepts, nor is it anything we come to by theorizing. Education is something that one grows into, by getting older and meeting younger human beings. Only when one has grown older and stands before younger people, and—through this meeting of younger people and through having been young once oneself—one draws near to the "I," can education become natural.

Many suggestions about education today seem to me no different from the content—horrible dictums—of the book of the once famous Knigge, who also gave directions as to how adults should be approached. It is the same with books on good form and breeding. Therefore, what I have said and written about education, and what is attempted practically in the Waldorf School, aims only at saying as much as possible about the characteristics of human beings, in order to learn to know the human being, and not to give directions: "You should do this in such-and-such a way." Knowledge of the human being is what must be striven for, and the rest left to God, if I may use this religious expression. True knowledge of the human being makes the human being into a teacher. For we should really get the feeling that we are ashamed to talk about education. But under the cultural conditions of today, we have to do many things that ought to make us ashamed. The time will come, however, when we shall no longer need to talk about education.

Today these ways of thinking are lacking, but only since a little more than a hundred years. For, read Fichte or Schiller thoughtfully. You will find in their writings what seems quite disturbing to modern people. They have spoken, for example, about the state and about all kinds of arrangements to make the state into what it should be. And they have spoken about the aim of the state, saying: Morality must be such that the state becomes superfluous, that human beings are capable out of themselves of becoming free agents, capable through their morality of making the state superfluous. Fichte said that the state should be an institution which gives over the reins and gradually becomes entirely superfluous. Today this would make a similar impression as the following incident on a troupe of actors. A play had been performed for the fiftieth time by a traveling company, and the director said, "Now that we have performed this for the fiftieth time, the prompter's box can be dispensed with." But the actors were quite terrified at the idea. Finally one of them pulled himself together and said, "But, sir, then one will see the prompter!" This is about what would happen with human beings today. They do not see that the prompter, too, can be dispensed with. The state will have found its best constitution when it makes itself superfluous. Yes, but what would all the government officials and the chancellors and the private councilors say to such a thing?

We must bring ourselves out of the everyday practice and set ourselves within this great change going on in the depths of modern souls, if we are to realize that we must come to the point where talk about education is as superfluous as it was in older cultural epochs. Education was not talked about in earlier days. The science of education first arose when people could no longer educate out of the primal forces of their beings. But this is more important than is supposed. Boys or girls, seeing the teacher come into the classroom, must not have the feeling that the teacher is teaching according to theoretical principles because he or she does not grasp the subconscious. They want a human relation with the teacher. That is, however, destroyed when educational principles are introduced. Therefore, if we are to get back to a natural condition of authority between young and old, it is of infinite importance and an absolute necessity, that education shall not be talked about so much. There is no need to talk or think about education as much as is done today. For there are still many spheres in which education is conducted according to quite sound principles, although they are also already being undermined.

You see, theoretically it is all quite clear, and theoretically people know how to handle the matter, just as it is handled by the academic opinion of the present day. But in practice it is quite good if there should happen to anyone what happened to me. A friend had scales by his plate and weighed the different foods, in order to take the right quantity of each into his organism. From the physiological point of view, this may be quite correct. However, picture this transposed into the realm of education. Unfortunately, it does happen, even if in a primitive way. It is more wholesome when this happens intuitively, if parents, instead of buying some special physiological work on nourishment, judge how to feed their children through the feeling for how they themselves ate as children. And so in pedagogy, we must overcome everything that lays down rules, such as how much food should be taken into the stomach, and strive in the sphere of education for real insight into the nature and being of the human being. This insight into the nature of the human being will have consequences for the whole of human life.

Whoever comes to an understanding of the human being in the way I have been describing during these days, and thereby imbues this knowledge with an artistic attitude, will remain young. For there is some truth in it that once we have grown up, we are actually impoverished human beings. Yet, the most important thing for the human being is that we have forces of growth within us. What we have in us as a child is of the utmost importance for the human being. We are led back to this in inner experience through true knowledge of the human being. We really become childlike when we acquire the right knowledge of the human being and become thereby suited to meet young people and children in the right way.

We must strive, not in an egoistical sense as often happens today, to say: Except ye become as little children, ye cannot enter the Kingdom of Heaven. We must seek for this in practical life. If we were not imbued with an active human force that worked in us during childhood, we could never teach. Pedagogy is not enough, if it makes the teachers or educators merely clever. I do not say that it should make them empty of thought, but in this way, one does not become empty of thought. Pedagogy that make teachers merely clever is not of the right kind. The right kind of pedagogy makes teachers inwardly alive and fills them with a lifeblood of the soul that pours itself actively into their physical lifeblood. And if there is anything by which we can recognize true teachers or educators, it is that their pedagogical art has not made them pedants.

Now, my dear friends, that you can find a pedant working in some place is perhaps only a myth or a legend. If teachers are pedants, if these myths and legends are founded on truth, then we may be sure that the pedagogy has taken a wrong road. To avoid giving offense I must assume these legends and myths to be hypothetical and say: If pedants and philistines were to be found in the teaching profession, it would be a sign that our education is going under. Education is on the ascent only when, in its experience and whole way of working, pedantry and philistinism are driven right out of the human being. The true teacher can be no philistine, can be no pedant.

In connection with this, so that you may be able to check what I have been saying, I ask you to consider from what vocation in life the word pedant is derived. Then, perhaps, you will be able to contribute to the recognition of the reality of what has been indicated. I do not want to elaborate on it, because already much that I have said is being taken amiss. It is only on this condition that we can have a right pedagogy. Otherwise, it would have to become a pedagogy in accordance with what I have been giving you in these lectures. Thus, in the lecture tomorrow I will attempt to bring these talks to some conclusion.

13

STUTTGART, OCTOBER 15, 1922

NATURALLY, a great deal more could be said in conclusion to what I have put before you here. In speaking, one is obliged to explain things in words and ideas. What is intended, however, is the unity of character and the unity of force, which one would like to make stream through the words and ideas. Let me sum up by using a half-pictorial form to convey what I still wish to say to you. You will work it out for yourselves and will perhaps understand better what I mean.

From various sides I have drawn your attention to how every civilized human being today lives in intellectualism, in a life of concepts, which in our epoch has developed in the most intense, penetrating way. Humanity has worked itself up to the most abstract concepts. You need only compare, for instance, how in an age preceding our own, Dante received descriptions of the world from his teacher. Everything was still permeated with soul; everything was still spiritual. It wafted like a breath of magic through the whole of Dante's great poem. Then came the time when humanity wanted to pour what was experienced inwardly into abstract concepts. People have always had concepts, but as I have already explained to you, they were revealed concepts, rather than concepts that no longer corresponded to inner revelations of the soul. Only when human beings had wrestled through to concepts no longer springing from revelations did they evolve concepts from observation of external nature, and from outer experiments. Then they allowed validity only to what was received from outside through observation.

If we go deeply into the old world of thought, into that of the twelfth, thirteenth and fourteenth centuries, we have the feeling that it was united with the inner being of the soul. There was still an inner life then, a living from within outwards, an experiencing which arose, because the human being had united with this life.

The conceptual system even of the most primitive human being is acquired from outside today, from external nature observed by the senses. And even those who still cling to the older concepts no longer hold to this belief with any depth of conviction, not even the farmer. To pass on something from outside, something established scientifically and verified by nature, is the ideal towards which people strive. But concepts or ideas, arising out of the inner life of the soul, have the characteristic that, because they wrestle their way out of the soul, as I have already explained, they die as concepts. And human beings feel it right that, in so far as they are born out of their inner being, these concepts die. But the strange thing that has come to pass during the last few centuries, reaching its culmination in the nineteenth century, is that the concepts dying in the inner being took on fresh life from the outer world. It can actually be proved by a historical phenomenon. Think how Goethe built up a whole conception of evolution out of his inner being. It reached its zenith in his concept of metamorphosis. We have the feeling that we are working out of the living into the dead, but that the human being has to work into what is dead because the living is coercion. Freedom could only arise by concepts becoming dead. Yet these concepts have taken on new life from outer nature. Inasmuch as Darwinism, for instance, has come upon the scene—even in our Middle European civilization—we have concepts and ideas which acquire new life from outer nature. But it is a life which devours the human being.

Today we must feel the full intensity of being surrounded by a thinking bound to nature, which gained life-force from nature, but which devours the human being. How does it devour the human being? With the ideas the most advanced kind of thinking draws from nature, we can never understand the human being. What does our magnificent theory of evolution provide? It gives us a survey of how animals evolve from animals. Then the human beings stand before us, but only as the culminating point in the ranks of the animal kingdom, and not as what we are as human beings.

This is what modern civilization tells us. Previous civilizations understood the kingdoms of nature as arising out of humanity. Modern civilization grasps humanity as arising out of nature, as the highest animal. It does not grasp to what extent animals are imperfect humans. If we fill our soul with what our thinking has become through nature, there appears in the picture of the human-devouring dragon that which is the most potent factor in modern civilization. Humanity feels itself confronting a being who is devouring them.

Consider how this devouring has taken effect. Whereas, from the fifteenth century onwards, natural science has been triumphantly progressing, knowledge of the human being has been declining more and more. Human beings could only hold out, with great difficulty, against the dragon devouring their inner life, by preserving and handing on the old, no-longer living ideas and traditions. And in the last third of the nineteenth century, the dragon stood with particular intensity before the human being, threatening in the most terrible way to devour the individual soul life. Those who still had within themselves a full soul life, felt how the dragon, who was destined for death, acquired fresh life in the new age of development through observation and experiment; but it is a life that devours the human being.

In more ancient times people played a part in producing the dragon, but had been given the necessary amount of death forces, so they could master it. In those days people contributed to their experience only as much intellectuality as they could master through forces of the heart. Now, the dragon has become sternly objective and meets us from outside and devours us as soul-beings.

This is the essential characteristic of civilization from the fifteenth century on into the nineteenth. We see it correctly only when we consider the picture of the dragon. In olden times it had a prophetic meaning and pointed to what would come in the future. However, those of olden times were conscious of having given birth to the dragon, and also, on the other side, of having given birth to Michael or St. George, to forces capable of overcoming the dragon.

But from the fifteenth century and on into the nineteenth, humanity was powerless against the dragon. It was the epoch that has gradually succumbed to belief in the material world. As a result, the inner soul life of that epoch was killed to the point that, in respect of the deepest treasures of the soul, there was no more truthfulness. An era which made the world arise out of the Kant-Laplace primeval nebula,† which densifies into a globe, and in this process engenders living beings and finally human beings, could but say: Ultimately such activity must disappear into death by warmth. However, that will also be the death of everything human beings have developed in the moral sphere! Though people have ever again sought to prove that the moral world order could find a place in a world that began out of the Kant-Laplace primeval nebula and ending with death through warmth, such a view is not sincere. And by no means sincere, and by no means honest, is the view that considers moral development to originate in the evolving and dividing of the animal kingdom and to disappear when the death through warmth brings about complete annihilation.

Why did such a view of the world ever arise? Why does it live fundamentally in all souls today? Because the dragon penetrates even to the remotest country cottage—though not consciously recognized—and slays the heart. Why is this so? It comes about because human beings can no longer understand the human being.

What happens then in the human being? In every moment something is happening in the human being which occurs nowhere else in our earthly surroundings. Human beings take in the foodstuff from the surrounding world. They take this foodstuff from the kingdom of the living and only to a small extent from what is dead. However, as it passes through the digestive system, it is completely destroyed. We take in living substance and completely destroy it, in order to infuse it with our own life. And not until the foodstuff passes into the lymph ducts is the dead made living again in our inner being.

One can see, if one grasps the nature of the human being totally, that in the soul-and-spirit-permeated organic process, matter is completely destroyed and then created anew. In the human organism we have a continual process of destruction of matter, so that matter can be newly created. Matter is continually being changed into nothingness and newly created in us.

The door to this knowledge was firmly sealed in the nineteenth century, when people arrived at the law of the conservation of matter and of energy, and believed that matter is also conserved in the human organism. The establishment of the law of the conservation of matter is clear proof that the human being is no longer inwardly understood.

But now consider how infinitely difficult it is today not to be considered a fool if one fights against what is regarded in modern physics as a definite fact. The law of the conservation of matter and of energy simply means that science has entirely barred the path leading to the human being. The dragon has entirely devoured human nature. However, the dragon must be conquered and therefore, the knowledge must gain ground that the picture of Michael overcoming the dragon is not merely an ancient picture, but that it has reached the highest degree of reality in our time! It was created in ancient times because people still felt Michael within themselves, permeating their unconscious and bringing about that they unconsciously overcame what arose out of intellectualism. Today the dragon has become quite external. Now the dragon encounters us from outside, threatening continually to kill the human being. But the dragon must be conquered. It can be conquered only through our becoming aware of how Michael, or St. George, also comes from outside. And Michael, or St. George, who comes from outside, who is able to conquer the dragon, is nothing other than a true spiritual knowledge that conquers this center of life, which for our inner being is a center of death—the so-called law of the conservation of energy—so that right into knowledge itself, the human being can again be human being. Today we are not allowed to accomplish this, for as long as there is a law of the conservation of matter and of energy, moral law dissolves and runs off into the universal death through warmth, and then the Kant-Laplace theory is no mere empty phrase!

Human beings shrinking away from this consequence is the fearful untruth that has penetrated right into the human heart, into the human soul, and has seized hold of everything, making them untrue human beings upon the Earth. We must acquire the vision of Michael, who shows us that what is material on Earth does not merely pass through the universal death through warmth, but will at some time actually disperse and vanish. He shows us that, by uniting ourselves with the spiritual world, we can bring life again into a dead world through our moral impulses. Thus, what is in the Earth begins to be transformed into the new life, into the moral. For the reality of the moral world-order is what Michael, who is approaching, can give. The old religions cannot do this, for they have allowed themselves to be conquered by the dragon. They simply accept the dragon, which kills humanity, and by the side of the dragon, they establish some special, abstractly moral divine order. But the dragon does not tolerate this. The dragon must be conquered. It does not suffer human beings to found something alongside it. What we need is the force that we can gain from victory over the dragon.

You see how deeply this problem must be grasped. But what has modern civilization given us? Every science has become a metamorphosis of the dragon; all external culture, too, is an outcome of the dragon. Certainly, the outer world-mechanism, which lives not only in the machine, but also in our social organism, is rightly called a dragon. But besides, the dragon meets us everywhere, where modern science tells us about the origin of life, about the transformation of living beings, about the human soul, or even in the field of history. Everywhere the results proceed from the dragon. This had become so acute in the last third of the nineteenth century, at the turn of the nineteenth century and on into the twentieth, that growing human beings, who longed to know what the older people knew, saw the dragon coming towards them in botany, zoology, history, and so on. Out of every science, they saw themselves confronted by the dragon waiting to devour the most inner being of their souls.

First in our own epoch has the battle of Michael with the dragon become real to the highest degree. When we penetrate into the spiritual texture of the world, we find that with the culmination of the dragon's power there also came, at the turn of the nineteenth century, the intervention by Michael, with whom we can unite ourselves. Human beings can have, if they will, spiritual science. That is to say, Michael actually penetrates from spiritual realms into our earthly realm. He does not force himself upon us, for today everything must spring out of human freedom. The dragon pushes itself forward, demanding the highest authority. The authority of science is the most powerful that has ever been exercised in the world. Compare it to the authority of the Pope; it is almost as powerful. A person can be ever so ignorant and yet say, "Science has established that." People are silenced by science, even if they say something that is true. There is no more overwhelming power of authority in the whole of human evolution than that of modern science. Everywhere the dragon rears up to meet one.

There is no other remedy against this than to unite ourselves with Michael; that is to say, to permeate ourselves with real knowledge of the spiritual weaving and being of the world. Only now does this picture of Michael truly stand before us. For the first time it has become our essential concern as human beings. In olden times this picture was still seen in imagination. That is not possible today for external consciousness. Hence, any fool can say that it is not true that external science is the dragon. Yet, it is the dragon all the same.

Those, who grew up with science and were not so bewitched by the dragon that they quietly let themselves be devoured, who reacted against the soul being investigated by all kinds of apparatus for testing the memory, and who found no answer to their search for the human being, because the dragon devoured it, those people saw themselves confronting the dragon but were not yet able to see Michael. This lived in the hearts of many human beings at the beginning of the twentieth century. They felt instinctively that they saw the dragon, but could not see Michael. Hence, they removed themselves as far as possible from the dragon. They sought a land which could not be reached by the dragon, because they did not want to know anything more of it. And so, we see that the young are running away from the old, because they want to escape from the region of the dragon. That also is an aspect of the youth movement. The young wanted to flee from the dragon, because they saw no possibility of conquering it. They wanted to go somewhere where the dragon was not.

However, there is a mystery, and it consists of the fact that the dragon can exercise its power everywhere, even where it is not spatially present. And when it does not succeed in killing the human being directly through ideas and intellectualism, it succeeds by so rarefying the air everywhere in the world that one can no longer breathe. And this will certainly be the essential thing, that the young people who ran from the dragon so as not to be damaged by it, and who came into such rarefied air that they could not breathe the future, felt intensely the nightmare of the past, because the air had become unwholesome there where it was formerly possible to escape the immediate influence of the dragon. The nightmare that comes from within is, as regards human experience, not very different from the pressure that comes from without, from the dragon.

Thus, in the last third of the nineteenth century, the older generation felt direct exposure to the dragon, and the young people experienced the nightmare of the air so corrupted by the dragon that it could not be breathed. Here, the only help is to find Michael who conquers the dragon. Human beings need the power of the dragon conqueror, for the dragon receives its life out of a world quite different from that in which the human soul can live. The human soul cannot live in the world out of which the dragon receives its lifeblood. But in the overcoming of the dragon, the human being must acquire the strength to be able to live. The epoch from the fifteenth century to the nineteenth, which has developed human beings so that they have become quite empty, must be overcome. The age of Michael who conquers the dragon must now begin, for the power of the dragon has become great!

It is this, above all, that we must accomplish, if we want to become true leaders of the young. For Michael needs, as it were, a chariot by means of which to enter our civilization. And this chariot reveals itself to the true educator as coming forth from the young, growing human being, yes, even from the child. Here the power of the pre-earthly life is still working. Here we find, if we nurture it, what becomes the chariot by means of which Michael will enter our civilization. By educating in the right way we are preparing Michael's chariot for his entrance into our civilization.

We must no longer nurture the dragon by cultivating a science with thought-forms whereby we are unconcerned that they want to penetrate into the human souls, into human bodies, into human beings themselves, in order to develop them. We must build the vehicle for Michael. For this we need living humanity such as flows out of the supersensible worlds into the earthly life and manifests there precisely in the early periods of human life. However, for such an education, we must have a heart. We must learn—speaking pictorially—to make ourselves companions of the approaching Michael, if we want to become proper teachers. More is accomplished for the art of education than by any theoretical principles, if what we receive into ourselves works so that we feel ourselves Michael's companions; allies of the spiritual being who is entering the Earth, for whom we prepare a vehicle by carrying out a living artistic education of the young. What can come out of this impulse is far better than all the theoretical educational principles. We must manage to lift up our eyes to Michael, who has been striving to enter our outworn dragon-civilization since the last third of the nineteenth century.

This is the fundamental impulse of all educational doctrine. We must not take up this art of education as a theory or as something we can learn. We should take it as something with which we would unite ourselves, the advent of which we welcome, and as something which comes to us not as dead concepts but as a living spirit-being to whom we offer our services because we must do so, if humanity is to progress in its evolution. This means to bring knowledge to life again. It means to call forth in full consciousness what once was there in the human unconscious.

My dear friends, in olden times when an atavistic clairvoyance was still natural to human beings, there were Mystery centers. In these Mystery centers, which were at the same time church, school, and art center, the pupils, who went through their development there, sought also for knowledge, though more in a soul way. Many things could be found in such centers, but libraries, in our sense, did not exist. Do not misunderstand me—no library in our own sense. Something like a library did indeed exist. That is to say, things were written down, but everything that was written down was there to be read, so that it could work upon the soul. Today a great deal of what constitutes a library is only there to be stored, not to be read. The bulk is used only when a thesis or dissertation must be written, because one must take such things into account. But people would prefer to eliminate livingness entirely. What is supposed to come into these theses or dissertations must be quite mechanical. The aim is for the human being to enter into them as little as possible. Human beings' participation in spirituality has been wrested from them.

Spirituality must become living again, but now in full consciousness, so that we do not merely experience what can be perceived by the senses, but experience once more what can be perceived by the spirit. The age of Michael must begin. Basically, everything that has been granted to the human being since the fifteenth century has come from outside. In the age of Michael human beings will have to find their own relation to the spiritual world. Learning and knowledge will acquire value in a quite different way.

What was in the libraries from the ancient Mysteries was more of the nature of monuments upon which was inscribed what was intended to pass into human memory. The contents of these libraries cannot be compared in any way with our books. For all leaders in the Mysteries directed their pupils to a different kind of reading. They said: There is a library, and this library is made up of the human beings walking about. Learn to read them! Learn to read the mysteries that are inscribed in every person. We must return to this. Only we must come to it, as it were, from another side, so that as teachers we know: All accumulation of learning, of knowledge, is worthless. As such, it is dead and gets its life only from the dragon. We should have the feeling that in wishing "to know," knowledge cannot be stored up here or there, for then it would fall apart at once. We must learn that in literature, what spirit is, can only be hinted at or intimated.

How can you really find within a book what spirit is? The spiritual is something living! The spiritual is not like the bones, but rather like the blood. And the blood needs vessels in which to flow. What we recognize as the spiritual needs vessels. These vessels are the human beings who are growing up. Into these vessels we must pour the spiritual, in order that it may hold together. Otherwise, we shall have the spirit as something that is so alive that it immediately flows away. We must so preserve our knowledge, that it can flow in the developing human beings. Then we shall build the chariot for Michael. Then we shall be able to become Michael's companions. And what you seek, my dear friends, you will best attain through being conscious of wishing to become companions of Michael.

You must once again be able to follow a purely spiritual being who is not incarnated on the Earth. And you will have to learn to have faith in a human being who shows you the way to Michael. Humanity must understand in a new and living way the words of Christ: My Kingdom is not of this world. For it is just through this that it is in the true sense "of this world!" For the task of the human being is to make the spirit, which without [the Christ] would not be on Earth, into a living content of this world. The Christ himself came down to Earth. He did not take the human being away to an earthly life in the heavens. Human beings must permeate their earthly lives with a mediating spirituality which gives them power to conquer the dragon.

This must be understood so thoroughly that one can answer the question: Why did human beings tear each other to pieces during the second decade of the twentieth century? They tore each other to pieces, because they carried the battle into a region where it does not belong. They did not see the real enemy, the dragon. To the conquest of the dragon belong the forces which, only when developed in the right way, will bring peace upon Earth.

In short, we must take seriously our entrance into the Michael age. With the means available at present, we shall have to guide human beings again to the experience of being surrounded by the picture of Michael, powerful and radiant. For Michael, through the forces developing in human beings towards a full life of soul, can overcome the dragon preying on humanity. Only when human beings take this picture into their souls in a more living way than formerly, will the forces come for the development of inner activity, because they know themselves to be in the company of Michael. Only then shall we participate in what can lead to progress and bring peace between the generations, in what can guide the young to listen to the old, and in what brings it about that the old have something to say which the young long to receive and know.

Because the older generation held the dragon up to the youth, they fled to regions with poor air. A true youth movement will only reach its goal when, instead of being offered the dragon, the younger generation finds in Michael the forces to exterminate the dragon. This will show itself by older and younger generations having something to say to each other and something to receive from each other. For, in fact, if educators are proper human beings, they receive as much from the children as they give to the children. Whoever cannot learn from the children the message they bring down from the spiritual world, cannot teach them about the mysteries of earthly existence. Only when the children become our educators by bringing their message to us from the spiritual world, will they be ready to receive tidings of earthly life from us.

It was not for the sake of mere symbolism that Goethe sought everywhere for things that suggest a breathing—out-breathing, inbreathing; out-breathing, inbreathing—rather, Goethe saw the whole of life as a picture of taking, or receiving, and giving. Everyone receives, and everyone gives. Every giver becomes a receiver. But for the receiving and the giving to find a true rhythm, it is necessary that we enter the Michael Age.

So I want to conclude with this picture for you to see how the preceding lectures were actually meant. Their aim was that you should not merely carry away in your heads what I have said here, and ponder it. What I would prefer is for you to have something in your hearts and then to transform what you carry in your hearts into activity. What human beings carry in their heads will be lost along the way. But what they receive into their hearts, their hearts will preserve and carry into all spheres of activity in which they are involved. May what I have ventured to say to you not be carried away merely in your heads—for then it will certainly be lost—but if it is carried away in your hearts, in the whole of your being, then, my dear friends, we have been talking together in the right way.

Out of this feeling, let me give you my farewell greeting today by saying: Take what I have tried to express as if I had wanted, above all, to let something that cannot be uttered in words penetrate into your hearts. If hearts have found some connection with what is meant here by the *living spirit*, then, at least in part, what we wanted to achieve in these gatherings will have been fulfilled. We want to take this feeling with us when we separate today. With this feeling, however, we want also to come together again. Thus we shall find connection in the spirit, even though we work apart in different spheres of life. The chief thing will be that in our hearts we have found each other. Then the spiritual, all that belongs to Michael, will also flow into our hearts.

EDITORIAL AND REFERENCE NOTES

Page xv, *"The Philosophy of Freedom"*
This is the original title given by Rudolf Steiner in 1894. Other editions bear the following titles: *Intuitive Thinking as a Spiritual Path* and *The Philosophy of Spiritual Activity*.

Page 3, "we have forgotten Goethe"
Rudolf Steiner's reference to the unique importance of Goethe and the Goethe generation is a recurrent and important feature of his view of European development. It is not, however, unique to Steiner. The concept of "Goethezeit" [Goethe's time or generation] has been and remains a productive way of looking at this hybrid "time," spanning several philosophical and artistic waves (late Enlightenment, "Sturm und Drang," Classicism, early Romanticism, Idealism), loosely connected by the overarching presence of Goethe's long productive life, the power of his personality, and a heroic vision of the self.

Page 4, "Jacob Grimm"
Jacob Grimm (1785-1863), German philologist, jurist and mythologist. A linguist and scholar of early German history, he studied under the legal historian Savigny. He wrote a far-reaching *History of the German Language*; he is one of the authors of Grimm's Law on the correspondence of consonants between Indo-European languages and the Saxon and German languages. He is best known worldwide as one of the Brothers Grimm.

Page 8, "Giordano Bruno"
Giordano Bruno (1548-1600), philosopher, astronomer, occultist. An early proponent of the idea of extrasolar planets and extraterrestrial life, he was brought in front of the Inquisition under 130 separate charges. The charges included: his heliocentric theory of the movement of the Earth, as well as his views of an infinite universe, formed of an infinite number of solar systems, separated by vast regions full of ether; his belief that heavenly bodies are made up of the same materials as the Earth—each star was a permanent celestial body, formed of the four elements; his doubt that the stellar region was finite, or that all stars were equidistant from a single center of the universe; God was as present on Earth as in the Heavens, an immanent God rather than a remote heavenly deity. Urged to recant, he repeatedly refused to do so and was burnt at the stake. He is considered a martyr in the cause of free-thinking.

Page 8, "Julius Robert Mayer"
Julius Robert Mayer (1814-1878), German physician and physicist. Between 1840 and 1843, Mayer, James Prescott Joule and Ludwig Colding independently came to hypothesize the mutual equivalence of heat and energy. They encountered

initially vigorous resistance to the idea. In 1851, William Thomson (later Lord Kelvin) published an article in favor of their theory, crediting both Joule and Mayer. By then Mayer had become ill. Strictly speaking, Steiner's anecdote is inaccurate (Mayer's breakdown was probably caused by a familial tragedy), but the controversies about the timing of the three scientists' discovery had been a source of great distress and the granting of a nobiliary "von" particle to his name, when he emerged from ten years of incarceration was poor consolation. In any case, Joule's later collaboration with Thomson in further experimental work ensured that he received full credit, as symbolized by the fact that a unit of work is called the *joule*. Ten years later, Wilhelm Helmholtz was to expand the theory by establishing that gravity, electrical force, magnetic force and heat all can perform mechanical work, and that heat in turn is a by-product of all mechanical work.

Page 16, "Scotus Erigena"
John Scotus Erigena (ca. 816-880?), Irish theologian, philosopher, and poet, best known as the translator of Pseudo-Dionysius into Latin, which brought him some prominence. He appeared in France at the court of Charles the Bald about 847, was received favorably and appointed head of the palace school. Although he did not interact directly with the great scholastic teachers, his radical neoplatonism and his pantheism were repeatedly condemned. But requests to send him to Rome for examination were never followed through. By the thirteenth century, mystics were interested in his work and drew on him. Meister Eckhart was influenced by him. His influence revived the nominalist-realist debates. Lost a second time, his work was found again and printed in Oxford in 1681. In the nineteenth century, Schopenhauer saw in him a kindred spirit, putting him side by side with the Vedas.

Page 16, "Savigny"
Friedrich Carl von Savigny (1779-1861) founded the German *historical school* of law. His 1803 treatise on the *Law of Property* remains a prominent landmark in the history of jurisprudence. An 1814 pamphlet protested the movement for legal codification on the ground that there was great risk of the "so-called natural law," with its "infinite arrogance," and its "shallow philosophy," which would ruin workable laws that had evolved organically, out of historical practice. Rights do not belong to the human being as such, Savigny maintained, they are the result of positive laws. Law has its source in custom, in people going about their ordinary business. Their mores and beliefs express the nature and needs of a particular people in response to its environment-writ-large, it is the result of long-lasting forces, a mysterious and sometimes obscure "History" of which they are the outgrowth. Laws can be understood by going back to their sources, i.e., the conditions of their appearance.

Page 17, "Klopstock"
Friedrich Gottlieb Klopstock (1747-1803), German poet, with a profound influence upon the Sturm und Drang Movement. His style served as a (positive or

negative) point of reference for young authors. An emotional Lutheran piety and classical aesthetics were dominant intellectual influences in his life. His huge Christian epic, *The Messiah* created a literary storm when it first appeared, giving credence to Klopstock's contention that the German language was capable of the highest literary achievements, with works equal to, and even superior to those of the classical tradition. Until then, respect had been reserved for German translations of the Bible or the Greco-Roman authors. Its vigorous religiosity, expressed in German hexameters, united German Christians of all denominations. The young people of Goethe's generation grew up memorizing large parts of it. Although its emotional style soon came to feel excessive and in bad taste, some of his poems remain part of the "folk-culture" of Germany, often set to music.

Page 17, "Boethius"
Anicius Manlius Severinus Boethius (ca. 480-526), Roman philosopher, translator of Aristotle and Plato, successful politician during the reign of the Ostrogoth king Theodoric and role model for several generations of Europeans. He is best known for his "dialogue" in alternating verse and prose on the *Consolations of Philosophy*, written in jail while awaiting his execution, perhaps as the result of false accusations, during the violent confrontations between Arian and Athanasian Christians. Over the centuries, the reading of the *Consolations* consoled many Europeans from the vicissitudes of unjust fortune. Its memorized passages sustained many political prisoners.

Page 21, "clever enough to perceive contradictions in the Gospels"
This is a reference to the *"radical criticism"* school of biblical studies, centered in Tübingen. Starting in the late eighteenth century, these scholars analyzed Middle Eastern historical archives of early Christian and Biblical times, looking for independent confirmation of events related in the Gospels and Old Testament.

Page 37, "Spencer's *Principle of Ethics*"
Herbert Spencer (1820-1903), British philosopher and sociologist. A proponent of evolutionary theory, he was initially known for applying evolutionary theory to the human sciences: he coined the phrase "survival of the fittest," which Darwin later adopted, but disagreed with Darwin on the idea of evolution being based on a simple principle of natural selection. *Principle of Ethics* (1892) argued that there was in human beings a natural mechanism—a "moral sense"—by which they arrive at moral intuitions and from which laws of conduct might be deduced. Natural sympathy and mutual concern, the recognition of common interests were the effect of accumulated instinctual and inherited experiences.

Page 38, "*Intuitive Thinking as a Spiritual Path*"
Also titled *The Philosophy of Freedom* and *The Philosophy of Spiritual Activity*.

Page 39, "Friedrich Nietzsche"
Friedrich Nietzsche (1844-1900), perhaps the most influential philosopher of

modern times, began his career under three influences: the study of classical, especially Greek texts; music, especially through his friendship with the composer Richard Wagner; and the turbulent, atheistic work of the philosopher Arthur Schopenhauer. These coalesced in his first work, *The Birth of Tragedy from the Spirit of Music* (1872). In 1873, he wrote an unpublished essay "On Truth and Lies in a Nonmoral Sense," which contained some of the key ideas he would develop through the rest of his career. Universal constants are rejected and truth becomes a "mobile army of metaphors, metonyms, and anthropomorphisms." He completed his early period by writing a number of books on Germany and German Culture. In his middle period (1878-1882), he developed his mature, aphoristic style in which philosophy became at the same time literature. In a series of six books—including *Human, All Too Human* (1878), *Daybreak: Reflections on Moral Prejudice* (1881), and *The Gay Science* (1882)—he laid the ground for what Martin Heidegger would later call the "end of metaphysics" (or Platonism, understood as dualism) and the beginning of philosophy or true thinking. This was the period when he proclaimed his ideas of the "death of God" and "eternal recurrence"—spiritual insights near-fatally contaminated by materialism, as Steiner would remark. In his last period came the celebrated *Thus Spoke Zarathustra* (1883-5), *Beyond Good and Evil* (1886), and *On the Genealogy of Morals* (1887). In 1888, his last creative year, he produced, among others, *Twilight of the Idols, or How One Philosophizes with a Hammer, The Antichrist,* and *Ecce Homo: How One Becomes What One is.* In January 1889, while in Turin, Nietzsche collapsed, experiencing a mental breakdown from which he never recovered. It was in this state that Rudolf Steiner, who felt close to Nietzsche and recognized his greatness visited him. Following the visit, he wrote his book *Nietzsche, Fighter for Freedom.*

Page 40, "Schopenhauer's philosophical pessimism"
Arthur Schopenhauer (1788-1860) was born in Danzig, Poland, of Dutch stock. His father was a successful merchant. As a youth he traveled extensively with his family throughout Europe. In 1805, after the death of his father, his mother moved to Weimar, where she was a friend of Goethe and became a well-known writer. In 1809, Schopenhauer began his university studies at Göttingen, first in medicine, then philosophy, which he studied under Fichte, among others. Other influences include Plato and Kant, as well as Friedrich Schleiermacher (1768-1834), founder of hermeneutics and a philosophy of "feeling" and the skeptical philosopher Schulze (1761-1833). Out of this mix, he formulated a kind of quasi-skeptical and pessimistic Kantian irrationalism, with which he opposed what he called the "charlatanism" of German idealism. His main work is *The World as Will and Representation* (1819). Later, he encountered Eastern philosophy—especially Upanishadic and Buddhist—and thought he found in them confirmation of his views.

Page 42, "David Friedrich Strauss"
David Friedrich Strauss (1808-1874), member of the "Radical Criticism" school

of biblical studies, centered in Tübingen. He created a scandal when he used these methods deconstructing the Gospels in his *Life of Jesus Critically Examined* (translated by English novelist George Eliot). One point of controversy was his analysis of the miraculous elements in the Gospels as being mythical in character. Strauss dispelled the actuality of the stories and reads them solely on a mythic level. Moving from miracle to miracle, he showed them to be the product of the early Christians' use of Jewish ideas about what the Messiah would be like, in order to express the conviction that Jesus was indeed the Messiah.When he was elected to a Chair of Theology in Zürich, the appointment provoked such a storm of controversy that the authorities decided to pension him before he began his duties.

Page 42, "Paul Rée"

Paul Rée (1849-1901), German author, best remembered nowadays for his friendship with and early influence on Nietzsche. Studies of philosophy and law, Darwin, Schopenhauer, and the French *moralistes* led to a doctorate on Aristotle's *Ethics*. The friendship with Rée was a decisive turning point in Nietzsche's development. Rée's *Psychological Observations*, combining aphorisms and literary/philosophical exegesis, precipitated Nietzsche's radical break with an idealized "German tradition." Eventually, Nietzsche's mature self-proclaimed "immoralist" philosophy in turn left behind Rée and the French *moralistes*, as he broke through to a post-national *On the Genealogy of Morals* from which all great human figures descend.

Page 51, "Anselm of Canterbury"

Anselm of Canterbury (1033-1109), father of medieval scholasticism. Born in Piedmont, he left home early to live in Burgundy and France as a monk. He then became an abbot and, eventually, archbishop of Canterbury. Caught in the continual struggle between king and archbishop, he sent several fruitless embassies to Rome, and went there himself for three years. Anselm was a Realist, and one of his earliest works, *De fide Trinitatis*, was an attack on the doctrine of the Trinity as expounded by the nominalist Roscelin.

Page 54, "DuBois-Reymond"

Emil DuBois-Reymond (1818-1896), German physiologist, discoverer of electrophysiology, the electrical properties of nervous and muscular tissue, and the existence of blood electrolytes. He is often remembered and was immortalized by Steiner as the coiner of the phrase *Ignorabimus* (meaning "We do not know and *we will not know*"), which he proposed in his 1872 speech the "Boundaries of Our Knowledge of Nature"; he argued that while experimental science might achieve remarkable results, the nature of matter and energy and the concept of consciousness would remain unknowable by the means of experimental science. For Steiner, his name was the symbol of the defeatism/cowardice of modern science in the face of the phenomena of consciousness.

Page 55, "Spenglerism"
Oswald Spengler (1880-1936), German author of *The Decline of the West* in which he puts forth a cyclical theory of the rise and fall of civilizations. Published in 1917, the book was evoking the inevitable decay of Germany, but given the ravages of World War I, it became and remained popular throughout Europe among people of the most diverse political persuasions. It offered a rational explanation for the great European disaster of WWI as part of cyclical world-historic process; and it furthermore provided a rationale for many of the events later in the century. The book was widely discussed, even by those who had not read (or understood) it. While professional scholars dismissed Spengler's amateur effort, *Decline of the West* became an important foundation for popular theorists of cyclical history. Spengler's views of cultures as "organic," following a "life pattern" of growth, maturity and decay, his definition of Western culture as "Faustian," became part and parcel of the European self-image.

Page 59, "Bergson"
Henri Bergson (1859-1941), French philosopher. Deeply influenced by Spencer, Mill, and Darwin during his youth, his own philosophy was a reaction against their systems. He attempted to integrate the findings of biological science with a theory of consciousness. Bergson's work was considered the main challenge to the mechanistic view of nature. His concept of *élan vital*, "creative impulse" or "living energy," was developed in *Creative Evolution*, his most famous book. Although the existence of *élan vital* cannot be scientifically verified, it provides the vital impulse that continuously shapes all life. He argued that this creative urge, not the Darwinian concept of natural selection, is at the heart of evolution. He believed that "there is nothing in philosophy which could not be said in everyday language," and the public responded: Bergson enjoyed the status of a world-class cult figure in the years between the two world wars.

Page 67, "to the conception of ethical individualism"
Steiner wrote about the origins and meaning of ethical individualism in his 1900 piece "Moral und Christentum" (Morality and Christianity) published in several installments in the *Magazin für Literatur*, July 28 and August 4, 11, 18, and 25, 1900 (translated by Mado Spiegler, available from the Rudolf Steiner Library, Ghent, New York.)

Page 70, "Paracelsus"
Paracelsus (1493-1541), Swiss chemist and physician, a father of experimental medicine, and great innovator in surgical procedures. His name is associated with the theory of "signatures," which makes him a precursor of homeopathy. Taught by a physician and alchemist father, he went on to study under the Benedictine monk Trithemius (alchemist, astrologer, and student of the Cabbala). This was followed by extensive travels, observing and learning on and off the beaten paths; his discovery of Hippocrates' medical philosophy along the way was the bridge that allowed his synthesizing genius to fully express itself.

Page 75, "Albertus Magnus"

Albertus Magnus (1200?-1280), whose given name was Albert de Groot [the Great], was often called *doctor universalis*. He left a monumental work covering all areas of science and philosophy. His interpretations of Greek and Arabic philosophers were essential to the latter's diffusion in the Christian West. He was the first Scholastic philosopher to systematically study all the works by Aristotle available in his time, and was eventually followed and surpassed by his student Thomas Aquinas, whom he defended against accusations of heresy. He wrote massive compendia of observations about hundreds of minerals, Northern European fauna and flora, the reproduction of birds and mammals, the role of sunlight in plant development, human physiology, meteorology, and astronomy. A student and teacher of alchemy, public rumor often alleged he was a magician, or that he had found the philosopher's stone.

Page 75, "Herbart"

Johann Friedrich Herbart (1776-1841), German philosopher, psychologist, and founder of pedagogy as an academic discipline.

Page 89, "Kepler"

Johannes Kepler (1571-1630) was a German Lutheran mathematician, astronomer, and astrologer, and a key figure in the seventeenth-century astronomical revolution. He is best known for his eponymous laws of planetary motion, codified by later astronomers based on his works *Astronomia Nova* (1609), *Harmonice Mundi* (1619), and *Epitome Astronomiae* (1621). Kepler's laws also provided one of the foundations for Isaac Newton's theory of universal gravitation.

During his career Kepler was a mathematics teacher at a Graz seminary school, an assistant to Tycho Brahe, the court mathematician to Emperor Rudolf II, a mathematics teacher in Linz, Austria, and an adviser to General Wallenstein. He also did fundamental work in the field of optics and helped to legitimize the telescopic discoveries of his contemporary Galileo Galilei.

Page 89, "Henle or Burdach"

Friedrich Gustav Jakob Henle (1809-1885), German physician, pathologist and anatomist, discoverer of the loop of Henle in the kidney. His innovative *Manual of Rational Pathology* treated physiology and pathology as branches of one science, and the facts of disease were systematically treated by reference to physiology. His *Handbook of Systematic Human Anatomy* was notable for the minute details of its descriptions and illustrations.

Karl Friedrich Burdach (1776-1847), anatomist and physiologist. He may be one originator of the word "biologie." He identified the *fasciculus cuneatus* (tract of Burdach) and other features of the thalamus.

Page 90, "Hyrtl"

Josef Hyrtl (1810-1894), Austrian anatomist, acquired a great reputation as a teacher of anatomy. His *Handbook of Topographic Anatomy* (1850) was the first textbook of applied anatomy of its kind ever issued. He came to be looked upon as the special glory of the University of Vienna. His 1865 inaugural address as Rector argued that the resurrection of the old materialistic view of Epicurus and Lucretius was untenable on scientific grounds and that its hold over modern thinking would eventually disappear. In the early 1880s, Rudolf Steiner may have attended his extremely popular lectures.

Page 95, "Life is brought down from the cosmos"
The scientific idea of an extra-terrestrial origin of life, which had ancient roots, underwent a revival during Steiner's early life, the idea being widely broached in both popular and scientific literature. Mainstream scientists, like Joens Berzelius, H.E. Richter, William Thomson (Lord Kelvin), and Hermann von Helmholtz, laid the ground for a more detailed hypothesis formulated in 1903 by the Swedish chemist Svante Arrhenius.

Page 110, "Zeller"
Eduard Zeller (1814-1908), German philosopher and historian of Greek culture. His *Philosophie der Griechen* (1844-52), translated into most European languages, became for a long time the key textbook on Greek philosophy. He initiated the periodization of Greek culture conventionally adopted in modern times. One of his interests was the history of monotheism. The journal *Theologische Jahrbücher*, which he founded, played an important role in diffusing David Strauss's and Christian Baur's historical critique and periodization of the Bible.

Page 110, "Michelet"
Jules Michelet (1798-1874), French historian, ardent propagandist of Romantic nationalist republicanism, scholar, and popularizer. Although scholar and university teacher, most of his many books were specifically written as textbooks or for popular consumption. In 1848, his lectures were considered so incendiary that they were banned by the monarchist government. His monumental *Histoire de France*, which took thirty years to complete was accompanied by a multitude of companion books on all aspects of social and personal life, as well as natural history. His lively writing, the encyclopedic sweep of his mind and his historical flair made him for almost a hundred years a source of inspiration to readers by its inspired combinations of visionary imagination and solid research.

Page 110, "Eduard von Hartmann"
Eduard von Hartmann (1842-1906), German philosopher. Intended for a military career, health reasons forced him to change course. He became a philosopher. His reputation was established by his first book, *The Philosophy of the Unconscious* (1869). This success was largely due to the originality of its title, the diversity of its contents, its radical pessimism and the lucidity of its style. Rudolf Steiner admired him, disagreed with him and greatly valued his opinion of his work. He first wrote about him in 1891 in the newspaper *Deutsche Worte* (see GA 30, 288-302, translation available at the Rudolf Steiner Library).

Page 122, "Johann Gottlieb Fichte"

Johann Gottlieb Fichte (1762-1814), the first of the great triad of "German idealists" (Hegel and Schelling are the others) after Kant, developed his own "system of transcendental philosophy" (*Wissenschaftslehre*), which greatly influenced his contemporaries, as well as Rudolf Steiner. Born poor, Fichte began his career as a tutor. In 1790, responding to a student's need for instruction, he immersed himself in Kant's critical philosophy. It changed his life. He went to Königsburg to meet the Master, who was not impressed. To prove his philosophical expertise, Fichte immediately composed *An Attempt at the Critique of all Revelation*, a Kantian work, which did impress Kant, who saw to its publication in 1792. In fact, because his name was mysteriously omitted from the title page, readers thought it was by Kant. Thus Fichte's career was launched. In 1794, he was called to the Chair of Philosophy at Jena. There he wrote *The Scholar's Vocation*, among others, and began work on his system. Going beyond Kant, and in any way undoing him, Fichte took as his starting point or foundation, not consciousness, but "the 'I' positing itself absolutely." The "I" as "act"—not static, but a self-producing process—thus became primary, the ground of all experience. [See *The Science of Knowledge* (1794/5/7)] His work (and the rest of his life) then became a phenomenology of the "I"'s continuous "transcendental" construction of itself and what followed from this in all spheres of life (law, ethics, etc.).

Page 148, "arise out of the Kant-Laplace primeval nebula"

This refers to the Kant-Laplace nebula theory of the origins of the solar system, proposed by Immanuel Kant in 1755 and combined with Pierre-Simon de Laplace's 1796 theory. It is the basis of all current theories accounting for the formation and presence of the Sun; the orbits of the planets around it; the origin of the terrestrial and gaseous planets; the origin of satellites; and the reasons for the distribution of mass and momentum between the planets and the Sun, also known as the problem of angular momentum. According to this theory, the solar system began as a cloud of dispersed particles. He assumed that the mutual gravitational attractions of the particles caused them to start moving and colliding, at which point chemical forces kept them bonded together. As some of these aggregates became larger than others, they grew still more rapidly, ultimately forming the planets. (See also http://www.astro.utoronto.ca/~bclarke/AST199M/SS_Origin.htm.)

RUDOLF STEINER'S COLLECTED WORKS

The German Edition of Rudolf Steiner's Collected Works (the Gesamtausgabe [GA] published by Rudolf Steiner Verlag, Dornach, Switzerland) presently is 354 titles. It is organized either by type of work (written or spoken), chronology, audience (public or other), or subject (education, art, etc.). For ease of comparison, the Collected Works in English (CW) is based on the German organization.

A complete listing of the CWs follows. The volumes that are not yet translated have been given a literal translation of the German title. For ease of identification and to avoid confusion, readers looking for a title should do so by the CW number.

Because the work of creating the Collected Works of Rudolf Steiner in English is an ongoing process, with new titles being published every year, we have not indicated in this listing which books are presently available. To find out what titles in the Collected Works are currently in print, please check our website at www.steinerbooks.org.

A. Written Works

I. Writings 1884–1925

CW 1	Nature's Open Secret. Introductions to Goethe's Scientific Writings
CW 2	Goethe's Theory of Knowledge. An Outline of the Epistemology of His Worldview
CW 3	Truth and Knowledge (Truth and Science)
CW 4	The Philosophy of Freedom (The Philosophy of Spiritual Activity; Intuitive Thinking as a Spiritual Path)
CW 4a	Documents on "The Philosophy of Freedom"
CW 5	Friedrich Nietzsche: A Fighter against His Own Time
CW 6	Goethe's Worldview
CW 7	Mystics at the Dawn of the Modern Age
CW 8	Christianity as Mystical Fact and the Mysteries of Antiquity
CW 9	Theosophy. An Introduction to the Spiritual Processes in Human Life and in the Cosmos
CW 10	How to Know Higher Worlds (Knowledge of the Higher Worlds and its Attainment)
CW 11	Cosmic Memory. The Story of Atlantis, Lemuria, and the Division of the Sexes

CW 12	The Stages of Higher Knowledge: Imagination, Inspiration, Intuition
CW 13	An Outline of Esoteric Science (Occult Science, An Outline)
CW 14	Four Mystery Dramas
CW 15	The Spiritual Guidance of the Individual and Humanity
CW 16	A Way of Self-Knowledge
CW 17	The Threshold of the Spiritual World
CW 18	The Riddles of Philosophy
(CW 19)	in CW 24
CW 20	The Riddle of Man
CW 21	Riddles of the Soul
CW 22	Goethe's Spiritual Nature and Its Revelation in *Faust* and through the "Fairy Tale of the Green Snake and the Beautiful Lily"
CW 23	Towards Social Renewal. Basic Issues of the Social Question
CW 24	The Renewal of the Social Organism
CW 25	Cosmology, Religion, and Philosophy
CW 26	Anthroposophical Leading Thoughts. Anthroposophy as a Path of Knowledge. The Michael Mystery
CW 27	Extending Practical Medicine. Fundamental Principles Based on the Science of the Spirit
CW 28	Autobiography. Chapters in the Course of My Life 1861-1907

II. Collected Essays

CW 29	Collected Essays on Dramaturgy, 1889-1900
CW 30	Methodical Foundations of Anthroposophy: Collected Essays on Philosophy, Natural Science, Aesthetics and Psychology, 1884-1901
CW 31	Collected Essays on Culture and Current Events, 1887-1901
CW 32	Collected Essays on Literature, 1884-1902
CW 33	Biographies and Biographical Sketches, 1894-1905
CW 34	Lucifer-Gnosis: Foundational Essays on Anthroposophy and Reports from the Periodicals "Lucifer" and "Lucifer-Gnosis," 1903-1908
CW 35	Philosophy and Anthroposophy: Collected Essays, 1904-1923
CW 36	The Goetheanum-Idea in the Middle of the Cultural Crisis of the Present: Collected Essays from the Periodical "Das Goetheanum," 1921-1925
(CW 37)	Now in CW 251 and CW 260a

III. Publications from the Literary Estate

CW 38	Letters, Vol. 1: 1881-1890
CW 39	Letters, Vol. 2: 1890-1925
CW 40	Truth-Wrought Words (Includes: The Calendar of the Soul)
CW 40a	Verses and Meditations
CW 41b	Translations and Free Renderings from Various Works
(CW 42)	Now in CWs 264-266
CW 43	Stage Adaptations (planned in GA)
CW 44	On the Four Mystery Dramas. Sketches, Fragments and Paralipomena on the Four Mystery Dramas
CW 45	Anthroposophy: A Fragment
CW 46	Treatments and Fragments out of the Estate

B. Lectures

I. Public Lectures

CW 51	On Philosophy, History, and Literature
CW 52	Spiritual Teachings about the Soul and Observation of the World
CW 53	The Origin and Goal of the Human Being
CW 54	Riddles of the World and Anthroposophy
CW 56	Knowledge of the Soul and of the Spirit
CW 57	Where and How Does One Find the Spirit?
CW 58	Transforming the Soul, Vol. 1 (formerly: Metamorphoses of the Soul, Vol. 1)
CW 59	Transforming the Soul, Vol. 2 (formerly: Metamorphoses of the Soul, Vol. 2)
CW 60/61	Turning Points in Spiritual History
CW 62	Results of Spiritual Research
CW 63	Spiritual Science as a Treasure for Life
CW 64	From Destiny-burdened Times
CW 65	Out of Central European Spiritual Life
CW 66	Spirit and Matter, Life and Death
CW 67	The Eternal in the Human Soul. Immortality and Freedom
CW 68	Public Lectures in Various Cities, 1906-1918 (planned in GA)
CW 68c	Goethe and the Present
CW 69a	Truths and Errors in Spiritual Research. Spiritual Science and the Future of Humanity

CW 69b	Knowledge and Immortality
CW 69c	The New Christ Experience
CW 69d	Death and Immortality in the Light of Spiritual Science
CW 69e	Spiritual Science and the Spiritual Goals of Our Time
CW 70	Public Lectures in Various Cities, 1906-1918 (planned in GA)
CW 71	Public Lectures in Various Cities, 1906-1918 (planned in GA)
CW 72	Freedom – Immortality – Social Life
CW 73	Anthroposophy Has Something to Add to Modern Science
CW 73a	Specialized Fields of Knowledge and Anthroposophy
CW 74	The Redemption of Thinking
CW 75	Anthroposophy and Science
CW 76	The Fructifying Effect of Anthroposophy on Specialized Fields
CW 77a	The Task of Anthroposophy in Relation to Science and Life. The Darmstadt College Course
CW 77b	Art and Anthroposophy
CW 78	Fruits of Anthroposophy
CW 79	Self-Consciousness
CW 80	Public Lectures in Various Cities, 1922 (planned in GA)
CW 80a	The Nature of Anthroposophy
CW 80b	The Nature of Anthroposophy
CW 81	Reimagining Academic Studies. Science, Philosophy, Education, Social Science, Theology, Theory of Language
CW 82	So that the Human Being Can Become a Complete Human Being
CW 83	The Tension Between East and West
CW 84	What Did the Goetheanum Intend and What Should Anthroposophy Do?

II. Lectures to the Members of the Anthroposophical Society

CW 88	Concerning the Astral World and Devachan
CW 89	Awareness – Life – Form
CW 90a	Self-Knowledge and Knowledge of the Divine, Vol. I
CW 90b	Self-Knowledge and Knowledge of the Divine, Vol. II
CW 91	Participant Notes from the Lectures during the Years 1903–1905

CW 92	The Occult Truths of Ancient Myths and Saga
CW 93	The Temple Legend
CW 93a	Fundamentals of Esotericism
CW 94	An Esoteric Cosmology
CW 95	Founding a Science of the Spirit (formerly: At the Gates of Theosophy)
CW 96	Origins of Spiritual Science
CW 97	The Christian Mystery. Early lectures
CW 98	Nature Beings and Spirit Beings – Their Effects in Our Visible World
CW 99	Rosicrucian Wisdom (formerly: Theosophy of the Rosicrucian)
CW 100	True Knowledge of the Christ. Theosophy and Rosicrucianism. The Gospel of John.
CW 101	Myths and Legends. Occult Signs and Symbols
CW 102	Good and Evil Spirits and Their Influence on Humanity
CW 103	The Gospel of John
CW 104	The Apocalypse of John
CW 104a	Reading the Pictures of the Apocalypse
CW 105	Universe, Earth, and Man
CW 106	Egyptian Myths and Mysteries
CW 107	Disease, Karma, and Healing. Spiritual-Scientific Enquiries into the Nature of the Human Being
CW 108	Answering the Questions of Life and the World through Anthroposophy
CW 109/111	The Principle of Spiritual Economy
CW 110	The Spiritual Hierarchies and the Physical World. Zodiac, Planets, and Cosmos
CW 112	The Gospel of John in Relation to the Other Gospels
CW 113	The East in the Light of the West
CW 114	According to Luke (The Gospel of Luke)
CW 115	A Psychology of Body, Soul, and Spirit
CW 116	The Christ Impulse and the Development of Ego-Consciousness
CW 117	The Deeper Secrets of the Development of Humanity in Light of the Gospels
CW 117a	The John Gospel and the Other Three Gospels: A Supplement
CW 118	The Second Coming of Christ
CW 119	Macrocosm and Microcosm
CW 120	Manifestations of Karma
CW 121	The Mission of the Folk Souls
CW 122	Genesis. Secrets of Creation
CW 123	According to Matthew (The Gospel of Matthew)

CW 124 Background to the Gospel of Mark
CW 125 Paths and Goals of the Spiritual Human Being. Life Questions in the Light of Spiritual Science
CW 126 Occult History. Historical Personalities and Events in the Light of Spiritual Science
CW 127 The Mission of the New Spiritual Revelation. The Christ-Event as the Middle-Point of Earth Evolution
CW 128 An Occult Physiology
CW 129 Wonders of the World, Ordeals of the Soul, and Revelations of the Spirit
CW 130 Esoteric Christianity
CW 131 From Jesus to Christ
CW 132 Inner Experiences of Evolution
CW 133 Earthly and the Cosmic Man
CW 134 The World of the Senses and the World of the Spirit
CW 135 Reincarnation and Karma
CW 136 Spiritual Beings in the Heavenly Bodies and in the Kingdoms of Nature
CW 137 Man in the Light of Occultism, Theosophy, and Philosophy
CW 138 Initiation, Eternity, and the Passing Moment
CW 139 The Gospel of Mark
CW 140 Life between Death and Rebirth
CW 141 Between Death and Rebirth
CW 142/146 The Bhagavad Gita and the West. The Esoteric Significance of the Bhagavad Gita and Its Relation to the Epistles of Paul
CW 143 Experiences of the Supersensible. Three Paths of the Soul to Christ
CW 144 The Mysteries of the East and of Christianity
CW 145 The Effects of Esoteric Development
CW 147 Secrets of the Threshold
CW 148 The Fifth Gospel
CW 149 Christ and the Spiritual World and the Search for the Holy Grail
CW 150 How the Spiritual World Projects into Physical Existence. The Influence of the Dead
CW 151 Human and Cosmic Thought
CW 152 Approaching the Mystery of Golgotha
CW 153 The Inner Nature of Man
CW 154 The Presence of the Dead on the Spiritual Path
CW 155 Christ and the Human Soul / The Spiritual Foundation of Morality
CW 156 Inner Reading and Inner Hearing and How to Achieve Existence in the World of Ideas

CW 157 The Destinies of Individuals and of Nations
CW 157a Spiritual Life Now and after Death
(formerly: The Forming of Destiny and Life After Death)
CW 158 Our Connection with the Elemental World. Kalevala – Olaf Åsteson – the Russian People. The World as the Result of Balancing Influences
CW 159 The Mystery of Death. The Nature and Significance of Middle Europe and the European Folk Spirits
CW 161 Artistic Sensitivity as a Spiritual Approach to Knowing Life and the World
CW 162 Questions of Art and Life in Light of Spiritual Science
CW 163 Chance, Providence, and Necessity
CW 164 The Value of Thinking for a Knowledge That Satisfies the Human Being. The Relationship of Spiritual Science to Natural Science
CW 165 Unifying Humanity Spiritually through the Christ Impulse
CW 166 Necessity and Freedom
CW 167 The Human Spirit. Past and Present. Occult Fraternities and the Mystery of Golgotha
CW 168 The Connection between the Living and the Dead
CW 169 Toward Imagination
CW 170 The Riddle of Humanity
CW 171 Inner Impulses of Evolution
CW 172 The Karma of Vocation
CW 173 The Karma of Untruthfulness, Vol. 1
CW 174 The Karma of Untruthfulness, Vol. 2
CW 174a Middle Europe between East and West. Cosmic and Human History, Vol. 6
CW 174b The Spiritual Background of the First World War. Cosmic and Human History, Vol. 7
CW 175 Building Stones for an Understanding of the Mystery of Golgotha. Human Life in a Cosmic Context
CW 176 The Karma of Materialism / Inner Aspects of Evolution
CW 177 The Fall of the Spirits of Darkness
CW 178 Secret Brotherhoods and the Mystery of the Human Double
CW 179 The Influence of the Dead on Destiny
CW 180 Ancient Myths and the New Isis Mystery
CW 181 Dying Earth and Living Cosmos. The Living Gifts of Anthroposophy. The Need for a New Form of Consciousness
CW 182 Death as Metamorphosis of Life. Including "What Does the Angel Do in Our Astral Body?" and "How Do I Find the Christ?"

CW 183 Human Evolution. A Spiritual-Scientific Quest
CW 184 Eternal and Transient Elements. The Cosmic Past of Humanity and the Mystery of Evil
CW 185 From Symptom to Reality in Modern History
CW 185a Historical-Developmental Foundations for Forming a Social Judgment
CW 186 The Challenge of the Times
CW 187 How Can Mankind Find the Christ Again? The Threefold Shadow Existence of Our Time and the New Light of Christ
CW 188 Goetheanism, a Transformation-Impulse and Resurrection-Thought. Science of the Human Being and Science of Sociology
CW 189 Conscious Society. Anthroposophy and the Social Question
CW 190 Impulses of the Past and the Future in Social Occurrences. The Spiritual Background of the Social Question, Vol. 2
CW 191 Understanding Society through Spiritual-Scientific Knowledge. Social Threefolding, Christ, Lucifer, and Ahriman
CW 192 Spiritual-Scientific Treatment of Social and Pedagogical Questions
CW 193 Problems of Society: An Esoteric View. From Luciferic Past to Ahrimanic Future
CW 194 Michael's Mission. Revealing the Essential Secrets of Human Nature
CW 195 Cosmic New Year. Thoughts for the New Year 1920
CW 196 What is Necessary in These Urgent Times
CW 197 Polarities in the Evolution of Mankind
CW 198 Healing Factors for the Social Organism
CW 199 Spiritual Science as a Foundation for Social Forms
CW 200 The New Spirituality and the Christ-Experience of the Twentieth Century
CW 201 Mystery of the Universe. The Human Being, Model of Creation (formerly: Man: Hieroglyph of the Universe)
CW 202 Universal Spirituality and Human Physicality. Bridging the Divide. The Search for the New Isis and the Divine Sophia
CW 203 The Responsibility of Human Beings for the Development of the World through their Spiritual Connection with the Planet Earth and the World of the Stars
CW 204 Materialism and the Task of Anthroposophy
CW 205 Human Development, World-Soul, and World-Spirit. Part One: The Human Being as a Being of Body and Soul in Relationship to the World

CW 206	Human Development, World-Soul, and World-Spirit. Part Two: The Human Being as a Spiritual Being in the Process of Historical Development
CW 207	Cosmosophy, Vol. 1
CW 208	Cosmosophy, Vol. 2
CW 209	Nordic and Central European Spiritual Impulses. The Festival of the Appearance of Christ
CW 210	Old and New Methods of Initiation
CW 211	The Sun Mystery and the Mystery of Death and Resurrection. Exoteric and Esoteric Christianity
CW 212	Life of the Human Soul and Its Relation to World Evolution
CW 213	Human Questions and World Answers
CW 214	The Mystery of the Trinity (English edition is not complete)
CW 215	Philosophy, Cosmology, and Religion
CW 216	The Fundamental Impulses of the World-Historical Development of Humanity
CW 217	Becoming Michael's Companions. Rudolf Steiner's Challenge to the Younger Generation (formerly: The Younger Generation)
CW 217a	Youth and the Etheric Heart. Rudolf Steiner Speaks to the Younger Generation
CW 218	Spirit as Sculptor of the Human Organism
CW 219	Man and the World of Stars
CW 220	Awake! For the Sake of the Future
CW 221	Earthly Knowledge and Heavenly Wisdom
CW 222	The Driving Force of Spiritual Powers in World History
CW 223	The Cycle of the Year as Breathing Process of the Earth / Michaelmas and the Soul Forces of Man
CW 224	The Human Soul and Its Connection with Divine-Spiritual Individualities. The Internalization of the Festivals of the Year
CW 225	Three Perspectives of Anthroposophy. Cultural Phenomena Observed from a Spiritual-Scientific Perspective
CW 226	Man's Being, His Destiny, and World Evolution
CW 227	The Evolution of Consciousness
CW 228	Initiation Science and the Development of the Human Mind
CW 229	The Experiencing of the Course of the Year in Four Cosmic Imaginations
CW 230	Harmony of the Creative Word. The Human Being and the Elemental, Animal, Plant, and Mineral Kingdoms (formerly: Man as Symphony of the Creative Word)
CW 231	At Home in the Universe
CW 232	Mystery Knowledge and Mystery Centres

CW 233	World History in the Light of Anthroposophy
CW 233a	Mystery Sites of the Middle Ages: Rosicrucianism and the Modern Initiation-Principle
CW 234	Anthroposophy and the Inner Life (formerly: Anthroposophy: An Introduction)
CW 235	Karmic Relationships: Esoteric Studies, Vol. I
CW 236	Karmic Relationships: Esoteric Studies, Vol. II
CW 237	Karmic Relationships: Esoteric Studies, Vol. III
CW 238	Karmic Relationships: Esoteric Studies, Vol. IV
CW 239	Karmic Relationships: Esoteric Studies, Vol. V / Karmic Relationships: Esoteric Studies, Vol. VII
CW 240	Karmic Relationships: Esoteric Studies, Vol. VI / Karmic Relationships: Esoteric Studies, Vol. VIII
CW 243	True and False Paths in Spiritual Investigation
CW 245	Guidance in Esoteric Training
CW 250	The Building-up of the Anthroposophical Society. From the Beginning to the Outbreak of the First World War (planned in GA)
CW 251	The History of the Goetheanum Building Union (planned in GA)
CW 252	Life in the Anthroposophical Society from the First World War to the Burning of the First Goetheanum
CW 253	Sexuality, Inner Development, and Community Life. Ethical and Spiritual Dimensions of the Crisis in the Anthroposophical Society in Dornach, 1915
CW 254	The Occult Movement in the Nineteenth Century and Its Relation to Modern Culture
CW 255	Rudolf Steiner during the First World War
CW 255a	Anthroposophy and the Reformation of Society. On the History of the Threefold Movement (planned in GA)
CW 255b	Anthroposophy and Its Opponents, 1919-1921
CW 256	How Can the Anthroposophical Movement Be Financed? (planned in GA)
CW 256a	Futurum Inc./International Laboratories (planned in GA)
CW 256b	The Coming Day Inc. (Der Kommende Tag A.G.) (planned in GA)
CW 257	Awakening to Community
CW 258	The Anthroposophic Movement
CW 259	The Year of Destiny 1923 in the History of the Anthroposophical Society. From the Burning of the Goetheanum to the Christmas Conference

CW 260 The Christmas Conference for the Founding of the General Anthroposophical Society, 1923/1924
CW 260a The Constitution of the School for Spiritual Science (English edition is incomplete)
CW 261 Our Dead: Memorial, Funeral, and Cremation Addresses, 1906-1924
CW 262 Correspondence and Documents, 1901-1925 (Letters and Documents, 1901-1925))
CW 263/1 Rudolf Steiner and Edith Maryon: Correspondence: Letters, Verses, Sketches, 1912-1924
CW 264 From the History and Contents of the First Section of the Esoteric School. Letters, Documents, and Lectures: 1904-1914
CW 265 Freemasonry and Ritual Work: The Misraim Service
CW 266/1 Esoteric Lessons 1904-1909. From the Esoteric School. Lectures, Notes, Meditations, and Exercises by Rudolf Steiner. Notes of Esoteric Lerssons from Memory by the Participants
CW 266/2 Esoteric Lessons 1910-1912. From the Esoteric School. Notes Written from Memory by the Participants and Meditation Verses by Rudolf Steiner
CW 266/3 Esoteric Lessons 1913-1923. From the Esoteric School. Notes Written from Memory by the Participants and Meditation Verses by Rudolf Steiner
CW 267 Soul Exercises. Word and Symbol Meditations, 1903-1924
CW 268 Mantric Sayings. Meditations, 1903-1925
CW 269 Ritual Texts for the Celebration of the Free Christian Religious Instruction. The Collected Verses for Teachers and Students of the Waldorf School
CW 270 The First Class Lessons and Mantras (19 Lessons) and The First Class of the Michael School (7 Recapitulation Lessons)

III. Lectures and Courses on Specific Areas of Life

Lectures on Art

CW 271 Art and Knowledge of Art. Foundations of a New Aesthetic
CW 272 Anthroposophy in the Light of Goethe's *Faust*
CW 273 Goethe's *Faust* in the Light of Anthroposophy
CW 274 Addresses for the Christmas Plays from the Old Folk Traditions
CW 275 Art as Seen in the Light of Mystery Wisdom
CW 276 The Arts and Their Mission
CW 277a An Introduction to Eurythmy

CW 277b The Early History of Eurythmy
CW 277c The Early History of Eurythmy
CW 278 Eurythmy as Visible Singing
CW 279 Eurythmy as Visible Speech
CW 280 Creative Speech
CW 281 The Art of Recitation and Declamation
CW 282 Speech and Drama
CW 283 The Nature of Music and the Experience of Tone in the Human Being
CW 284 Rosicrucianism Renewed. The Unity of Art, Science, and Religion. The Theosophical Congress of Whitsun 1907
CW 286 Architecture as a Synthesis of the Arts
CW 287 Architecture as Peacework. The First Goetheanum, Dornach, 1914
CW 288 Architecture, Sculpture, and Painting of the First Goetheanum
CW 289 The Building-Idea of the Goetheanum. Lectures with Slides from the Years 1920-1921
CW 290 Toward a New Theory of Architecture. The First Goetheanum in Pictures
CW 291 Colour
CW 291a Knowledge of Colors. Supplementary Volume to Colour
CW 292 Art History as a Reflection of Inner Spiritual Impulses

Lectures on Education

CW 293 Foundations of Human Experience (Study of Man)
CW 294 Practical Advice to Teachers
CW 295 Discussions with Teachers
CW 296 Education as a Force for Social Change (formerly: Education as a Social Problem)
CW 297 The Spirit of the Waldorf School
CW 297a Education, Teaching, and Practical Life
CW 298 Rudolf Steiner in the Waldorf School
CW 299 The Genius of Language
CW 300a Faculty Meetings, Vol. 1
CW 300b Faculty Meetings, Vol. 2
CW 300c Faculty Meetings, Vol. 3
CW 301 The Renewal of Education
CW 302 Education for Adolescents
CW 302a Balance in Teaching
CW 303 Soul Economy
CW 304 Waldorf Education and Anthroposophy I

CW 304a Waldorf Education and Anthroposophy II
CW 305 The Spiritual Ground of Education
CW 306 The Child's Changing Consciousness
CW 307 A Modern Art of Education
CW 308 Essentials of Education
CW 309 The Roots of Education
CW 310 Human Values in Education
CW 311 The Kingdom of Childhood

Lectures on Medicine

CW 312 Introducing Anthroposophical Medicine (formerly Spiritual Science and Medicine)
CW 313 Illness and Therapy. Spiritual-Scientific Aspects of Healing
CW 314 Physiology and Healing. Treatment, Therapy, and Hygiene
CW 315 Eurythmy Therapy (formerly Curative Eurythmy)
CW 316 Understanding Healing. Meditative Reflections on Deepening Medicine through Spiritual Science
CW 317 Education for Special Needs. The Curative Education Course
CW 318 Broken Vessels (formerly: Pastoral Medicine)
CW 319 The Healing Process. Spirit, Nature, and Our Bodies

Lectures on Natural Science

CW 320 The Light Course. First Course in Natural Science: Light, Color, Sound – Mass, Electricity, Magnetism
CW 321 The Warmth Course. Second Course in Natural Science. The Theory of heat
CW 322 The Boundaries of Natural Science
CW 323 Interdisciplinary Astronomy. Third Scientific Course
CW 324 Nature Observation, Mathematics, and Scientific Experimentation and Results from the Viewpoint of Anthroposophy
CW 324a The Fourth Dimension. Sacred Geometry, Alchemy, and Mathematics
CW 325 Natural Science and the World-Historical Development of Humanity since Ancient Times
CW 326 The Origins of Natural Science
CW 327 Agriculture: Spiritual Foundations for the Renewal of Agriculture (Agricultural Course: The Birth of the Biodynamic method))

CW 328 The Social Question. Lectures on Social Life and the Threefolding of the Social Organism
CW 329 The Liberation of the Human Being as the Foundation for a New Social Form
CW 330 From the Unified State to the Threefold Division of the Social Organism
CW 331 Cultural Councils and Socialization
CW 332 Total Reform of Society and the Union for Threefolding. Advice on Culture and the Liberation of the Spiritual Life (planned in GA)
CW 332a The Social Future. Culture, Equality, and the Economy
CW 333 Freedom of Thought and Societal Forces. Implementing the Demands of Modern Society
CW 334 Social Issues. Meditative Thinking and the Threefold Social Order (English translation incomplete)
CW 335 The Crisis of the Present and the Path to Healthy Thinking
CW 336 The Great Questions of the Times and Anthroposophical Spiritual Knowledge
CW 337a Social Ideas, Social Reality, Social Practice. Vol. 1: Question and Answer Evenings and Study Evenings of the Alliance for the Threefold Social Organism in Stuttgart, 1919-1920
CW 337b Social Ideas, Social Realities, Social Practice. Vol. 2: Discussion Evenings of the Swiss Alliance for theThreefold Social Organism
CW 338 Communicating Anthroposophy. The Course for Speakers to Promote the Idea of Threfolding
CW 339 The Art of Lecturing
CW 340/341 Rethinking Economics. Lectures and Seminars on World Economics

LECTURES AND COURSES ON CHRISTIAN RELIGIOUS WORK

CW 342 First Steps in Christian Religious Renewal. Preparing the Ground for The Christian Community (Vol.1)
CW 343 Lectures and Courses on Christian Religious Work. Vol. 2: Spiritual Knowledge – Religious Feeling – Ritual Deeds
CW 344 Lectures and Courses on Christian Religious Work. Vol. 3: Lectures at the Founding of the Christian Community
CW 345 Lectures and Courses on Christian Religious Work. Vol. 4: Concerning the Nature of the Working Word
CW 346 The Book of Revelation and the Work of the Priest

Lectures for the Workers at the Goetheanum

CW 347 From Crystals to Crocodiles
CW 348 From Comets to Cocaine (formerly: Health and Illness)
CW 349 From Limestone to Lucifer
CW 350 From Mammoths to Mediums
CW 351 Bees
CW 352 From Elephants to Einstein
CW 353 From Beetroot to Buddhism
CW 354 From Sunspots to Strawberries

SIGNIFICANT EVENTS IN THE LIFE OF RUDOLF STEINER

1829: June 23: birth of Johann Steiner (1829-1910)—Rudolf Steiner's father—in Geras, Lower Austria.

1834: May 8: birth of Franciska Blie (1834-1918)—Rudolf Steiner's mother—in Horn, Lower Austria. "My father and mother were both children of the glorious Lower Austrian forest district north of the Danube."

1860: May 16: marriage of Johann Steiner and Franciska Blie.

1861: February 25: birth of *Rudolf Joseph Lorenz Steiner* in Kraljevec, Croatia, near the border with Hungary, where Johann Steiner works as a telegrapher for the South Austria Railroad. Rudolf Steiner is baptized two days later, February 27, the date usually given as his birthday.

1862: Summer: the family moves to Mödling, Lower Austria.

1863: The family moves to Pottschach, Lower Austria, near the Styrian border, where Johann Steiner becomes stationmaster. "The view stretched to the mountains...majestic peaks in the distance and the sweet charm of nature in the immediate surroundings."

1864: November 15: birth of Rudolf Steiner's sister, Leopoldine (d. November 1, 1927). She will become a seamstress and live with her parents for the rest of her life.

1866: July 28: birth of Rudolf Steiner's deaf-mute brother, Gustav (d. May 1, 1941).

1867: Rudolf Steiner enters the village school. Following a disagreement between his father and the schoolmaster, whose wife falsely accused the boy of causing a commotion, Rudolf Steiner is taken out of school and taught at home.

1868: A critical experience. Unknown to the family, an aunt dies in a distant town. Sitting in the station waiting room, Rudolf Steiner sees her "form," which speaks to him, asking for help. "Beginning with this experience, a new soul life began in the boy, one in which not only the outer trees and mountains spoke to him, but also the worlds that lay behind them. From this moment on, the boy began to live with the spirits of nature...."

1869: The family moves to the peaceful, rural village of Neudorfl, near Wiener-Neustadt in present-day Hungary. Rudolf Steiner attends the village school. Because of the "unorthodoxy" of his writing and spelling, he has to do "extra lessons."

1870: Through a book lent to him by his tutor, he discovers geometry: "To grasp something purely in the spirit brought me inner happiness. I know that I first learned happiness through geometry." The same tutor allows him to draw, while other students still struggle with their reading and writing. "An artistic element" thus enters his education.

1871: Though his parents are not religious, Rudolf Steiner becomes a "church child," a favorite of the priest, who was "an exceptional character." "Up to the age of ten or eleven, among those I came to know, he was far and away the most significant." Among other things, he introduces Steiner to Copernican, heliocentric cosmology. As an altar boy, Rudolf Steiner serves at Masses, funerals, and Corpus Christi processions. At year's end, after an incident in which he escapes a thrashing, his father forbids him to go to church.

1872: Rudolf Steiner transfers to grammar school in Wiener-Neustadt, a five-mile walk from home, which must be done in all weathers.

1873-75: Through his teachers and on his own, Rudolf Steiner has many wonderful experiences with science and mathematics. Outside school, he teaches himself analytic geometry, trigonometry, differential equations, and calculus.

1876: Rudolf Steiner begins tutoring other students. He learns bookbinding from his father. He also teaches himself stenography.

1877: Rudolf Steiner discovers Kant's *Critique of Pure Reason*, which he reads and rereads. He also discovers and reads von Rotteck's *World History*.

1878: He studies extensively in contemporary psychology and philosophy.

1879: Rudolf Steiner graduates from high school with honors. His father is transferred to Inzersdorf, near Vienna. He uses his first visit to Vienna "to purchase a great number of philosophy books"— Kant, Fichte, Schelling, and Hegel, as well as numerous histories of philosophy. His aim: to find a path from the "I" to nature.

October 1879-1883: Rudolf Steiner attends the Technical College in Vienna—to study mathematics, chemistry, physics, mineralogy, botany, zoology, biology, geology, and mechanics—with a scholarship. He also attends lectures in history and literature, while avidly reading philosophy on his own. His two favorite professors are Karl Julius Schröer (German language and literature) and Edmund Reitlinger (physics). He also audits lectures by Robert Zimmerman on aesthetics and Franz Brentano on philosophy. During this year he begins his friendship with Moritz Zitter (1861-1921), who will help support him financially when he is in Berlin.

1880: Rudolf Steiner attends lectures on Schiller and Goethe by Karl Julius Schröer, who becomes his mentor. Also "through a remarkable combination of circumstances," he meets Felix Koguzki, an "herb gatherer" and healer, who could "see deeply into the secrets of nature." Rudolf Steiner will meet and study with this "emissary of the Master" throughout his time in Vienna.

1881: January: "... I didn't sleep a wink. I was busy with philosophical problems until about 12:30 a.m. Then, finally, I threw myself down on my couch. All my striving during the previous year had been to research whether the following statement by Schelling was true or not: *Within everyone dwells a secret, marvelous capacity to draw back from the stream of time—out of the self clothed in all that comes to us from outside—into our innermost being and there, in the immutable form of the Eternal, to look into ourselves.* I believe, and I am still quite certain of it, that I discovered this capacity in myself; I had long had an inkling of it. Now the whole of idealist philosophy stood before me in modified form. What's a sleepless night compared to that!"

Rudolf Steiner begins communicating with leading thinkers of the day, who send him books in return, which he reads eagerly.

July: "I am not one of those who dives into the day like an animal in human form. I pursue a quite specific goal, an idealistic aim—knowledge of the truth! This cannot be done offhandedly. It requires the greatest striving in the world, free of all egotism, and equally of all resignation."

August: Steiner puts down on paper for the first time thoughts for a "Philosophy of Freedom." "The striving for the absolute: this human yearning is freedom." He also seeks to outline a "peasant philosophy," describing what the worldview of a "peasant"—one who lives close to the earth and the old ways—really is.

1881-1882: Felix Koguzki, the herb gatherer, reveals himself to be the envoy of another, higher initiatory personality, who instructs Rudolf Steiner to penetrate Fichte's philosophy and to master modern scientific thinking as a preparation for right entry into the spirit. This "Master" also teaches him the double (evolutionary and involutionary) nature of time.

1882: Through the offices of Karl Julius Schröer, Rudolf Steiner is asked by Joseph Kurschner to edit Goethe's scientific works for the *Deutschen National-Literatur* edition. He writes "A Possible Critique of Atomistic Concepts" and sends it to Friedrich Theodore Vischer.

1883: Rudolf Steiner completes his college studies and begins work on the Goethe project.

1884: First volume of Goethe's *Scientific Writings* (CW 1) appears (March). He lectures on Goethe and Lessing, and Goethe's approach to science. In July, he enters the household of Ladislaus and Pauline Specht as tutor to the four Specht boys. He will live there until 1890. At this time, he meets Josef Breuer ((1842-1925), the coauthor with Sigmund Freud of *Studies in Hysteria*, who is the Specht family doctor.

1885: While continuing to edit Goethe's writings, Rudolf Steiner reads deeply in contemporary philosophy (Edouard von Hartmann, Johannes Volkelt, and Richard Wahle, among others).

1886: May: Rudolf Steiner sends Kurschner the manuscript of *Outlines of Goethe's Theory of Knowledge* (CW 2), which appears in October, and which he sends out widely. He also meets the poet Marie Eugenie Delle Grazie and writes "Nature and Our Ideals" for her. He attends her salon, where he meets many priests, theologians, and philosophers, who will become his friends. Meanwhile, the director of the Goethe Archive in Weimar requests his collaboration with the *Sophien* edition of Goethe's works, particularly the writings on color.

1887: At the beginning of the year, Rudolf Steiner is very sick. As the year progresses and his health improves, he becomes increasingly "a man of letters," lecturing, writing essays, and taking part in Austrian cultural life. In August-September, the second volume of Goethe's *Scientific Writings* appears.

1888: January-July: Rudolf Steiner assumes editorship of the "German Weekly" (*Deutsche Wochenschrift*). He begins lecturing more intensively, giving, for example, a lecture titled "Goethe as Father of a New Aesthetics." He meets and becomes soul friends with Friedrich Eckstein (1861-1939), a vegetarian, philosopher of symbolism, alchemist, and musician, who will introduce him to various spiritual currents (including Theosophy) and with whom he will meditate and interpret esoteric and alchemical texts.

1889: Rudolf Steiner first reads Nietzsche (*Beyond Good and Evil*). He encounters Theosophy again and learns of Madame Blavatsky in the Theosophical circle around Marie Lang (1858-1934). Here he also meets well-known figures of Austrian life, as well as esoteric figures like the occultist Franz Hartman and Karl Leinigen-Billigen (translator of C.G. Harrison's *The Transcendental Universe.*) During this period, Steiner first reads A.P. Sinnett's *Esoteric Buddhism* and Mabel Collins's *Light on the Path*. He also begins traveling, visiting Budapest, Weimar, and Berlin (where he meets philosopher Edouard von Hartman).

1890: Rudolf Steiner finishes volume 3 of Goethe's scientific writings. He begins his doctoral dissertation, which will become *Truth and Science* (CW 3). He also meets the poet and feminist Rosa Mayreder (1858-1938), with whom he can exchange his most intimate thoughts. In September, Rudolf Steiner moves to Weimar to work in the Goethe-Schiller Archive.

1891: Volume 3 of the Kurschner edition of Goethe appears. Meanwhile, Rudolf Steiner edits Goethe's studies in mineralogy and scientific writings for the *Sophien* edition. He meets Ludwig Laistner of the Cotta Publishing Company, who asks for a book on the basic question of metaphysics. From this will result, ultimately, *The Philosophy of Freedom* (CW 4), which will be published not by Cotta but by Emil Felber. In October, Rudolf Steiner takes the oral exam for a doctorate in philosophy, mathematics, and mechanics at Rostock University, receiving his doctorate on the twenty-sixth. In November, he gives his first lecture on Goethe's "Fairy Tale" in Vienna.

1892: Rudolf Steiner continues work at the Goethe-Schiller Archive and on his *Philosophy of Freedom*. *Truth and Science*, his doctoral dissertation, is published. Steiner undertakes to write introductions to books on Schopenhauer and Jean Paul for Cotta. At year's end, he finds lodging with Anna Eunike, née Schulz (1853-1911), a widow with four daughters and a son. He also develops a friendship with Otto Erich Hartleben (1864-1905) with whom he shares literary interests.

1893: Rudolf Steiner begins his habit of producing many reviews and articles. In March, he gives a lecture titled "Hypnotism, with Reference to Spiritism." In September, volume 4 of the Kurschner edition is completed. In November, *The Philosophy of Freedom* appears. This year, too, he meets John Henry Mackay (1864-1933), the anarchist, and Max Stirner, a scholar and biographer.

1894: Rudolf Steiner meets Elisabeth Förster Nietzsche, the philosopher's sister, and begins to read Nietzsche in earnest, beginning with the as yet unpublished *Antichrist*. He also meets Ernst Haeckel (1834-1919). In the fall, he begins to write *Nietzsche, A Fighter against His Time* (CW 5).

1895: May, *Nietzsche, A Fighter against His Time* appears.

1896: January 22: Rudolf Steiner sees Friedrich Nietzsche for the first and only time. Moves between the Nietzsche and the Goethe-Schiller Archives, where he completes his work before year's end. He falls out with Elisabeth Förster Nietzsche, thus ending his association with the Nietzsche Archive.

1897: Rudolf Steiner finishes the manuscript of *Goethe's Worldview* (CW 6). He moves to Berlin with Anna Eunike and begins editorship of the *Magazin fur Literatur*. From now on, Steiner will write countless reviews, literary and philosophical articles, and so on. He begins lecturing at the "Free Literary Society." In September, he attends the Zionist Congress in Basel. He sides with Dreyfus in the Dreyfus affair.

1898: Rudolf Steiner is very active as an editor in the political, artistic, and theatrical life of Berlin. He becomes friendly with John Henry Mackay and poet Ludwig Jacobowski (1868-1900). He joins Jacobowski's circle of writers, artists, and scientists—"The Coming Ones" (*Die Kommenden*)—and contributes lectures to the group until 1903. He also lectures at the "League for College Pedagogy." He writes an article for Goethe's sesquicentennial, "Goethe's Secret Revelation," on the "Fairy Tale of the Green Snake and the Beautiful Lily."

1888-89: "This was a trying time for my soul as I looked at Christianity. . . . I was able to progress only by contemplating, by means of spiritual perception, the evolution of Christianity . . . . Conscious knowledge of real Christianity began to dawn in me around the turn of the century. This seed continued to develop. My soul trial occurred shortly before the beginning of the twentieth century. It was decisive for my soul's development that I stood spiritually before the Mystery of Golgotha in a deep and solemn celebration of knowledge."

1899: Rudolf Steiner begins teaching and giving lectures and lecture cycles at the Workers' College, founded by Wilhelm Liebknecht (1826-1900). He will continue to do so until 1904. Writes: *Literature and Spiritual Life in the Nineteenth Century; Individualism in Philosophy; Haeckel and His Opponents; Poetry in the Present;* and begins what will become (fifteen years later). *The Riddles of Philosophy* (CW 18). He also meets many artists and writers, including Käthe Kollwitz, Stefan

Zweig, and Rainer Maria Rilke. On October 31, he marries Anna Eunike.

1900: "I thought that the turn of the century must bring humanity a new light. It seemed to me that the separation of human thinking and willing from the spirit had peaked. A turn or reversal of direction in human evolution seemed to me a necessity." Rudolf Steiner finishes *World and Life Views in the Nineteenth Century* (the second part of what will become *The Riddles of Philosophy*) and dedicates it to Ernst Haeckel. It is published in March. He continues lecturing at *Die Kommenden*, whose leadership he assumes after the death of Jacobowski. Also, he gives the Gutenberg Jubilee lecture before 7,000 typesetters and printers. In September, Rudolf Steiner is invited by Count and Countess Brockdorff to lecture in the Theosophical Library. His first lecture is on Nietzsche. His second lecture is titled "Goethe's Secret Revelation." October 6, he begins a lecture cycle on the mystics that will become *Mystics after Modernism* (CW 7). November-December: "Marie von Sivers appears in the audience...." Also in November, Steiner gives his first lecture at the Giordano Bruno Bund (where he will continue to lecture until May, 1905). He speaks on Bruno and modern Rome, focusing on the importance of the philosophy of Thomas Aquinas as monism.

1901: In continual financial straits, Rudolf Steiner's early friends Moritz Zitter and Rosa Mayreder help support him. In October, he begins the lecture cycle *Christianity as Mystical Fact* (CW 8) at the Theosophical Library. In November, he gives his first "Theosophical lecture" on Goethe's "Fairy Tale" in Hamburg at the invitation of Wilhelm Hubbe-Schleiden. He also attends a tea to celebrate the founding of the Theosophical Society at Count and Countess Brockdorff's. He gives a lecture cycle, "From Buddha to Christ," for the circle of the *Kommenden*. November 17, Marie von Sivers asks Rudolf Steiner if Theosophy does not need a Western-Christian spiritual movement (to complement Theosophy's Eastern emphasis). "The question was posed. Now, following spiritual laws, I could begin to give an answer...." In December, Rudolf Steiner writes his first article for a Theosophical publication. At year's end, the Brockdorffs and possibly Wilhelm Hubbe-Schleiden ask Rudolf Steiner to join the Theosophical Society and undertake the leadership of the German section. Rudolf Steiner agrees, on the condition that Marie von Sivers (then in Italy) work with him.

1902: Beginning in January, Rudolf Steiner attends the opening of the Workers' School in Spandau with Rosa Luxemberg (1870-1919). January 17, Rudolf Steiner joins the Theosophical Society. In April, he is asked to become general secretary of the German Section of the Theosophical Society, and works on preparations for its founding. In July, he visits London for a Theosophical congress. He meets Bertram

Keightly, G.R.S. Mead, A.P. Sinnett, and Annie Besant, among others. In September, *Christianity as Mystical Fact* appears. In October, Rudolf Steiner gives his first public lecture on Theosophy ("Monism and Theosophy") to about three hundred people at the Giordano Bruno Bund. On October 19-21, the German Section of the Theosophical Society has its first meeting; Rudolf Steiner is the general secretary, and Annie Besant attends. Steiner lectures on practical karma studies. On October 23, Annie Besant inducts Rudolf Steiner into the Esoteric School of the Theosophical Society. On October 25, Steiner begins a weekly series of lectures: "The Field of Theosophy." During this year, Rudolf Steiner also first meets Ita Wegman (1876-1943), who will become his close collaborator in his final years.

1903: Rudolf Steiner holds about 300 lectures and seminars. In May, the first issue of the periodical *Luzifer* appears. In June, Rudolf Steiner visits London for the first meeting of the Federation of the European Sections of the Theosophical Society, where he meets Colonel Olcott. He begins to write *Theosophy* (CW 9).

1904: Rudolf Steiner continues lecturing at the Workers' College and elsewhere (about 90 lectures), while lecturing intensively all over Germany among Theosophists (about a 140 lectures). In February, he meets Carl Unger (1878-1929), who will become a member of the board of the Anthroposophical Society (1913). In March, he meets Michael Bauer (1871-1929), a Christian mystic, who will also be on the board. In May, *Theosophy* appears, with the dedication: "To the spirit of Giordano Bruno." Rudolf Steiner and Marie von Sivers visit London for meetings with Annie Besant. June: Rudolf Steiner and Marie von Sivers attend the meeting of the Federation of European Sections of the Theosophical Society in Amsterdam. In July, Steiner begins the articles in *Luzifer-Gnosis* that will become *How to Know Higher Worlds* (CW 10) and *Cosmic Memory* (CW 11). In September, Annie Besant visits Germany. In December, Steiner lectures on Freemasonry. He mentions the High Grade Masonry derived from John Yarker and represented by Theodore Reuss and Karl Kellner as a blank slate "into which a good image could be placed."

1905: This year, Steiner ends his non-Theosophical lecturing activity. Supported by Marie von Sivers, his Theosophical lecturing—both in public and in the Theosophical Society—increases significantly: "The German Theosophical Movement is of exceptional importance." Steiner recommends reading, among others, Fichte, Jacob Boehme, and Angelus Silesius. He begins to introduce Christian themes into Theosophy. He also begins to work with doctors (Felix Peipers and Ludwig Noll). In July, he is in London for the Federation of European Sections, where he attends a lecture by Annie Besant: "I have seldom seen Mrs. Besant speak in so inward and heartfelt a manner...." "Through Mrs. Besant I have found the way to H.P. Blavatsky."

September to October, he gives a course of thirty-one lectures for a small group of esoteric students. In October, the annual meeting of the German Section of the Theosophical Society, which still remains very small, takes place. Rudolf Steiner reports membership has risen from 121 to 377 members. In November, seeking to establish esoteric "continuity," Rudolf Steiner and Marie von Sivers participate in a "Memphis-Misraim" Masonic ceremony. They pay forty-five marks for membership. "Yesterday, you saw how little remains of former esoteric institutions." "We are dealing only with a 'framework'... for the present, nothing lies behind it. The occult powers have completely withdrawn."

1906: Expansion of Theosophical work. Rudolf Steiner gives about 245 lectures, only 44 of which take place in Berlin. Cycles are given in Paris, Leipzig, Stuttgart, and Munich. Esoteric work also intensifies. Rudolf Steiner begins writing *An Outline of Esoteric Science* (CW 13). In January, Rudolf Steiner receives permission (a patent) from the Great Orient of the Scottish A & A Thirty-Three Degree Rite of the Order of the Ancient Freemasons of the Memphis-Misraim Rite to direct a chapter under the name "Mystica Aeterna." This will become the "Cognitive Cultic Section" (also called "Misraim Service") of the Esoteric School. (See: *From the History and Contents of the Cognitive Cultic Section* (CW 264). During this time, Steiner also meets Albert Schweitzer. In May, he is in Paris, where he visits Edouard Schuré. Many Russians attend his lectures (including Konstantin Balmont, Dimitri Mereszkovski, Zinaida Hippius, and Maximilian Woloshin). He attends the General Meeting of the European Federation of the Theosophical Society, at which Col. Olcott is present for the last time. He spends the year's end in Venice and Rome, where he writes and works on his translation of H.P. Blavatsky's *Key to Theosophy*.

1907: Further expansion of the German Theosophical Movement according to the Rosicrucian directive to "introduce spirit into the world"—in education, in social questions, in art, and in science. In February, Col. Olcott dies in Adyar. Before he dies, Olcott indicates that "the Masters" wish Annie Besant to succeed him: much politicking ensues. Rudolf Steiner supports Besant's candidacy. April-May: preparations for the Congress of the Federation of European Sections of the Theosophical Society—the great, watershed Whitsun "Munich Congress," attended by Annie Besant and others. Steiner decides to separate Eastern and Western (Christian-Rosicrucian) esoteric schools. He takes his esoteric school out of the Theosophical Society (Besant and Rudolf Steiner are "in harmony" on this). Steiner makes his first lecture tours to Austria and Hungary. That summer, he is in Italy. In September, he visits Edouard Schuré, who will write the introduction to the French edition of *Christianity as Mystical Fact* in Barr, Alsace. Rudolf Steiner writes the autobiographical statement known as the "Barr Document." In *Luzifer–Gnosis*, "The Education of the Child" appears.

1908: The movement grows (membership: 1150). Lecturing expands. Steiner makes his first extended lecture tour to Holland and Scandinavia, as well as visits to Naples and Sicily. Themes: St. John's Gospel, the Apocalypse, Egypt, science, philosophy, and logic. *Luzifer-Gnosis* ceases publication. In Berlin, Marie von Sivers (with Johanna Mücke (1864-1949) forms the *Philosophisch-Theosophisch* (after 1915 *Philosophisch-Anthroposophisch*) *Verlag* to publish Steiner's work. Steiner gives lecture cycles titled *The Gospel of St. John* (CW 103) and *The Apocalypse* (104).

1909: *An Outline of Esoteric Science* appears. Lecturing and travel continues. Rudolf Steiner's spiritual research expands to include the polarity of Lucifer and Ahriman; the work of great individualities in history; the Maitreya Buddha and the Bodhisattvas; spiritual economy (CW 109); the work of the spiritual hierarchies in heaven and on Earth (CW 110). He also deepens and intensifies his research into the Gospels, giving lectures on the Gospel of St. Luke (CW 114) with the first mention of two Jesus children. Meets and becomes friends with Christian Morgenstern (1871-1914). In April, he lays the foundation stone for the Malsch model—the building that will lead to the first Goetheanum. In May, the International Congress of the Federation of European Sections of the Theosophical Society takes place in Budapest. Rudolf Steiner receives the Subba Row medal for *How to Know Higher Worlds*. During this time, Charles W. Leadbeater discovers Jiddu Krishnamurti (1895-1986) and proclaims him the future "world teacher," the bearer of the Maitreya Buddha and the "reappearing Christ." In October, Steiner delivers seminal lectures on "anthroposophy," which he will try, unsuccessfully, to rework over the next years into the unfinished work, *Anthroposophy (A Fragment)* (CW 45).

1910: New themes: *The Reappearance of Christ in the Etheric* (CW 118); *The Fifth Gospel; The Mission of Folk Souls* (CW 121); *Occult History* (CW 126); the evolving development of etheric cognitive capacities. Rudolf Steiner continues his Gospel research with *The Gospel of St. Matthew* (CW 123). In January, his father dies. In April, he takes a month-long trip to Italy, including Rome, Monte Cassino, and Sicily. He also visits Scandinavia again. July-August, he writes the first mystery drama, *The Portal of Initiation* (CW 14). In November, he gives "psychosophy" lectures. In December, he submits "On the Psychological Foundations and Epistemological Framework of Theosophy" to the International Philosophical Congress in Bologna.

1911: The crisis in the Theosophical Society deepens. In January, "The Order of the Rising Sun," which will soon become "The Order of the Star in the East," is founded for the coming world teacher, Krishnamurti. At the same time, Marie von Sivers, Rudolf Steiner's coworker, falls ill. Fewer lectures are given, but important new ground is broken. In Prague, in March, Steiner meets Franz Kafka (1883-1924) and Hugo Bergmann (1883-1975). In April, he delivers his paper to the

Philosophical Congress. He writes the second mystery drama, *The Soul's Probation* (CW 14). Also, while Marie von Sivers is convalescing, Rudolf Steiner begins work on *Calendar 1912/1913*, which will contain the "Calendar of the Soul" meditations. On March 19, Anna (Eunike) Steiner dies. In September, Rudolf Steiner visits Einsiedeln, birthplace of Paracelsus. In December, Friedrich Rittelmeyer, future founder of the Christian Community, meets Rudolf Steiner. The *Johannes-Bauverein*, the "building committee," which would lead to the first Goetheanum (first planned for Munich), is also founded, and a preliminary committee for the founding of an independent association is created that, in the following year, will become the Anthroposophical Society. Important lecture cycles include *Occult Physiology* (CW 128); *Wonders of the World* (CW 129); *From Jesus to Christ* (CW 131). Other themes: esoteric Christianity; Christian Rosenkreutz; the spiritual guidance of humanity; the sense world and the world of the spirit.

1912: Despite the ongoing, now increasing crisis in the Theosophical Society, much is accomplished: *Calendar 1912/1913* is published; eurythmy is created; both the third mystery drama, *The Guardian of the Threshold* (CW 14) and *A Way of Self-Knowledge* (CW 16) are written. New (or renewed) themes included life between death and rebirth and karma and reincarnation. Other lecture cycles: *Spiritual Beings in the Heavenly Bodies and the Kingdoms of Nature* (CW 136); *The Human Being in the Light of Occultism, Theosophy, and Philosophy* (CW 137); *The Gospel of St. Mark* (CW 139); and *The Bhagavad Gita and the Epistles of Paul* (CW 142). On May 8, Rudolf Steiner celebrates White Lotus Day, H.P. Blavatsky's death day, which he had faithfully observed for the past decade, for the last time. In August, Rudolf Steiner suggests the "independent association" be called the "Anthroposophical Society." In September, the first eurythmy course takes place. In October, Rudolf Steiner declines recognition of a Theosophical Society lodge dedicated to the Star of the East and decides to expel all Theosophical Society members belonging to the order. Also, with Marie von Sivers, he first visits Dornach, near Basel, Switzerland, and they stand on the hill where the Goetheanum will be. In November, a Theosophical Society lodge is opened by direct mandate from Adyar (Annie Besant). In December, a meeting of the German section occurs at which it is decided that belonging to the Order of the Star of the East is incompatible with membership in the Theosophical Society. December 28: informal founding of the Anthroposophical Society in Berlin.

1913: Expulsion of the German section from the Theosophical Society. February 2-3: Foundation meeting of the Anthroposophical Society. Board members include: Marie von Sivers, Michael Bauer, and Carl Unger. September 20: Laying of the foundation stone for the *Johannes Bau* (Goetheanum) in Dornach. Building begins immediately. The third mystery drama, *The Soul's Awakening* (CW 14), is completed.

Also: *The Threshold of the Spiritual World* (CW 147). Lecture cycles include: *The Bhagavad Gita and the Epistles of Paul* and *The Esoteric Meaning of the Bhagavad Gita* (CW 146), which the Russian philosopher Nikolai Berdyaev attends; *The Mysteries of the East and of Christianity* (CW 144); *The Effects of Esoteric Development* (CW 145); and *The Fifth Gospel* (CW 148). In May, Rudolf Steiner is in London and Paris, where anthroposophical work continues.

1914: Building continues on the *Johannes Bau* (Goetheanum) in Dornach, with artists and coworkers from seventeen nations. The general assembly of the Anthroposophical Society takes place. In May, Rudolf Steiner visits Paris, as well as Chartres Cathedral. June 28: assassination in Sarajevo ("Now the catastrophe has happened!"). August 1: War is declared. Rudolf Steiner returns to Germany from Dornach—he will travel back and forth. He writes the last chapter of *The Riddles of Philosophy*. Lecture cycles include: *Human and Cosmic Thought* (CW 151); *Inner Being of Humanity between Death and a New Birth* (CW 153); *Occult Reading and Occult Hearing* (CW 156). December 24: marriage of Rudolf Steiner and Marie von Sivers.

1915: Building continues. Life after death becomes a major theme, also art. Writes: *Thoughts during a Time of War* (CW 24). Lectures include: *The Secret of Death* (CW 159); *The Uniting of Humanity through the Christ Impulse* (CW 165).

1916: Rudolf Steiner begins work with Edith Maryon (1872-1924) on the sculpture "The Representative of Humanity" ("The Group"—Christ, Lucifer, and Ahriman). He also works with the alchemist Alexander von Bernus on the quarterly *Das Reich*. He writes *The Riddle of Humanity* (CW 20). Lectures include: *Necessity and Freedom in World History and Human Action* (CW 166); *Past and Present in the Human Spirit* (CW 167); *The Karma of Vocation* (CW 172); *The Karma of Untruthfulness* (CW 173).

1917: Russian Revolution. The U.S. enters the war. Building continues. Rudolf Steiner delineates the idea of the "threefold nature of the human being" (in a public lecture March 15) and the "threefold nature of the social organism" (hammered out in May-June with the help of Otto von Lerchenfeld and Ludwig Polzer-Hoditz in the form of two documents titled *Memoranda*, which were distributed in high places). August-September: Rudolf Steiner writes *The Riddles of the Soul* (CW 20). Also: commentary on "The Chemical Wedding of Christian Rosenkreutz" for Alexander Bernus (*Das Reich*). Lectures include: *The Karma of Materialism* (CW 176); *The Spiritual Background of the Outer World: The Fall of the Spirits of Darkness* (CW 177).

1918: March 18: peace treaty of Brest-Litovsk—"Now everything will truly enter chaos! What is needed is cultural renewal." June: Rudolf Steiner visits Karlstein (Grail) Castle outside Prague. Lecture cycle: *From Symptom to Reality in Modern History* (CW 185). In mid-November,

Emil Molt, of the Waldorf-Astoria Cigarette Company, has the idea of founding a school for his workers' children.

1919: Focus on the threefold social organism: tireless travel, countless lectures, meetings, and publications. At the same time, a new public stage of Anthroposophy emerges as cultural renewal begins. The coming years will see initiatives in pedagogy, medicine, pharmacology, and agriculture. January 27: threefold meeting: " We must first of all, with the money we have, found free schools that can bring people what they need." February: first public eurythmy performance in Zurich. Also: "Appeal to the German People" (CW 24), circulated March 6 as a newspaper insert. In April, *Toward Social Renewal* (CW 23)—"perhaps the most widely read of all books on politics appearing since the war"—appears. Rudolf Steiner is asked to undertake the "direction and leadership" of the school founded by the Waldorf-Astoria Company. Rudolf Steiner begins to talk about the "renewal" of education. May 30: a building is selected and purchased for the future Waldorf School. August-September, Rudolf Steiner gives a lecture course for Waldorf teachers, *The Foundations of Human Experience (Study of Man)* (CW 293). September 7: Opening of the first Waldorf School. December (into January): first science course, the *Light Course* (CW 320).

1920: The Waldorf School flourishes. New threefold initiatives. Founding of limited companies *Der Kommenden Tag* and *Futurum A.G.* to infuse spiritual values into the economic realm. Rudolf Steiner also focuses on the sciences. Lectures: *Introducing Anthroposophical Medicine* (CW 312); *The Warmth Course* (CW 321); *The Boundaries of Natural Science* (CW 322); *The Redemption of Thinking* (CW 74). February: Johannes Werner Klein—later a cofounder of the Christian Community—asks Rudolf Steiner about the possibility of a "religious renewal," a "Johannine church." In March, Rudolf Steiner gives the first course for doctors and medical students. In April, a divinity student asks Rudolf Steiner a second time about the possibility of religious renewal. September 27-October 16: anthroposophical "university course." December: lectures titled *The Search for the New Isis* (CW 202).

1921: Rudolf Steiner continues his intensive work on cultural renewal, including the uphill battle for the threefold social order. "University" arts, scientific, theological, and medical courses include: *The Astronomy Course* (CW 323); *Observation, Mathematics, and Scientific Experiment* (CW 324); the *Second Medical Course* (CW 313); *Color*. In June and September-October, Rudolf Steiner also gives the first two "priests' courses" (CW 342 and 343). The "youth movement" gains momentum. Magazines are founded: *Die Drei* (January), and—under the editorship of Albert Steffen (1884-1963)—the weekly, *Das Goetheanum* (August). In February-March, Rudolf Steiner takes his first trip outside Germany since the war (Holland). On April 7, Steiner receives a letter regarding "religious renewal," and May 22-23, he agrees to address the question in a practical way. In June, the Klinical-Therapeutic Institute opens in Arlesheim under the direction of Dr. Ita Wegman. In August, the Chemical-Pharmaceutical Laboratory opens in Arlesheim (Oskar Schmiedel and Ita Wegman, directors). The Clinical Therapeutic Institute is inaugurated in Stuttgart (Dr. Ludwig Noll, director); also the Research Laboratory in Dornach (Ehrenfried Pfeiffer and Gunther Wachsmuth, directors). In November-December, Rudolf Steiner visits Norway.

1922: The first half of the year involves very active public lecturing (thousands attend); in the second half, Rudolf Steiner begins to withdraw and turn toward the Society—"The Society is asleep." It is "too weak" to do what is asked of it. The businesses—*Die Kommenden Tag* and *Futura A.G.*—fail. In January, with the help of an agent, Steiner undertakes a twelve-city German tour, accompanied by eurythmy performances. In two weeks he speaks to more than 2,000 people. In April, he gives a "university course" in The Hague. He also visits England. In June, he is in Vienna for the East-West Congress. In August-September, he is back in England for the Oxford Conference on Education. Returning to Dornach, he gives the lectures *Philosophy, Cosmology, and Religion* (CW 215), and gives the third priest's course (CW 344). On September 16, The Christian Community is founded. In October-November, Steiner is in Holland and England. He also speaks to the youth: *The Youth Course* (CW 217). In December, Steiner gives lectures titled *The Origins of Natural Science* (CW 326), and *Humanity and the World of Stars: The Spiritual Communion of Humanity* (CW 219). December 31: Fire at the Goetheanum, which is destroyed.

1923: Despite the fire, Rudolf Steiner continues his work unabated. A very hard year. Internal dispersion, dissension, and apathy abound. There is conflict—between old and new visions—within the society. A wake-up call is needed, and Rudolf Steiner responds with renewed lecturing vitality. His focus: the spiritual context of human life; initiation science; the course of the year; and community building. As a foundation for an artistic school, he creates a series of pastel sketches. Lecture cycles: *The Anthroposophical Movement; Initiation Science* (CW 227) (in England at the Penmaenmawr Summer School); *The Four Seasons and the Archangels* (CW 229); *Harmony of the Creative Word* (CW 230); *The Supersensible Human* (CW 231), given in Holland for the founding of the Dutch society. On November 10, in response to the failed Hitler-Ludendorf putsch in Munich, Steiner closes his Berlin residence and moves the *Philosophisch-Anthroposophisch Verlag* (Press) to Dornach. On December 9, Steiner begins the serialization of his *Autobiography: The Course of My Life* (CW 28) in *Das Goetheanum*. It will continue to appear weekly, without a break, until his death. Late December-early January: Rudolf Steiner refounds the Anthroposophical Society (about 12,000 members internationally) and takes over its leadership. The new board members are: Marie Steiner, Ita Wegman, Albert Steffen, Elizabeth Vreede, and Guenther Wachsmuth. (See *The Christmas Meeting for the Founding of the General Anthroposophical Society* (CW 260). Accompanying lectures: *Mystery Knowledge and Mystery Centers* (CW 232); *World History in the Light of Anthroposophy* (CW 233). December 25: the Foundation Stone is laid (in the hearts of members) in the form of the "Foundation Stone Meditation."

1924: January 1: having founded the Anthroposophical Society and taken over its leadership, Rudolf Steiner has the task of "reforming" it. The process begins with a weekly newssheet ("What's Happening in the Anthroposophical Society") in which Rudolf Steiner's "Letters to Members" and "Anthroposophical Leading Thoughts" appear (CW 26). The next step is the creation of a new esoteric class, the "first class" of the "University of Spiritual Science" (which was to have been followed, had Rudolf Steiner lived longer, by two more advanced classes). Then comes a new language for Anthroposophy—practical, phenomenological, and direct; and Rudolf Steiner creates the model for the second Goetheanum. He begins the series of extensive "karma" lectures (CW 235-40); and finally, responding to needs, he creates two new initiatives: biodynamic agriculture and curative education. After the middle of the year, rumors begin to circulate regarding Steiner's health. Lectures: January-February, *Anthroposophy* (CW 234); February: *Tone Eurythmy* (CW 278); June: *The Agriculture Course* (CW 327); June-July: Speech [?] Eurythmy (CW 279); *Curative Education* (CW 317); August: (England, "Second International Summer School"), *Initiation Consciousness: True and False Paths in Spiritual Investigation* (CW 243); September: *Pastoral Medicine* (CW 318). On September 26, for the first time, Rudolf Steiner cancels a lecture. On September 28, he gives his last lecture. On September 29, he withdraws to his studio in the carpenter's shop; now he is definitively ill. Cared for by Ita Wegman, he continues working, however, and writing the weekly installments of his *Autobiography* and *Letters to the Members/Leading Thoughts* (CW 26).

1925: Rudolf Steiner, while continuing to work, continues to weaken. He finishes *Extending Practical Medicine* (CW 27) with Ita Wegman. On March 30, around ten in the morning, Rudolf Steiner dies.

INDEX